Citizenshi

Key Themes in Sociology

This outstanding introductory series covers major theoretical perspectives and key concepts reflecting contemporary society. Written in an engaging style and accessible format, these concise volumes are designed to stimulate student discussion and thought. Pedagogical features such as primary readings, chapter summaries, key terms, and further suggested reading ensure these student-friendly volumes will be an essential aid to the study of the key themes in sociology.

Published

The Sociology of Gender: An Introduction to Theory and Research
Amy S. Wharton

Science and Technology in Society: From Biotechnology to the Internet
Daniel Lee Kleinman

Citizenship: Discourse, Theory, and Transnational Prospects
Peter Kivisto and Thomas Faist

Citizenship

Discourse, Theory, and Transnational Prospects

Peter Kivisto and Thomas Faist

Blackwell
Publishing

© 2007 by Peter Kivisto and Thomas Faist

BLACKWELL PUBLISHING
350 Main Street, Malden, MA 02148-5020, USA
9600 Garsington Road, Oxford OX4 2DQ, UK
550 Swanston Street, Carlton, Victoria 3053, Australia

The right of Peter Kivisto and Thomas Faist to be identified as the Authors of this Work
has been asserted in accordance with the UK Copyright, Designs, and Patents Act 1988.

First published 2007 by Blackwell Publishing Ltd

2   2008

Library of Congress Cataloging-in-Publication Data

Kivisto, Peter, 1948–
   Citizenship : discourse, theory, and transnational prospects / Peter Kivisto and
Thomas Faist.
      p. cm. – (Key themes in sociology)
   Includes bibliographical references and index.
   ISBN 978-1-4051-0551-4 (hardback : alk. paper)
   ISBN 978-1-4051-0552-1 (pbk. : alk. paper)
   1. Citizenship. I. Faist, Thomas, 1959– II. Title.

   JF801.K57 2007
   323.601–dc22

                                                                    2006034413

A catalogue record for this title is available from the British Library.

Set in 10 on 12 pt Sabon
by SNP Best-set Typesetter Ltd, Hong Kong
Printed and bound in Singapore
by COS Printers Pte Ltd

The publisher's policy is to use permanent paper from mills that operate a sustainable
forestry policy, and which has been manufactured from pulp processed using acid-free
and elementary chlorine-free practices. Furthermore, the publisher ensures that the text
paper and cover board used have met acceptable environmental accreditation standards.

For further information on Blackwell Publishing, visit our website:
www.blackwellpublishing.com

Contents

1

Introduction

Citizenship was long a neglected subject in the social sciences, but in a dramatic reversal it has more recently become a focal point for wide-ranging and varied discussions concerning the democratic prospect in an increasingly global society. Indeed, it is fair to say that we are currently witnessing an efflorescence of interest in the future of citizenship, or what David Scobey (2001: 20) has referred to as the "'return of the citizen' in public and policy discourse." Moreover, this efflorescence is a reflection of a growing belief in many quarters that we are living in what sociologist and former President of Brazil Fernando Henrique Cardoso (2000) has referred to as "an age of citizenship."

This renewed concern stems from two interrelated and shared convictions on the part of those who have entered into the fray: first, citizenship is important, and second, citizenship is changing. However, commentators begin to part company with others when it comes to specifying in what ways citizenship is presumed to be important and similarly over identifying the changes that are thought to be transforming – for better or worse – its significance and character. Not surprisingly, the normative evaluations attached to various prognostications also vary considerably, as do the emotional reactions, which range from deep pessimism to a rather rosy optimism.

At one level, citizenship can be succinctly defined in terms of two component features. The first is that it constitutes membership in a polity, and as such citizenship inevitably involves a dialectical process between inclusion and exclusion, between those deemed eligible for citizenship and those who are denied the right to become members. In its earliest articulation in ancient Greece, the polity in question was the city-state. In the modern world, it was transformed into the nation-state. Second, membership brings with it a reciprocal set of duties and rights, both of which vary by place and time, though some are universal. Thus, paying taxes and obeying the law are among the duties expected of citizens in all polities, while the right to participate in the political process in various ways – by voting, running for office, debating, petitioning, and so forth – is an inherent feature of democracy.

However, at another level, when one begins to look more closely at the substance of citizenship in the world today, it quickly becomes quite clear that there is no singularly agreed-upon answer to the question Derek Heater (1999) posed in the title of his book *What is Citizenship?* A rather cursory review of the literature reveals something of the capacious nature of recent discussions about contemporary citizenship. In an effort to capture that which is deemed to be novel about the present situation, a proliferation of adjectives are evident in that literature aimed as describing peculiar features of citizenship today. Thus, we find treatments of world citizenship (Heater 2002), global citizenship (Falk 1994), universal citizenship (Young 1989), cosmopolitan citizenship (Linklater 1998), multiple citizenship (Held 1995), postnational citizenship (Soysal 1994), transnational citizenship (Johnston 2001), dual citizenship (Miller 1991), nested citizenship (Faist 2000a and 2000b), multilayered citizenship (Yuval-Davis 2000), cultural citizenship (Stevenson 1997), multicultural citizenship (Delgado-Moreira 2000), cyber-citizenship (Tambini 1997), environmental citizenship (Jelin 2000), feminist citizenship (Lister 1997), gendered citizenship (Seidman 1999), flexible citizenship (Ong 1999), traditional citizenship (Bloemraad 2004), intimate citizenship (Plummer 2003), and protective citizenship (Gilbertson and Singer 2003). And the list could go on.

To further illustrate the multiplicity of terms used to depict citizenship today, one can simply turn to Isin and Wood's *Citizenship and Identity* (1999), where the authors describe a contemporary multifaceted citizenship that they characterize as being at once modern, diasporic, aboriginal, sexual, cosmopolitan, ecological, cultural, and radical. All of this clearly signals a conviction on the part of these two scholars that citizenship today is vital, malleable, in many ways novel, and inherently complex. Without necessarily agreeing with all of the particulars of this framing of the contemporary situation, many others concur with this general sensibility regarding an increasingly complex and variegated character of citizenship.

Others, however, offer a considerably less sanguine assessment. From their perspective, citizenship is being threatened by one of a variety of perceived forces that are seen as undermining its salience. The list of culprits is varied, including changes in the nation-state itself, which some have depicted as withering, while for others it is brought about by the shift from welfare capitalism to neoliberalism. Some point to changes in the citizenry itself, claiming that as a consequence of the individualistic tendencies of modern societies, increasing numbers of people no longer possess a willingness to become involved in public life. Still others would locate the source of the problem in larger, macro-level factors generally depicted in terms of the effects of globalization (Putnam 2000; Touraine 2001; Turner 2001; Dower 2003). In contrast to the vibrancy inherent in the preceding perspective, scholars operating with a conviction that citizenship is in trouble typically describe it as anemic, thin, or as merely instrumental.

EXPANSION OR EROSION?

As we sifted through the large – and rapidly growing – body of recent scholarly work on citizenship, largely from the interrelated fields of sociology, political science, philosophy, and cultural studies, we initially distinguished what we identified as two major discourses on the topic: as noted above, the first is concerned with the erosion of citizenship, the second with its expansion. We have also been struck by the fact that spokespersons for each of these positions seem deaf to the other discourse. Thus, at the outset we saw it as our intention in this brief inquiry into the problems and prospects of contemporary citizenship to bring the two discourses into fruitful dialogue, a task we realized was far more easily stated than achieved. To accomplish this objective, we thought that we would first subject each of the two discourses to critical analysis. Next, we would attempt to bring the two into contact with each other. This would lead to our final task, which would have been to distil from these first two tasks our own assessment of the future of citizenship.

However, our self-defined task proved to be more intricate and complicated than we had anticipated. As we looked at the erosion camp, we became increasingly aware that there are in fact two different, though sometimes interconnected, concerns that have been voiced about what is seen as a decline in the efficacy and salience of citizenship: one concerns the rights that accrue to individuals as citizens and the other attends to issues surrounding the obligations of citizenship. In terms of rights, a lively debate is currently underway that addresses the assault on social citizenship brought about by the rise of neoliberal political regimes since the 1970s. Appropriately, this debate is usually framed in terms of T. H. Marshall's (1964) paradigm of the evolution of citizenship that is linked to the rise and expansion of the modern welfare state. Less explicit in Marshall's account, but there nonetheless, is a view of the citizen in the modern welfare state as essentially passive – a recipient of rights due to the evolution of an expanded view of what citizenship entails, but not an active participant in democratic decision making (Turner 1993; 2001).

This touches on the obligation side of the coin. Generally without reflecting on Marshall, a number of contemporary theorists have raised concerns about what they perceive to be the steady decline in involvement in public life by ordinary people. This particular topic has been of major concern to those interested in the fate of the public sphere or civil society. Thus, a rather disparate group of thinkers – including but certainly not limited to Benjamin Barber, Robert Bellah, Amitai Etzioni, Anthony Giddens, Jürgen Habermas, Robert Putnam, Theda Skocpol, Alain Touraine, and Bryan Turner – have raised in different ways, from different political perspectives, and with different valences, concerns about the decline in civic participation.

If the erosion of citizenship discourse generally offers a rather pessimistic prognosis for the future (even when various nostrums are proposed to combat the problem), the other discourse views citizenship, not as anemic, but as expanding, vibrant, and susceptible to reinvention in ways appropriate to the dictates of globalization. But here too, we discovered that there are actually two, though again sometimes interconnected, discourses. On the one hand, the expansion of citizenship is seen in terms of the progressive inclusion of heretofore marginalized and excluded groups. This particular aspect of expansion pays primary attention to the changing significance of gender and race in shaping an understanding of who is to be incorporated into full membership in the body politic.

One account, seen most explicitly in Talcott Parsons's (1971) evolutionary functionalism, suggests that among the master trends shaping modern societies is a growing capacity and societal interest in inclusivity. From such a perspective, citizenship serves as a particularly significant mode of identity and solidarity in modern pluralist societies. A competing account, especially evident among social movement scholars, stresses the struggles of marginalized groups in gaining entrée to the public sphere as equals possessing all of the rights of citizens. Be it a focus on the women's movement, the black civil rights movement in the United States, or similar struggles elsewhere on the part of excluded racial or religious minorities, the main thrust of this approach tends to be reflective of what the American labor leader and civil rights activist A. Philip Randolph once said: "Rights must be taken."

Both of these accounts of inclusion share one thing in common: they presuppose that the locus of citizenship is the nation-state. This assumption has been increasingly challenged by scholars who have raised questions about what they claim to be the erosion in the efficacy of the nation-state while simultaneously pondering whether various trans-state entities such as the United Nations or, at a more regional level, the European Union might be capable of developing notions of citizenship that, in effect, burst the boundaries of the nation-state (Jacobson 1996; Soysal 1994). In part, the argument draws a parallel between the premodern and the modern loci of citizenship. In the former, it was the city-state, while in the latter it became the nation-state. The assumption underpinning this argument is that as we enter what some see as late or advanced modernity (Giddens 1990) and others as the postmodern (Harvey 1989), a similar shift occurs in the locus of citizenship regimes. Given the embryonic character of these emergent trends, it is not surprising that there is little agreement about whether the future suggests the development of a global state (Heater 1999, 2002) or what John Hoffman (2004) refers to as "citizenship beyond the state" – by which he means not only beyond the nation-state, but beyond any sort of trans-state.

The discussions about transcending the boundaries of the nation-state can be seen in the wide-ranging discussions today, not only among scholars but also among politicians and policy makers, about dual or multiple citizenship. Given the reality of expanding numbers of dual citizens residing around the world, it is not surprising that this topic has been of particular interest of late. Much of this discussion is about individuals going beyond the boundaries of any particular nation-state by becoming members of two or more states. As such, at one level the legitimacy or efficacy of the existing global order of states is assumed and not questioned.

A topic that has received somewhat less attention, but is nonetheless equally central to this general line of inquiry, is nested citizenship. It has received less attention because it is a concrete phenomenon only in Europe at the moment, and does not appear relevant to North America, Asia, or elsewhere. However, it should be recalled that the European Community as it was conceived at its founding in the post-World War II period was primarily an economic entity designed to give Western Europe greater clout in world markets, particularly in response to American economic hegemony. It was over the course of several decades that its potential political implications began to emerge, and with it the idea that one might be a citizen of a particular European nation while simultaneously being a citizen of Europe. One question nested citizenship theory raises is whether, for example, the North American Free Trade Agreement (NAFTA), which is in its early years and is at the moment viewed solely as an economic treaty, might over time evolve into something resembling the European Union (EU). Likewise, might something similar occur elsewhere, be it in the form of pan-Africanism, strategic alliances among the economic powerhouses of East Asia, or in Latin America? These are questions that the idea of nested citizenship raises.

At another level, the transcendence of the nation-state is seen to open up the prospects of world citizenship (Heater 2002). While much of this particular conversation occurs at the philosophical level, the impact of universal human rights regimes and the idea that organizations such as the United Nations have a role to play in insuring the protection of those rights – including the interventions of various sorts into nations accused of rights violations – also gives it real-world evidence to examine and interpret.

FOUR THEMES

The objective we have staked out for this book is in our estimation both modest and important. It is modest insofar as we do not seek to lay out alternative explanations, develop new types of citizenship to add to the already expansive list, or provide a lengthy and sustained argument about what we think the future of citizenship in the next quarter of a century or so is likely to be. Rather, our purpose is, first, to offer an analytical assessment that is useful in locating and making sense of the various thematic discourses on citizenship, and, second, to provide guidance in pulling together those discrete themes into a larger, more comprehensive framework of analysis that is capable of taking all of them into account. We think this is important insofar as it permits a more constructive dialogue across these various discourses.

To that end, the following four chapters will take up the concerns discussed above, structured into the following broad themes: (1) inclusion, (2) erosion, (3) withdrawal, and (4) expansion. In each instance, we make no effort to provide a comprehensive account of the body of scholarship dealing with each theme. Rather, the focus is on the main contours of the state of the argument, and to get at those contours, we have intentionally selected what we think are among the most important works to date – works that have become touchstones for others working in the area. In some cases, we will stay close to the texts themselves by providing exegeses of these works, seeking not only to identify and critically evaluate that which the authors say, but also to point to authorial silences. Some of the texts in question are theoretical while others are chiefly the products of empirical research. There is a decided focus on the Anglo-American world, and in some instances, as with the first half of the chapter on inclusion and the chapter on erosion, the focus is primarily on the United States. In other places, such as the discussion of dual citizenship, we will make use of a somewhat broader range of sources and will survey the current state of the literature. While this might suggest to some readers an arbitrariness in our selections, we think we have managed to tap into the most salient works available to help us to capture each theme's key features.

Inclusion

Inclusion, the first major theme we address, is an expansive topic that concerns itself both with, on the one hand, the incorporation of people into the ranks of citizens and, on the other, the terms of incorporation. What E. J. Hobsbawm (1962) called the "age of revolution" – framed by the French Revolution and the failed revolutionary upheavals of 1848 – resulted in the triumph of bourgeoisie democracy. Who precisely was to be included in the system as citizens varied by country, but in general there were efforts – sometimes more successful, sometimes less successful – to effect closure in order to prevent certain categories of persons from achieving full citizenship. In some places, this meant that the working class and the poor were to be excluded. In other places, racial criteria were used to differentiate citizens from those who were excluded from full societal membership. In all instances, women were denied the rights of full citizenship by being denied access to the public sphere. Thus, part of the issue of inclusion involves the manner by, and extent to which, heretofore-excluded categories of people have managed to gain entrée into the polity by being accorded full citizenship rights, while at the same time the state has preserved its monopoly on dictating the terms of inclusion and exclusion.

However, more recently, citizenship debates have concentrated on issues related to the terms of incorporation. Of particular significance is the conversation about multiculturalism as a mode of inclusion. Although its meaning is varied and contested, there is general consensus that multiculturalism involves valorizing ethnic and cultural diversity, induced by the presence and activities of ethnonational minorities and aboriginal groups within nation-states and by the impact of immigration. Related to this, considerable attention has been devoted to the matter of "group-differentiated rights" (Young 1989, 2000; see also Kymlicka 1995, 2001), which would include all categories of citizens that do not belong to the majority mainstream, which in the nations of the West has historically meant white males. Among the questions that advocates of group-differentiated rights must wrestle with is whether, to what degree, and for which categories of citizens should such rights be seen as a constitutive part of citizenship. In the somewhat narrower realm of cultural rights, central concerns involve claims pertaining to religion, language, and education. Even more contentious is the matter of granting rights that promote self-government and partial forms of political autonomy for recognized minorities.

Both exogenous and endogenous factors have played a role in stimulating tendencies towards the expansion of cultural rights. In the case of ethnonational minorities, for instance, European integration has in some cases fostered subnational tendencies towards regionalism (as can be seen, for instance, with the Scots and the Welsh in Britain, the Basques and Catalonians in Spain, and the *Lega Nord* in Italy). Endogenous factors likewise have had similar consequences. Over the past several decades, for example, religious exemption rights have been increasingly granted to members of various immigrant groups, be it exempting Sikhs from wearing motorcycle helmets in Canada or offering halal food in British state school cafeterias. Still, there is much controversy over the granting of such rights. This is evident in the controversy over whether the wearing of headscarves by Muslim schoolgirls in France and women teachers in Germany should be permitted. Both cases remain disputed at the moment. Overall, religious exemption rights are covered by the constitutions of the various liberal democracies, albeit somewhat differently from nation to nation. There is evidence of a path-dependent development towards a convergence of such rights. However, the situation is far less clear when it comes to rights associated with limited self-government, greater autonomy, or even the prospect of independence for ethnonational minorities.

Erosion

The second topic concerns the social rights aspect of citizenship – more specifically, the relationship between citizens and the welfare dimension of modern states. In all of the world's liberal democracies, providing for the well-being of citizens has entailed the creation of a wide range of enforceable rights that all citizens possess, including social security and pension provisions, unemployment schemes, health insurance, access to education, and so forth. Not only does the range of rights vary from nation to nation, but so does the scope of those rights. Some states – with the United States being the most obvious instance – created relatively thin welfare regimes, while others – with the Scandinavian countries serving as paradigmatic examples – established and have maintained comparatively thick ones. Nevertheless, in all of these nations, citizens have become more, not less, reliant on state protection (Béland 2005).

What is interesting for our purposes are the shifting assumptions about the current condition and the future prospects of the welfare state. As an examination of the relevant social scientific literature reveals, by the middle of the twentieth century the received wisdom was that the welfare state was here to stay, having managed to deal with the most negative effects of inequality while also succeeding in reducing previous levels of class conflict. A typical argument was that during the early phase of industrialization, the primary economic role played by the state involved the facilitation of capital accumulation, which yielded ever-increasing levels of economic productivity. In contrast, once an industrial society reached a mature state of development, this role for the state progressively gives way to a new role wherein the primary task becomes, as A. F. K. Organski, in an emblematic expression of modernization theory, *The Stages of Political Development* (1965), put it, "to protect the very people who were the greatest sufferers in [the earlier stage of industrial society]." In short, the welfare state was a path-dependent consequence of the internal logic of capitalist development. First, with the assistance of the state, economic structures were put in place to stimulate accumulation and enhance productive capacity. Once that had occurred, it became possible to begin to address the primary unintended consequence of industrialization, which is the generation of unacceptable levels of inequality (the matter of environmental degradation in the early period was not a major topic of concern for modernization theorists).

Within a decade of Organski's thesis, critics from both the left and right began to question the legitimacy and the economic viability of the welfare state. As the critics point out, the pressures on the welfare state are both exogenous and endogenous. Certainly, the pressure on state–citizen relations concerning social rights has been exacerbated by the effects of globalization on welfare states seeking to compete in international markets in a situation characterized by, as Saskia Sassen (1996: 6) put it, the "global footlooseness of corporate capital." Globalization has been identified as a factor contributing to the reduction of benefits and the general trend to constrict rather than expand or preserve existing social rights. In terms of endogenous factors, numerous critics of liberal democratic welfare states have contended that the pervasive provision of guaranteed benefits has resulted in an unwelcome and unintended side effect: namely, it has tended to undermine individual autonomy and the capacity of citizens to care for themselves and their families – becoming, in short, increasingly dependent on the various provisions which were designed to enable them to become independent.

In the midst of these intellectual and ideological challenges, the triumph of neoliberalism signaled the advent of a significant attack on existing welfare state policies and programs. While radical exponents of neoliberalism, such as the influential American neoconservative Grover Norquist, suggest in colorful language that their goal is to "strangle," "starve," or "drown" the welfare state, other neoliberals are content to cut away at it, reducing as much as is politically feasible its influence over the lives of citizens. In either case, the goal of neoliberalism is the erosion of the welfare state, a goal that has met various levels of success during the past few decades in all of the industrial nations.

Somewhat provocatively, Alain Touraine (2001: 9) has argued that *we have moved from a form of socialism to a form of capitalism, and that the market has replaced the state as the principal regulatory force* [italics in original] in neoliberal regimes. Clearly, neoliberalism calls into question the central claim of postindustrial theory, be it Touraine's leftist version or Bell's centrist account, about the central role accorded to the state in directing society. Neoliberal ideology, as Touraine points out, calls for replacing the state by corporate capitalism. Insofar as it succeeds in doing so, the question arises about the future of social rights. If the recent past has entailed the progressive erosion of such rights, does the future suggest more of the same, or is it possible, given the proper constellation of political forces emanating from the new social movements, for there to be a return of a welfare state, albeit a reformulated one, that takes us, in Touraine's words (2001), "beyond neoliberalism?"

Withdrawal

A third major field of public debate and contention concerning citizenship focuses on the matter of democratic participation and, underlying that, on the question of what it means to speak of the civic virtues of citizens. The first part of this debate is grounded in empirical observation. For decades, political scientists have pointed out that most citizens in representative democracies are neither well informed nor particularly interested in political matters. As the classic study *The American Voter* (Campbell et al. 1976 [1960]) revealed, citizens' familiarity with current political events and issues is severely limited. The United States is not all that unique in this regard. Given this general tendency to remain aloof from political engagement, the claim has been advanced that during the last quarter of the past century there has been a growing tendency to withdraw from the public sphere (Putnam 2000). It is quite clear that in many Western democracies, voter turnout has been decreasing in recent decades. Likewise, other sorts of involvements in both strictly political activities (writing letters to politicians, demonstrating, lobbying, etc.) and in more general sorts of civic activities (joining community organizations, volunteerism, etc.) have also experienced declines, sometimes quite dramatic ones.

While traditional political liberalism has been more concerned with protecting individual rights from unwarranted governmental intrusions, and not particularly or primarily concerned with the obligations of citizens to participate in public life, such is not the case with those who embrace classic republican ideals or, more recently, communitarianism. If today's liberal thinkers, such as those who self-identify as libertarians, express little concern about what the withdrawal of citizens from public life might mean to democratic practice, this has become a major preoccupation of contemporary thinkers who identify as republicans or communitarians. In their view, democracy is not possible without an informed and active citizenry. Thus, they are concerned that the foundation of democratic practice is endangered. Making sense of this particular claim involves two facets. First, it requires assessing the empirical adequacy of the case that is being made that the trend to withdraw from the civic arena is far more pronounced at present than in both the recent and distant past. Second, it entails a critical assessment of the causal factors that have been identified as the main culprits contributing to this withdrawal.

Expansion

Finally, it is the location of citizenship that is at stake. The most characteristic form of citizenship in modern democracies until the present has been single and exclusive citizenship in a nation-state. Some have argued that nation-states have become increasingly weakened and anachronistic as a consequence of globalization, and that we are now on the cusp of a new, postnational age (Soysal 1994). In such a novel set of circumstances, new loci for citizenship are seen to emerge. In a similar vein, among those who do not think the nation-state is in danger of disappearing (for better or worse), there is a growing sense that the typical form is increasingly coexisting with novel forms of citizenship located in some fashion beyond the nation-state. Given that much of the postnational discourse transpired before the events of 9/11 and the subsequent dramatic assertiveness of powerful nation-states, the dialogue at the moment is chiefly shaped by the question of whether and to what extent single-state, exclusive citizenship can coincide with other forms of citizenship.

The most common newer form of citizenship – with deeper roots than the other forms – is dual or multiple citizenship (as we shall see below, multiple is used in two distinct ways). It is defined as a form of overlapping membership in which an individual has full membership in at least two nation-states. A growing number of states have passed legislation permitting dual citizenship, and even in nations that do not permit it, except in limited circumstances, a growing tolerance of such identities is evident. At the very least, nations that do not officially legitimize dual or multiple citizenship are not inclined to prosecute people for holding two or more passports.

This development, it should be noted, marks a significant departure from the received understanding of dual citizenship, which was that it was to be avoided as much as possible in order to prevent the potential problem of dual loyalties. For example, such a view was enshrined in the nineteenth century in the Bancroft Treaties enacted between the United States and various European states and in the Hague Convention of 1930.

It was only three decades ago that Raymond Aron (1974: 638) pondered the question, "Is multinational citizenship possible?" His response was to conclude that he continued to believe "that my initial reaction – that the idea of multinational citizenship is a contradiction in terms – was correct." However, he added the following proviso that reflected his sense that this was not quite as simple a matter as he had thought: "Yet I admit that the question can arise: the various rights of citizenship are not all of a piece, and do not all relate to the state in the same way." Since Aron's speculative essay, the proliferation of dual citizenship regimes has meant that rather than contemplating the prospects of dual citizenship, social scientists today address its reality and the growing demand for its expansion. Not surprisingly, much that has been written in recent years about dual citizenship focuses on state policy making, with an extremely limited literature to date taking up the issue of what it is like to live as a dual citizen in an increasingly globalized world system.

The second new form of citizenship that has become a topic of interest, particularly among Europeans, is that of emerging forms of supranational citizenship. Thomas Faist (2000a: 13 and 2000b) has referred to this type as "nested citizenship." Describing this as resembling Russian dolls, citizenship is articulated at both the national and the supranational levels. Thus, a person is a French citizen and simultaneously a citizen of Europe – or more specifically of the European Union. David Held (1995) has used the term "multiple citizenship" to describe such a situation, a term that connotes full membership on multiple governance levels. Given that similar forms of citizenship have not arisen elsewhere, the European model has been the sole focus of scholarly attention.

As with dual citizenship, much attention has been devoted to the policy level. However, the idea of nested citizenship has also raised questions about the implications of European citizenship for the more emotive aspects of belonging to particular nations. It has also raised in some places the issue of the relationship between the nation-state and ethnonationalist movements within states. Scottish nationalists, for instance, have argued that they view Britain as an antiquated mode of identity. The goal of those in favor of an independent Scotland is to scuttle the relationship of the region to Britain and instead to embrace the ideal of locating Scotland within Europe. Thus, residents of Scotland would be at once citizens of Scotland and Europe, but no longer of the United Kingdom (Nairn 2000).

Related terms intended to reflect the expansive character of contemporary citizenship include transnational citizenship, global citizenship, cosmopolitan citizenship, and world citizenship. While the first of these most closely approximates dual or multiple citizenship – with a concern for definitions of belonging that involve one or more specific nation-states – the others in various ways are deemed to reflect the emergence of citizenship, or at least citizenship-like features, at a global level. The role of supranational organizations such as the United Nations and the proliferation of INGOs (international nongovernmental organizations) working to advance the idea of universal human rights points to the fact that people are increasingly inclined to turn to suprastate organizations to seek redress for perceived infringements of basic human rights (Tsutsui and Wotipka 2004). While many of these trends are in an early stage of development and much remains unclear about where they might lead, part of the discourse on the expansion of citizenship must reckon with them.

THE FUTURE OF CITIZENSHIP

These four themes – inclusion, erosion, withdrawal, and expansion – reflect the foci of contemporary discourses on citizenship. The renewal of concern in citizenship studies that we noted at the outset is reflected in the various ways that each of these themes has taken shape in recent decades. As the short sketches of these four main fields of debate indicate, citizenship is a pivotal contested concept in contemporary social science theory, but also in political practice. As is true of all contested concepts, discourses about citizenship inevitably have two dimensions, the normative (what should be) and the empirical (what actually is). Citizenship, as we have noted, is a relationship between a citizen and the state, or some entity that is state-like in key respects.

As will become evident in the following chapters, citizenship is at the moment undergoing a significant process of redefinition, following from the claims-making practices of ordinary people, the articulation of the obligations of citizens as prescribed by the state, and the recognition of various rights granted by the state. These three features in tandem point toward the idea of citizenship as status, defined in terms of legally enforceable rights accruing to citizens and a set of obligations, some but not all of which are legally mandated, that citizens are expected to fulfill.

Citizenship establishes the boundaries of the political community. It defines that which is public and that which is private. It also tells us who is in and who is outside of the political community. The boundaries of citizenship are set by the interactive combination of three pivotal dimensions of citizenship in a particular time and place: (1) democratic self-governance (including access to political life); (2) the particular constellation of citizens' rights and responsibilities; and (3) the matter of identity that comes with the sense of belonging to or being affiliated with a political community.

Finally, we make the following claim. Although all contemporary states define their legal inhabitants as citizens, it is our view that citizenship cannot be conceived without its twin sibling: democracy. In nondemocratic regimes, the legal residents of the state remain subjects rather than being citizens. They have membership and certain duties are required, but they lack the rights of democratic citizenship. Thus, just as manifestly anti-democratic nations have laid claim to the democratic label (witness the former Soviet Union and its Warsaw Pact satellites), so they have sought to view their inhabitants as citizens. We think the distinction is important: democracies alone have citizens. That being said, it is also true that real existing nations exist on a continuum, with some being more democratic than others. This clearly has implications for the form and especially the content of citizenship.

It is our sense that the four themes we have identified speak to the major issues pertaining to citizenship in liberal democracies. We are convinced that the discourses we will review in the following chapters are critical to any effort to make sense of the future of citizenship. At the same time, one of the unfortunate but perhaps inevitable consequences of the way these distinct discourses have developed is that there has been little effort to provide an overarching analysis of the condition of and prospects for citizenship, an analysis that incorporates the central thrust of each of the themes while bringing these discrete themes into contact with the other themes. For instance, what does the discourse on the withdrawal from civic involvement mean for the salience of dual citizenship? What does the discourse on the erosion of social rights mean to notions of global citizenship? While we do not propose to conclude this brief book with anything remotely meant to offer definitive answers to these and the multitude of related questions, we do hope to offer a framework that will help to make possible a more expansive and coherent discourse on the future of citizenship in an increasingly interconnected and interdependent world.

2

Inclusion

This chapter explores two distinct but nonetheless interrelated matters. The first involves the question of who is to be included among the ranks of citizens and (the reverse side of the coin) who is to be excluded. The second involves the matter of the terms or the modes of inclusion. Although there is considerable overlap between these two topics, it is also true that the first received substantially more attention during the nineteenth century and the first two-thirds of the twentieth century than the second, while with the rise of multiculturalism as a highly contested and variable type of incorporation the second has become a major theme in both academic discourse and in concrete social practices and public policies (Kivisto 2005).

As such, the first topic requires a look to the past, while the second more explicitly and evidently concerns the present and its implications for the future. Given that this book is concerned with contemporary citizenship, our examination of the past is not intended to offer anything resembling a comprehensive historical overview of the processes of exclusion or the movements aimed at advancing the cause of expanding inclusion. Rather its purpose is to indicate in what ways inclusion in the former sense of the term remains an unrealized goal and to understand the relevance of inclusion for the emergence of multiculturalism as a new mode of societal incorporation.

The democratic cultures that came to shape the modern nation-states in Western Europe and North America, certainly by the eighteenth century, revived and redefined the idea of citizenship. This involved, at the philosophical level, inheriting and embracing elements of citizenship's ancient origins in the Greek city-state and in the Roman Empire, while at the same time, at the political level, repudiating and replacing the autocratic model of subjecthood that characterized the feudal era with the idea of the citizen as an active agent in political decision making. It also held out the conviction that the status of the citizen *qua* citizen was an equal in spite of inequalities of wealth. At its core, despite nation-specific variations, the citizen was seen as an independent or free person engaged in the process of self-rule. Quentin Skinner (1998: 74) describes the system of self-rule as one, "in which the sole power of making laws remains with the people or their accredited representatives, and in which all individual members of the body politic – rulers and citizens alike – remain equally subject to whatever laws they choose to impose on themselves." Linda Kerber (1997: 34) concurs with this definition while pointing to the egalitarian character implicit in the concept of citizenship: " 'Citizen' is an equalizing word. It carries with it the activism of Aristotle's definition – one who rules and is ruled in turn."

In the modern democratic nation-state, the role of citizen came to constitute the central mode of belonging to the nation. It is thus implicated in the construction of modern conceptions of nationality. For this reason, the distinction between citizens and noncitizens, those who were for one reason or another excluded from full membership as citizens in these societies, served as a significant and consequential differential mark of identity (Heater 2004). It spoke to who could and who could not take part in the ongoing process of self-rule. The idea of full membership is crucial here insofar as while in some instances it was possible to distinguish the citizen from the alien – or in other words the member from the person who is unmistakably defined as a nonmember – in other instances the distinction is not quite so clear, as the idea of denizens attests (Hammar 1990).

What does the idea of full membership suggest? Likewise, what do we mean when we speak about second-class citizens, a phrase much in evidence during the American civil rights movement and parallel movements elsewhere? In other words, what do these adjectives tell us about those individuals who are in some ways members of a nation-state, but lack something possessed by those for whom this adjective is not attached to their citizenship status? This can be answered by considering one of the three crucial features that characterize the democratic political process. The three are: (1) the right to participate in the public sphere; (2) limitations on the power of government over the individual; and (3) a system based on the rule of law, not the arbitrary rule of rulers. The second two elements speak to the framework within which democratic participation by citizens who are in principle seen as equals is possible. Those who are seen as not possessing full membership in the polity because they are second-class citizens are legitimately seen as permanent residents of the nation, but do not have the right to fully participate in the political process. Such individuals are not permitted to vote, to engage in policy making, to run for elective office, and the like. They possess *formal* citizenship, but not *substantive* citizenship. Although their identities may be different from aliens, they share much in common insofar as both are denied certain fundamental rights that accrue to those possessing full membership in the society.

THE DIALECTIC OF INCLUSION AND EXCLUSION

The principal fault lines used to define the boundaries of inclusion versus exclusion have historically been based on three major social divisions: class, gender, and race. And, indeed, though much has changed, these divisions remain salient – and indeed tend to be intersecting (Kivisto and Hartung 2007). During the formative period of these fledgling democracies, the privileged white, property-owning male citizens were intent on disqualifying a majority of the nation's residents from citizenship rights. Confronted with a disjunction between the egalitarian ideals of democratic theory and the desire to exclude from full societal membership certain categories of persons who did not share their class, gender, or racial identities, they responded by erecting ideological justifications for exclusionary policies that resulted in, to borrow the language of Frank Parkin (1979: 44–73), "social closure as exclusion." For their part, the white working class, women, and nonwhites responded, always in difficult circumstances and with varying degrees of success, by creating social movements aimed at acquiring the political voice that had been denied them. We look briefly at some of the key features of these three movements, starting with the one that had the earliest impact, the working-class movement.

Working-class incorporation

There is no reason to assume that the development of citizenship unfolded in an inexorable historical teleology, as the Whig interpretation of history would have it. In the social sciences this perspective is nowhere more evident than in Parsonian social theory, which tended to view inclusion as the result of social structural changes rather than the agency of collective social actors, and which, by emphasizing inclusion, downplayed exclusion (Parsons 1971). Nonetheless, there is abundant evidence to suggest that the expansion and deepening of civil, political, and social rights during the nineteenth and twentieth centuries have been shaped by a number of developmental pressures shared by the world's liberal democracies. Beginning with the dual impacts of the American and French Revolutions, the array of rights conveyed to citizens *qua* citizens has expanded considerably. During this time democratic ideals took root, first among the middle classes in the nations of Western Europe and North America; however, over time they filtered throughout all segments of those societies and ultimately outward to the rest of the world (Glassman et al. 1993; Markoff 1996).

At the same time, persistent questions were posed in a variety of quarters about who ought to be eligible for citizenship, the result being the expansion of opportunities for the acquisition of citizenship status among those who had been historically excluded from consideration. In other words, if democracy was understood to mean rule of and by the people, the open question was who was included under the rubric "people." One of the ironies of democratic development is that among the main carriers of democratic ideals, those most responsible for challenging, to borrow from Tocqueville, the "old regime" were those equally intent on limiting the definition of who would qualify for citizenship in the new democratic regime. Specifically, the emerging bourgeoisie's definition of the situation circumscribed the boundaries of citizenship in class, gender, and race-specific terms. Thus, the ideal-typical citizen was construed as a white male property owner, who simultaneously embraced powerful democratic ideals while exhibiting an equally powerful concern for excluding those deemed to be unfit for the rights and obligations associated with democratic self-rule. The history of citizenship during the past two centuries can be viewed as a persistent struggle on the part of the "unfit," the disenfranchised, the marginalized, the dependent to be included in the ranks of "the citizen."

During the nineteenth century, the working-class movement, whether under the socialist banner or not, was motivated by a combination of economic grievances and political demands. This was clearly evident in Britain, the "cradle of the Industrial Revolution," where, as Eric Hobsbawm (1969: 91) has argued, "the two great social movements of this period" were Luddism and Chartism. The Luddites, whose machine-breaking activities extended over a two-decade period from around 1810 into the 1830s, are often regarded as an irrational rearguard movement. However, as Hobsbawm (1965: 9) makes clear in his discussion of these attempts at "collective bargaining by riot," the Luddites were not anti-technology romantics. They did not dream of a return to a preindustrial past; rather they were people seeking to have a say in how technological change was being introduced and what might be done to assist those most adversely impacted by capitalist industrialization. Deprived of a political voice, they had few options in their repertoire of protest other than machine breaking. In other words, the inherent weakness of the machine breakers was a consequence of the fact that they did not possess the political rights of the citizen that the propertied bourgeoisie possessed.

A generation later, the Luddites were replaced by the Chartists, a non-violent movement that, in its People's Charter, paved the way for the incorporation of working men in Britain into the ranks of the citizenry. The Charter contained six main points, calling for universal male suffrage, payment of Members of Parliament, the secret ballot, annual elections, equal electoral districts, and the abolition of property requirements for membership in the House of Commons. All of these demands were designed to provide working-class men not only with the right to vote but also with the ability and means to hold elective office. The implicit understanding of a movement committed to the expansion of democracy was that the acquisition of political rights was a prerequisite for promoting the evolutionary or parliamentary socialism that would redress the inequalities generated by the capitalist market.

On the Continent, the revolutionary upheavals of 1848 that swept across much of Western and Eastern Europe profoundly impacted France, Germany, Italy, and various flashpoints in the Habsburg Empire. They constituted a powerful but brief challenge to the status quo, but more significantly served as a symbolic expression of the new contested terrain brought about by the triumph of capitalist industrial society. As with the Chartists in Britain, the proponents of revolutionary change were motivated by the dual but interconnected goals of advancing the political representation of workers and other members of the lower classes and improving their economic circumstances. Not surprisingly, a key demand called for universal male suffrage, or, in other words, an expansion of the rights associated with citizenship.

Though not the whole story, both the transition from the Luddites to the Chartists and the events leading up to and beyond 1848 reveal the connection between the expansion of citizenship and the formation of the working class as, in Marx's terms, a class-in-itself (Thompson 1963; Katznelson and Zolberg 1986). Workers' gains in creating industrial unions and in achieving a political voice in the form of labor, social democratic, or democratic socialist political parties tended over time to mute the demand for revolution, the result being the institutionalization of parliamentary socialism. One can say that the incorporation of the working class into the British polity was completed with the electoral successes that elevated Ramsay MacDonald to prime minister in 1923 (Miliband 1964). At the same time on the Continent, according to Wolfgang Abendroth (1972: 86), "the social democratic parties represented the majority of the working class in the major European countries."

In the case of the United States, although militant challenges to capitalism – seen in such organizations as the Knights of Labor and the Industrial Workers of the World – were evident, for a variety of reasons that often fall under the rubric of "American exceptionalism," the pattern of development differed in some respects from that of Europe (Lipset and Marks 2000). For one thing, the ethnic and racial heterogeneity of the working class made difficult the development of class-consciousness, and thus America's working-class formation has a distinctive quality to it. The frontier served as a kind of safety valve, as disgruntled workers could seek to improve their circumstances by simply leaving one locale for another further west (often with the goal of landownership in mind). In addition, the class structure exhibited considerable fluidity. Moreover, the productivity of capitalism meant that over time the economic condition of the working class improved, so that by as early as 1906 Werner Sombart (1976: 119) could write that, "All socialist utopias came to nothing on roast beef and apple pie."

Perhaps the most fundamental difference between the European and American working classes was that in the case of the latter, the realms of worker and citizen were held to be distinct (Bodnar 1985; Katznelson and Zolberg 1986). In short, in a relatively brief period, the white male working class was incorporated into the political system. Lenin (n.d.: 51) attributed the general lack of revolutionary fervor among the American working class in part to the fact that there was an "absence of any big, nation-wide democratic tasks facing the proletariat." Put another way, American workers, having overcome property-right restrictions to citizenship at a relatively early point in the nineteenth century, came to distinguish their adversarial relationship with capitalism from their political involvements. After the last wave of union militancy on the part of the newly formed Congress of Industrial Organizations (CIO), no sector of the union movement sought a socialist alternative to capitalism. Rather, it represented the model of what Lenin disparagingly called "bread-and-butter trade union-ism." What this meant was that labor became an interest group – one among many. The purpose of organized labor was to seek to improve the lot of the working class. In many respects, workers assessed their situation by whether or not they experienced improvements in wages and fringe benefits, job security, and opportunities for home ownership. By the middle of the twentieth century, the historic compromise between capital and labor had created a situation where the working class was increasingly able to aspire to a middle-class lifestyle.

The United States was not qualitatively different from other advanced industrial societies in this regard. Thus, post-World War II sociologists elsewhere point to the rise of what Goldthorpe and his colleagues (1968) called the "affluent worker," while others signaled changes in the class structure that served to undermine working-class solidarity (Giddens 1973). If socialism failed early in the United States (Lipset and Marks 2000), rather than viewing this fact in terms of a presumed American exceptionalism, Lipset and Hausser (2001) have argued that what we are witnessing is the "Americanization of the European left." This is clearly evident in Tony Blair's New Labour, but it can be seen in somewhat less assertive form on the Continent as well. One way of explaining the decline of labor militancy is to point to the fact that citizenship has become a sufficiently powerful aspect of personal identity that it serves to militate against a militant anti-capitalist working-class identity. While this is clearly not the whole story, to the extent that this is the case it suggests that inclusion came at a price, one that workers are paying for in the era of neoliberal economic globalization as the weakness of the labor movement becomes increasingly evident.

The point of this discussion is that the working classes in the various industrializing nations of the nineteenth and early twentieth centuries became incorporated into the ranks of the citizenry, and insofar as they did, they came to share the political and civil rights previously monopolized by the more privileged classes. While the level of struggle and the intensity of opposition to incorporation differed by country, and thus the process occurred faster in some places and slower in others, nonetheless, by the end of the third decade of the twentieth century it had been completed.

There is one other aspect of this process of inclusion that needs mention. It is that white workingmen fighting for inclusion were prepared to prevent, or at least not support, the quest for inclusion of women and racial minorities. Much of the rhetoric and imagery employed by the working-class movement was decidedly masculine. Thus, in discussing the French working class near the end of the nineteenth century, Michelle Perrot (1986: 99) observed that working-class symbols were primarily "represented by the barrel-chested male worker with broad shoulders, swollen biceps, and powerful muscles," going on to note that this tendency was "by no means specifically French." Although the labor movement contained progressive elements that linked workers' and women's issues, there was considerable resistance to such efforts. In many respects, male members of the working class were as prepared as their middle- and upper-class counterparts to view women as appropriately located in the private sphere. The key concept here is the idea of independence. If citizenship was pivotal to achieving independence, and if by nature some categories of people – such as women – were incapable of independence, then it followed that they ought not to be granted citizenship status.

This was the logic that the white working class employed in its reaction to racial minorities. Given its legacy of slavery, this was especially apparent in the United States. With the abolition of property-ownership requirements in 1834, white American workers achieved citizenship rights. This occurred earlier for them than for their European counterparts (though some nations were not far behind; French male workers, for example, obtained the right to vote in 1848). The result, according to Judith Shklar (1991: 46), was that, "Like their enfranchised predecessors, they too now did not want to admit others to citizenship. The fear of being robbed and displaced by the social outsider came to haunt them too. It was an anxiety that was as impervious to solid, empirically grounded arguments as it was to moral reproof." This claim is reinforced by the work of contemporary labor historians, such as David Roediger (1991, 2005), who argue that the fear of economic competition alone cannot account adequately for white working-class racism; rather, racist ideology served various psychological needs that included but also transcended the quest for economic security. When turning to gender and race, it is not surprising that different historical inclusionary trajectories are evident, trajectories that continue to have an impact in the twenty-first century.

Women and the public sphere

In the early history of citizenship, women were excluded from the Greek *polis*. This exclusion would be a persistent feature of modern citizenship regimes until the twentieth century – in some instances until well into the century. Women, in short, waited considerably longer than the members of the white working class to obtain the franchise and to otherwise begin to be able to participate in the political arena on equal terms with their male counterparts (Pateman 1988; Lister 1997); this despite the fact that going back as far as the early phase of the French Revolution, the matter of women's suffrage was part of the larger political debates of the era. Women mobilized by creating political clubs that served as a vehicle for pressing their case in the court of public opinion. Their failure is illustrative of what happened elsewhere, although the French case is unique insofar as women did not win the right to vote until the aftermath of World War II in 1944–5.

Olwen Hufton (1992) has depicted what happened in France in terms of the construction of a rigid divide between the public and private spheres that was predicated on traditional notions of women's roles. Within this framework, it was possible to argue that women should be granted a variety of civil rights, including property rights such as rights of inheritance equal to those of men. This is because such rights pertained to women's place in the private realm. At the same time, women could appropriately be denied entrée to the public arena, which meant that their demands for the franchise could be rejected. Such a position became enshrined in the Constitution of 1791.

Women's clubs were suppressed in the wake of the Revolution. However, the women's movement resurfaced periodically and was particularly evident during periods of rapid social change. Thus, the demand for women's suffrage was again pressed in 1848. Although universal manhood suffrage was instituted at this time, women were again denied political rights. The same result played out in the rise and fall of the Paris Commune. How can one account for what Karen Offen (1997: 125) has called the "astonishing backwardness of a nation whose leaders portrayed it as the vanguard of civilization?" Offen's answer is that women ultimately could not count on the support of radical republicans committed to a secular state, precisely the sector of the political spectrum where one might have assumed their support to lie. While the forces of the political right – monarchists, the Roman Catholic Church, and other traditionalists – would be expected to oppose women's demands, why did the left fail women? Offen (1997: 132) contends that the opposition was based on radical republicans' "deep fear that enfranchised women would vote for the Catholic/right-wing ticket and thereby undermine the secular republic." In other words, they presumed women to be inherently traditional in their cultural outlook and therefore, so they thought, reactionary in their politics.

Although the movement for women's suffrage played out somewhat differently in each nation based on differing cultural conditions and socio-historical circumstances, nonetheless there was a similarity across cases insofar as in each instance the task of movement activists was to challenge the way that the private/public divide had isolated and constricted women to the domestic sphere. Not only did men need to be convinced of the injustice of such a divide, but so did many women. Indeed, the radical republicans in France were not entirely incorrect about the potential voting proclivities of many women should they obtain the franchise.

The resistance of women to the suffrage cause involved more than deeply conservative women. This fact was evident in what is generally seen as the starting point of the women's rights movement in the United States, the Seneca Falls Convention of 1848. A wide range of issues was addressed at this watershed event, including economic and legal issues such as those related to inheritance rights and occupational opportunities, educational opportunities, and gender roles within the family. Thus, the matter of political disenfranchisement was but one of a number of topics on the agenda. Moreover, as Steven Buechler (1990: 93) points out, it "generated substantial opposition . . . and the resolution demanding the ballot barely passed . . .". He goes on to point out that the reason that suffrage was seen as a quite different matter than the other issues preoccupying the assembled delegates was that it "was a reflection of the link between voting and independence." In other words, the demand for the vote, more than any other issue, got at the core of women's traditional dependent status and with it the presumption of the naturalness and rightness of male authority.

Despite these misgivings, the suffrage cause would become a persistent feature of late nineteenth-century and early twentieth-century American politics. Albeit slowly, the movement gained steam during this period, reflected in the introduction of a proposed constitutional amendment to the US Congress in 1878 and, beginning with Wyoming in 1890, the passage of state laws granting women the right to vote in state and local elections. The proposed amendment was overwhelmingly defeated. Although the vote was more favorable when reintroduced in 1914, it too failed to get anywhere near the required two-thirds majority. However, the situation changed quickly in the aftermath of World War I as both major political parties endorsed a constitutional amendment designed to grant women the right to vote. The measure passed both houses of Congress and shortly thereafter received the necessary two-thirds ratification by the individual states. Thus, the Nineteenth Amendment to the Constitution took effect in 1920 (Flexnor and Fitzpatrick 1996).

Although women's suffrage succeeded in the United States a quarter of a century earlier than in France, it, too, was a follower rather than a leader. In fact, the suffrage movement was a global campaign, at least in the world's liberal democracies. The first nation to grant women the right to vote was New Zealand, in 1893, followed by Australia in 1902. Canadian women won the right to vote two years earlier than their neighbors to the south. Meanwhile in Europe, the Scandinavian nations led the way, with Finland being the first European nation to legalize women's voting rights in 1906, followed by Sweden (1909), Norway (1913), and Denmark and Iceland (1915). World War I proved to be a significant turning point as a number of countries in addition to the United States passed universal suffrage legislation, including Britain, Ireland, the Netherlands, Germany, Austria, Hungary, Poland, and Czechoslovakia. Spain followed somewhat later, in 1931, during the era of republican rule. Similarly, in the aftermath of World War II a new wave of universal suffrage laws were passed. In addition to France, nations passing such legislation during the immediate postwar years included Italy, Belgium, and Greece. The US-drafted constitution of Japan also established women's voting rights. Of the remaining nations that had not passed such legislation, Portugal did in 1976 after it emerged from the long dictatorship of the Salazar regime. An anomaly in this regard is Switzerland, often regarded as a bastion of democracy. Women did not finally acquire the right to vote in all of the nation's cantons until 1990.

Although at present it would appear that, even in those cases where women won the right to vote relatively recently, the matter is now a closed book, in fact the right to vote constituted only an aspect of what is involved in political citizenship. In virtually all of the advanced industrial liberal democracies women remain significantly underrepresented in the ranks of elected officials and government ministers. Again, in the advanced industrial liberal democratic nations, the Scandinavian countries have taken the lead. Thus, in Sweden 45 percent of parliamentarians are women, while the figure is 38 percent in Denmark, 38 percent in Finland, 36 percent in Norway, and 30 percent in Iceland. Other nations with figures exceeding 30 percent include the Netherlands and New Zealand, while those between 20 and 30 percent include Germany, Spain, Switzerland, and Canada. The percentage of women in the US Congress currently is 14 percent. This is similar to the percentage of women in Australia's parliament, exceeding that of the United Kingdom, which hovers around 10 percent (www.ipu. org/press-e/gen62). What these figures reflect is the fact that although women have won the right to vote, they are far from achieving parity in terms of levels of active participation in political life.

There is another area where women's access to citizenship rights was historically circumscribed by the character of naturalization laws. This had to do with marital status. In an effort to prevent dual citizenships (the focus of Chapter 5), in the past a woman who married a citizen of another country typically lost her original citizenship and attained that of her husband. One of the rationales for such an approach to citizenship was that it insured that the children born into such families were citizens of only one nation and did not become dual citizens. The push for women's equality served to challenge this particular approach to citizenship assignment, viewing it as an expression of the dependency of women on the citizenship status of their spouses. Most liberal democracies have eliminated this feature of their citizenship laws, including the United States in 1932, Sweden in 1950, Denmark in 1951, Portugal in 1959, Italy in 1983, Belgium in 1984, Greece in 1984, and Israel as recently as 1996 (Weil 2001: 28; Spiro 2002: 20).

The racial divide and democratic citizenship

Standing alongside gender, race was the other limitation inscribed on the universalistic values of Enlightenment thinkers. This was evident in the varied social constructions of nation-specific definitions of citizenship during the eighteenth and nineteenth centuries. Although there was a universal character to citizenship status for all who possessed it, the general tendency was to deny membership to certain categories of people not only based on certain moral defects or defects of character (criminals and the insane), but on the ascribed identities of race and gender. Thus, the universal citizen was invariably a circumscribed identity insofar as it was only available to white males. As Evelyn Nakano Glenn (2002: 21) has pointed out, the argument for constructing this boundary rested to a large extent on the public–private and the independent–dependent dichotomies. As was indicated above, both loomed large in the rationales for the exclusion of women from the ranks of citizens. In the case of race, the public–private was less evident, while the idea of independence–dependence was central.

This could be seen in countries such as Germany that historically operated with a *jus sanguinis*, or, in other words, an ethnoracial conception of national identity. One could only be German if one's ancestors were German, and thus becoming German via naturalization was not possible. Underpinning this exclusionary policy was the racist belief that various non-German ethnic groups were incapable of the independence required of citizens. While useful as manual laborers, they were not capable of participating in collective self-rule. Such a conception shaped Germany from the founding of the modern state in 1871 until a new citizenship law – the most liberal in Europe – was passed in 1999, thereby ending one of Europe's most exclusionary citizenship policies (Kivisto 2002: 169). While in effect, the previous law prevented those who entered Germany due to labor shortages from becoming citizens, whether they be Slavs working in East German agriculture during the late nineteenth century and early twentieth century or Turks and Yugoslavs doing the nation's dirty, difficult, and dangerous work during the second half of the twentieth century. Germany was clearly not alone among the ethnonational civic regimes, but it did serve as a paradigmatic instance of this particular type.

One can find a parallel resistance to inclusionary policies via the granting of citizenship to those heretofore ineligible in other societies that did not embrace an explicitly ethnonational definition of national identity – or in other words in those nations that have been characterized as defining nationalism in civic rather than ethnic terms. For example, although the republican ideals of France ought to have made that nation far more open to absorbing diverse peoples into its ranks, provided they embraced the ideals of the republic, in practice France's civic nationalism was far from universal in its willingness to accept the racial other. One could see a similar racial exclusion in operation in settler societies. Australia, due to its status as part of the British Empire, at first viewed those eligible for citizenship as being limited only to British subjects. This was transformed into a "whites only" policy until the 1960s, after which time the nation became more receptive to redefining who was eligible for citizenship. Henceforth, the battle pitting those advocating an open society versus those promoting a restrictive version of national identity increasingly took place over immigration policy (Pearson 2001; Kivisto 2002: 109–12). In the end, labor shortages became sufficiently acute that economic considerations won out over the demands of cultural conservatives to preserve the nation's British character or at least to insure that new settlers were white (Pearson 2002: 996). Coincident with changes in naturalization policies regarding immigrants was a change in the relationship of the state to aboriginal peoples who had long been excluded from citizenship. Treated as wards of the state from the nineteenth century well into the twentieth, gradually over time some Aboriginals were permitted to seek naturalization. It was not until the 1948 National and Citizenship Act that all Aboriginals were to be defined as citizens, and only after a referendum held in 1967 did they receive the right to vote in federal elections.

Thus, racial exclusion shaped citizenship regimes widely. However, nowhere was its impact more consequential than in the United States, and for that reason this particular case is of unique importance in understanding racial exclusion; and therefore we concentrate on it in the following section. Judith Shklar (1991) is not alone in arguing that the existence of chattel slavery in a presumably democratic nation more than anything else shaped the ways Americans thought about race and racial exclusion. Shklar writes that she had not "forgotten how ungenerous and bigoted immigration and naturalization policies have often been, but [she argues] their effects and defects pale before the history of slavery and its impact upon our public attitudes" (Shklar 1991: 14). Indeed, the way that blacks were defined vis-à-vis the issue of citizenship served to frame the way that other groups defined as racially distinct were located in the scheme of things, as will be seen below in surveying the history of immigrant groups seeking citizenship.

Between independence and the immediate aftermath of the Civil War, the United States operated with a rather ill-defined conception of national independence. The states possessed considerable latitude in determining both who was and who was not eligible for citizenship, but also in defining the precise rights accruing to citizens. However, the Constitution did divide the nation's population into three categories: those defined as "the people," who were presumably candidates for citizenship; Indians, who were viewed as permanent aliens residing within the nation because they were members of tribal governments that had relations to the United States similar to the relations with foreign nations; and finally "others" referred to black slaves. In this scenario, Indians as members of various tribes and black slaves were treated as ineligible to become citizens (Ringer 1983).

However, there were ambiguities contained in this formulation, not the least of which had to do with the status of free people of color. Particularly in the wake of the American Revolution, when, as Bernard Bailyn (1967: 60) put it, a "contagion of liberty" swept the new republic, free blacks pressed for the right to become citizens. Glenn (2002: 32–3) has described their situation during the latter part of the eighteenth century as follows:

> More generally, blacks, especially free blacks, had fewer explicit restrictions on their rights at the beginning of the [nineteenth] century than by mid-century. Indeed, there was a brief period after the Revolution when some blacks were able to realize in a small way the status and rights of citizens.

> Blacks themselves had seized the initiative during the Revolution, taking advantage of the upheaval to escape from bondage. . . . In sum, though far from enjoying equality, for the first quarter-century after the Revolution free blacks were conceded to be citizens of a sort, and in many states could vote on the same terms as whites.

In other words, during this period, an extremely small minority of blacks, who were not only free people of color but also owned property, managed to achieve a second-class version of citizenship. But, as Glenn noted, even this limited access to citizenship eroded as the nation got closer to the Civil War. It was only in the aftermath of the war that blacks were formally accorded the rights to citizenship. In 1865, the passage of the Thirteenth Amendment to the Constitution abolished slavery, while in the following year the Fourteenth Amendment granted citizenship to all blacks and required equal treatment of all citizens under both federal and state laws, and the Fifteenth Amendment forbade denying the right to vote on the basis of race.

In the short-lived Reconstruction period, African Americans vigorously asserted their new political status. In the first place, they voted. But more than going to the polls, they entered the political process by running for office at the local, state, and federal levels. Numerous blacks were elected to various prominent positions, serving in various southern states as lieu-tenant governors, secretaries of state, state treasurers, and related high-ranking positions, while at the national level blacks were elected members of both the House of Representatives and the Senate (Foner 1988).

However, by the mid-1870s the federal government withdrew from its active engagement in the reconstruction of the South (where over 90 percent of blacks resided), thereby allowing whites in the region to reassert their supremacy. Emerging in the latter part of the nineteenth century and extending until the civil rights movement succeeded in dismantling it in the 1960s, this new era of white supremacy was known as the Jim Crow era. It involved two interrelated features: domination and segregation. There is a debate among scholars about whether the laws passed in the southern states merely codified the existing pattern of race relations or amounted to a significant structural change (Glenn 2002: 113; see also Fredrickson 1995; Glenn 2000).

Whatever the case, the result was the perpetuation of a caste system within a class society. While the impact of Jim Crow laws operated at all levels – cultural, economic, and political – we look here solely at the politi-cal consequences. More specifically, we concentrate on the formal aspects of inclusion/exclusion. Opposed to the political power of blacks, yet because of the Fifteenth Amendment unable to simply legally prohibit all blacks from voting, states sought to employ a variety of criteria whose sole purpose was to disenfranchise blacks. The two most widely used means for accomplishing this task were literacy tests and the poll tax.

The legislated basis of white supremacy was everywhere and in all instances backed up by the threat of extra-legal violence at the hands of a number of terrorist organizations, the most prominent and long-lived being the Ku Klux Klan. Lynching became a pervasive feature of southern life, serving as a constant form of intimidation of blacks. Although precise figures on the actual number of lynchings do not exist, one reliable source, the Tuskegee Institute, reported that 4,730 people were lynched between 1882 and the dawn of the civil rights movement in 1951. Another type of collective violence directed against blacks was the riot, whereby whites attacked blacks and their property – often burning homes and businesses to the ground (Olzak 1992; Litwack 1998: 284–98; Glenn 2002: 109–10). The peak of much of this activity occurred between 1890 and 1920, and the intended results were achieved. The percentage of blacks that were eligible to vote declined dramatically throughout the South. Thus, by the first decade of the twentieth century only 6 percent of blacks could vote in Mississippi, while the figures were 4 percent in Georgia and 1 percent in Louisiana (Glenn 2002: 112).

When blacks began to migrate to the North, beginning around World War I and again during and after World War II, they did so not only for economic reasons, but for political reasons as well. In effect, when they moved to what for a short time they called the Promised Land (until they discovered the northern version of racism), they were both economic migrants and political refugees. This situation would characterize the situation for blacks until the 1960s (Lemann 1992).

The civil rights movement constituted a watershed moment in the history of black–white relations. In particular, the passage of the Voting Rights Act of 1965 signaled a new effort on the part of the federal government to insure that blacks in the South would no longer be denied the franchise. At the same time, there are vestiges of efforts aimed at disenfranchisement. For example, in the post-Civil War period a number of laws were passed in southern states that denied the vote to convicted felons for life. Given that blacks were disproportionately imprisoned, the intent of such legislation was the same as that of literacy tests and poll taxes. Unlike these latter two, the laws directed at felons remain on the books in several states a half century after the civil rights movement. It is estimated that currently as many as 4 million ex-felons are barred for life from voting, and blacks are disproportionately represented among their ranks (Abramsky 2000).

Other people of color confronted barriers to inclusion. Thus, because they continued to be viewed as members of alien tribal nations, Native Americans did not acquire the right to citizenship until passage of the Indian Citizenship Act in 1924. However, the majority of nonblack people of color were immigrants, and for that reason the barriers they confronted were shaped chiefly by immigration and naturalization laws. Actually, as we shall see below, the phrase "people of color," a contemporary expression, can be ironically applied to immigrants from the late nineteenth and early twentieth centuries whose progeny have over the passage of time "become white" (Roediger 1991). At issue in a nation that was resource rich but population poor was that newcomers were needed because the demand for labor in an industrial economy could not be met by the native-born alone. At the same time, there was intense opposition to the entry of certain groups of people into the country, or, if they were to be admitted as temporary workers, nativists were adamant in their opposition to granting members of these groups citizenship.

Daniel Tichenor (2002) has pointed out that four collective actors have historically shaped immigration and naturalization policies. Two have favored liberal laws and two have historically supported restrictive ones. Promoters of a liberal approach include business interests seeking labor recruits and cultural cosmopolitans. The former often preferred open immigration laws but were not necessarily in favor of liberal naturalization laws, while the latter sought both liberal immigration and naturalization laws. Those embracing restrictive laws across the board included organized labor opposed to what they perceived to be a competitive threat by foreign workers who were presumed to undercut existing wage levels, and cultural conservatives who raised concerns about the presumed threat posed by newcomers to cultural values and societal cohesion. What has made coalitions among natural allies over this issue vexing is that business and cultural conservatives tend to be aligned with the Republican Party, while labor and cultural cosmopolitans tend to be Democratic Party stalwarts. Thus, effective coalitions required cross-party alliances. This situation shaped the politics of immigration control from the nineteenth century until very recently, when organized labor (though not necessarily the rank and file) has changed its stance and become an active advocate of new immigrants, whom they see as key to union growth.

In terms of immigration control, Asians were singled out earliest. More specifically, with the passage of the Chinese Exclusion Act of 1882, the Chinese were the first group to be denied admission to the United States. The Gentleman's Agreement of 1907 was designed to place strict limits on the number of Japanese that could enter the country. However, this was merely the beginning of a far more aggressive campaign of immigration restriction that arose during a period of unprecedented immigration.

Asians were not alone in being singled out, as increased attention was directed at the larger components of the new immigrants who originated from nations in Southern and Eastern Europe. As a variety of piecemeal laws passed around the turn of the century attests, nativists feared the newcomers for a variety of reasons. They were seen as a threat to the culture, advocates of political radicalism, morally and intellectually inferior, inclined to pauperism, and bearers of disease (Higham 1955; Daniels 2004: 27–58). The zenith of opposition to mass immigration occurred with the passage of the National Origins Act in 1924, which set admission quotas of 2 percent of the number of persons of a nationality as reflected in the 1890 census. In so doing, the law was intentionally structured along lines that privileged Western and Northern Europeans at the expense of other groups. The result was, in effect, to end mass immigration to the nation for the next four decades.

Naturalization laws likewise were shaped along racial lines. The earliest law, the Naturalization Act of 1790, defined those persons eligible to become citizens through a process of naturalization as limited to "free white persons" (Glenn 2002: 24). In the wake of the Civil War and the passage of the Fourteenth Amendment, the definition of who qualified for naturalization was redefined to include in addition to free persons of color, "persons of African nativity or African decent." Subsequently, as Stanford Lyman (1993a: 380) notes, both the Chinese and Japanese were denied the right to become citizens. Such would be the case for the Chinese from 1882 until 1943, when the exigencies of a world war would prompt the government to permit its Chinese ally's residents in the United States to naturalize. In the case of the Japanese, this would not occur until 1952, well after the cessation of hostilities.

Within this framework, where whites and blacks could naturalize but the two main immigrant groups from Asia could not, members of many groups found themselves located in an ambiguous situation. The law called for discerning what it meant to be nonwhite but not black. Actually, a number of both Chinese and Japanese immigrants raised this question in the courts. Thus in 1878 a Chinese immigrant, Ah Yup, who was identified in the court brief as a member of the Mongolian race, petitioned to become a citizen. His petition was rejected. The rationale offered by the court was that neither "in popular language, in literature, nor in scientific nomenclature, do we ordinarily, if ever, find the words 'white person' used in a sense so comprehensive as to include an individual of the Mongolian race" (quoted in Lyman 1991: 204; see also Lyman 1993b). In a 1922 Supreme Court case, a Japanese immigrant named Takao Ozawa claimed that anthropological evidence indicated that the Japanese were Caucasian and thus they ought to be considered eligible for citizenship. His argument, too, was rejected (Lyman 1991: 206–8).

This set the stage for numerous other groups to seek to be declared white in order to be accepted into the "white republic" (Saxton 1990). Thus, as Lyman (1991) has chronicled, among the groups declared ineligible for citizenship were the Burmese, Koreans, Hawaiians, Arabs, and East

Indians, while others such as Armenians and Syrians were declared to be white and therefore were permitted to become naturalized citizens. Race as it was deployed in some of these cases was linked to religion (thus, the designation "Hindoo" contained both religious and racial connotations) or politics. One of the more interesting instances of the latter occurred when 16 Finnish immigrants in northern Minnesota were denied their first citizenship papers on the grounds that Finns were Mongolians. This rejection took place in 1908, in the immediate aftermath of a bitter strike by iron miners on the Mesabi Range. The Finns singled out in this way were all activists in the Finnish Socialist Federation, and thus their involvement in what was described in court papers as an "East Asian philosophy" was meant to imply that their political views were reflective of their racial origins. This was a somewhat hard sell given that there was a growing sentiment at the time that European-origin immigrants were white. In fact, the case was soon thereafter thrown out, with the District Court judge concluding that although the ancient Finns had indeed been Mongols, nonetheless they had over the course of history mixed sufficiently with Teutonic peoples to be considered white (Kivisto 1984: 128).

Over the course of the twentieth century scientific racism progressively lost influence, with World War II serving as a watershed. The Nazi experience gave what was once respectable a bad name. However, this did not mean that racism simply evaporated; rather it persisted, albeit it in different guises. Thus, the Immigration and Naturalization Act of 1952 not only reaffirmed the national quota system of the 1924 National Origins Act but added new reasons for exclusion based on political ideology and sexual orientation. At the same time, the Jim Crow system, despite challenges, remained intact. It took a powerful civil rights movement in the 1950s and 1960s to finally dismantle that racial formation (McAdam 1982; Morris 1984; Omi and Winant 1986).

As the nation entered into the post-civil rights era, race and class began to intersect in new ways, making possible the expansion of a black middle class no longer rooted in the segregated black community. At the same time, however, it left behind in those communities the poor, or what William Julius Wilson (1987) described as "the truly disadvantaged." Thus, while one sector of black America came to acquire the various forms of capital – financial, social, and human – that permitted civic involvements as something other than second-class citizens, the other sector remained marginalized. High levels of persistent inequality intruded on their prospects of casting off the exclusionary legacy of Jim Crow. The concerted efforts to remove black voters from the rolls in Florida and elsewhere during the 2000 and 2004 presidential elections testifies to the fact that, four decades into the post-civil rights era, what Paul Sniderman and Thomas Piazza (1993) call "the scar of race" has not healed – cosmetic surgery notwithstanding.

It was in the heat of the civil rights struggle that a new immigration law, the Hart-Celler Act (1965), was passed (Schneider 2001). Its liberal sponsors sought to end the racist character of existing law by abolishing the national quotas system. Although its sponsors downplayed the significance of the law, and in particular its potential for creating a new period of mass migration, it is quite clear that the law was intended to open the nation's doors once again. In this it succeeded; indeed, the USA is now in a migratory wave that is having as significant an impact on American society as the earlier major wave from 1880 to 1930. Tichenor (2002: 217) summarizes the climate in which Hart-Celler was passed as follows:

> Tellingly, the demise of the national origins quota system came only at the zenith of the Great Society, when an extraordinary convergence of pro-immigration developments propelled an opening of the gates. In the final analysis, the expansive turn of national immigration policy in 1965 sprang from a familiar set of order-shattering forces: new international pressures, shifting group alliances, fresh expertise, and institutional change.

Some scholars (Freeman 1995; Joppke 2005) argue that this is part of a larger pattern in the world's liberal democracies, wherein the use of universal criteria for the terms of inclusion becomes an irreversible norm. We are more inclined to agree with Brubaker (1995) that there is no guarantee that such trends are historically contingent and potentially subject to reversal. That being said, at the moment, in terms of the ethnic composition of the nation, the consequence of the current migratory wave is that the Latino and Asian populations have grown significantly. Indeed, as the 2000 census revealed, Latinos now outnumber blacks. The nation is now considerably more diverse – ethnically, religiously, and linguistically – than it was in 1965. This has alarmed contemporary nativists. Thus, Samuel Huntington (2004: 181, 184) argues:

> In the contemporary world, the greatest threat to the societal security of nations comes from immigration. . . . Historically America has thus been a nation of immigration *and* assimilation, and assimilation has meant Americanization. Now, however, immigrants are different; the institutions and processes related to assimilation are different; and, most importantly, America is different. The great American success story may face an uncertain future.

This contention finds its counterpart elsewhere, though formulated somewhat differently based on differing historical experiences and understandings of nationalism and national identity. As we shall argue in the following section, this represents a serious misreading of present realities: it misrepresents the immigrants themselves (and one might add that it also misrepresents other minority groups – including ethnonational minorities and indigenous peoples), and it misinterprets the ways that contemporary liberal democracies are experimenting with novel modes of incorporating diversity (Kivisto 2005). In particular, it misconstrues multiculturalism. It is to this topic that we now turn. What follows is predicated on the conviction that modern industrial nations have until recently relied on a limited number of modes of incorporating heretofore marginalized groups that have tended to rely on the expectation that incorporation occurs at the individual, and not at the group level. Multiculturalism, in both practice and theory, is a recent mode of incorporation that challenges this assumption. In the process, it informs current discourses on the relationship between inclusion and citizenship.

It should be noted that this discussion of inclusion has concentrated on its formal aspect. But formal inclusion can entail the potential for creating societal solidarity based on egalitarian principles or it can lack such a commitment. Or, as Jeffrey Alexander (2005: 97) would frame it, what is at stake is whether or not the society in question promotes inclusion *and* justice. Although formal inclusion is a prerequisite for being in a position to have a voice in shaping the character of and relationship between the rights and duties of citizenship, it is no guarantee that the outsider enters into a just society as a genuine equal to those already on the inside. Rather, the terms of inclusion are crucial to determining whether this is the case, and it is with this in mind that the relevance of the following discussion of multiculturalism ought to be understood.

MULTICULTURALISM AS A MODE OF INCLUSION

Multiculturalism has generated during the past two decades a veritable cottage industry of scholarly and popular publications, primarily but not solely focusing on the advanced industrial nations of the globe. It has been widely used in various ways during this time, including in the depiction of interethnic relations, the defense of group rights, as a valorization of difference, and as a rationale for new state policies of incorporation. It has also generated intense ideological debates. Not long ago Nathan Glazer (1997) proclaimed that "we are all multiculturalists now," and others have argued that however fitfully and fraught with conflict and unease, the world's liberal democracies have imbibed what might be seen as a multicultural sensibility, even if it has not been translated into official policies or explicit endorsements of multiculturalism (Favell 1998; Modood 2001; Pearson 2001; Kivisto 2002; Joppke and Morawska 2003; Kymlicka 2003). However, even more recently this view has been challenged by those who contend that the multicultural moment is over as state policy, social practice, and perhaps as theoretical construct as well (Delanty 2000: 104; see also Barry 2001; Kelly 2002; Wolfe 2003; Joppke 2005).

Part of the reason for the widely divergent assessments of the short history and potential future of multiculturalism, as well as why it has been a flashpoint of political contestation, is that the word is often used with widely disparate meanings (Wieviorka 1998; Delanty 2000: 102–6; Delgado-Moreira 2000: 75–102; Joppke 2001; Sciortino 2003; Tiryakian 2004). In its typical articulation, it is generally presented in a fashion that manages to blend or blur its utility as an analytic concept with its expression as a normative precept. David Pearson (2001: 129) also noted the significance of context in coming to terms with the particular meaning attached to this "highly contested and chameleon-like neologism whose colours change to suit the complexion of local conditions." This is evident in a cursory glance at the major sites where multiculturalism as social policy or as a social sensibility has emerged as a significant factor. We turn to an examination of multiculturalism in practice in the four liberal democracies that, it can be argued (Kivisto 2002), represent the four nations most open to multiculturalism: Canada, Australia, the United States, and the United Kingdom (actually, one could add New Zealand to this list, though we won't examine this smaller nation below).

Multiculturalism as practice and social policy

It is generally agreed that the first nation to sketch out the contours of what has come to be defined as multiculturalism is Canada. In part, multiculturalism was conceived as an alternative to the assimilationist model of the United States. Multiculturalism's ideological roots are located in the popular understanding of the nation as a mosaic – with the idea of an identity based on discrete tiles constituting the constituent parts of a national portrait – rather than a melting pot (Porter 1965; Kymlicka 1998; Kivisto 2002: 85–101). The underlying historical context involved policy efforts on the part of the Canadian government to respond to an increasingly restive and militant Québecois nationalist movement.

Canadian national identity has historically been defined in terms of the distinctive identities of the nation's two "charter groups," the English and the French. According to Gilles Bourque and Jules Duchastel (1999: 185), the bifurcated model "made very poor use of the concept of nation; rather, it focused on the idea of a *community* of citizens," which contained an understanding of a shared system of universal entitlements brought about by the welfare state. However, the bifurcation was based on an asymmetrical relationship whereby the Anglophone community occupied a superordinate position vis-à-vis the Francophone community. This was the context in which the mobilization of the Francophone community began, with a movement of civil rights (influenced by the American model) known as the Quiet Revolution, which was quickly transformed into a more militant movement that called for the independence of Quebec. The left-of-center Canadian government reacted to this incipient ethnonationalist movement by promoting a policy of biculturalism. This included downplaying the hegemony of British influence in various symbolic forms, such as changing the Canadian flag from a modified Union Jack to an innocuous maple leaf. It also involved more substantive policy initiatives aimed at elevating the status of French-Canadian culture, seen most explicitly in the inauguration of official bilingualism.

Biculturalism was, however, short-lived due to the combined impact of mobilized First Nations people and the new immigrants arriving in Canada who revitalized what had become known as the Third Force – immigrant groups other than the English and the French. The latter had until the 1960s chiefly been composed of European immigrants, including large numbers of displaced persons from Eastern Europe who arrived in the immediate aftermath of World War II. However, a new wave began to arrive from the nations of the South and they transformed the ethnic dynamics of the nation, particularly in major cities. Thus, Canada was confronted not only by an ethnonationalist movement with a separatist agenda embraced by many Francophones, but also by an aboriginal rights movement and the presence of new immigrants demanding integration policies that respected their cultural backgrounds. In short order, bicultur-alism gave way to multiculturalism, particularly under the Trudeau admin-istration (Breton 1986).

Canada became the first nation in the developed world to officially enshrine multiculturalism into its constitution, doing so in 1982. In 1988 this multicultural provision took legislative form in the Multiculturalism Act. As part of a national identity-building project, multiculturalism meant that the official stance of the Canadian government was to repudiate the earlier valorization of a homogeneous Anglophone culture in favor of a plurality of cultures. To this end, unlike the United States, Canada appeared prepared to promote ethnic group rights as well as individual rights. However, from the point of view of elected officials and government bureaucrats, the purpose of multiculturalism was not to balkanize the nation, but rather to find a new modus vivendi for achieving national unity. At its most elemental, it was intended to insure that Québecois nationalism did not result in the break-up of Canada, but beyond ethnonationalism they saw in multiculturalism a way of dealing with what the left-of-center sector of the dominant culture saw as the legitimate grievances advanced by First Nations advocates and the need to find new tools to integrate the current wave of immigrants (Harles 1997). At the same time, Patricia Wood and Gilbert Liette (2005) have argued that to some extent multiculturalism emerged as an "accidental" discourse and its implications were not carefully considered by policy makers.

Multiculturalism in practice has meant that ethnic groups are permitted to maintain aspects of their ancestral heritages, and that at times the state will play an interventionist role in protecting ethnic group claims. Such has been the case in terms of federal legislation designed to elevate the status of French as one of the nation's two official languages. Multiculturalism led to the ill-fated effort to have Quebec defined in the Meech Lake Accord as a "distinct society." On the other hand, it has provided the rationale for funding a wide range of ethnic cultural pursuits, particularly such symbolic practices as ethnic festivals and the promotion of ethnic art, music, and so forth. In the case of aboriginal peoples, it led to the creation of Nunavut, a new political jurisdiction for the Inuit carved out of the Northwest Territory.

Canada was not alone in becoming a multicultural nation. Australia, though lacking an ethnonationalist separatist movement, was similar to Canada insofar as it confronted an increasingly restive aboriginal rights movement and the impact of mass immigration, particularly the migration of nonwhites – chiefly Asians. Patterning their legislation after the Canadian model, Australia became the second, and to date only other, developed nation to establish an official multicultural policy. In doing so, it replaced a short-lived policy of integration. While there are similarities between integration and multiculturalism, there were two significant differences. First, based on the assumption that multiculturalism necessitated a reduction in racism, the government assumed a more proactive role in the protection of the rights of individual minority members than it had in the past. Second, multiculturalism meant not merely tolerating the presence of difference, but viewing the core of Australian national identity as embedded in the notion of diversity. This implied that national identity was not to be construed as fixed in the past, but rather as fluid and future-oriented. Newcomers were not simply expected to fit into an existing and essentially static society, but rather were seen not only as agents of their own lives, but as actors who could be expected to take part in the nation's ongoing process of social construction.

Stephen Castles (1997: 15) has pointed out that multiculturalism in Australia did not promote minority group rights, but rather articulated at the level of the individual rights and obligations, and thus was premised on the commitment of the individual to the nation and its legal system, along with "the acceptance of basic principles such as tolerance and equality, English as the national language and the equality of sexes." As the new

Agenda of 1997 made clear, multiculturalism was to be understood in relation to "civic duty," which is the term used to locate cultural diversity within a framework of shared values and orientations of citizens. If we accept Russel Ward's (1978) thesis, underlying this articulation of democratic citizenship and solidarity is the frontier-based myth of "mateship." Multiculturalism in the Australian version encourages cultural pluralism or diversity, accepts structural pluralism, and necessitates civic assimilation. In so doing, it represents a willingness to reformulate what mateship means in a diverse and complex modern society. As is the case in all similar nations, multiculturalism has met with resistance in some quarters of the Australian public.

Although the United States did not become an officially state-sanctioned multicultural society, due to a number of causal variables, it increasingly came to exhibit a multicultural sensibility. Like Australia, the USA did not confront an ethnonationalist challenge, but was forced to deal with an increasingly mobilized indigenous population and a major new migratory wave. What made the US case distinctive (as noted in the preceding section) was the emergence of a civil rights movement from within the black community – a movement created by the only involuntary migrants in the nation. This movement originally pressed for equality and integration, but a more militant Black Power phase would question the desirability of the latter.

Criticism of Anglo-conformity as the appropriate model of incorporation into American society grew from the 1960s onwards, when it was challenged both by newly minted white ethnics from Southern and Eastern Europe (the "unmeltable ethnics" of Michael Novak's title) and by the rise of Black Nationalism. The Red Power and Chicano movements would also play roles in critiquing it. Even without multicultural legislation, the federal government, paralleling the attitudes of the general public, was increasingly willing to tolerate and even support manifestations of symbolic ethnicity (the proactive role of the federal government became especially evident with the passage of the Ethnic Heritage Studies Act in 1972).

However, multiculturalism was not merely advanced symbolically. Rather, it took more substantive form in policies that came to constitute "the minority rights revolution," which John Skrentny (2002: 4) depicts as rising very quickly during the 1960s as a result of a congeries of "federal legislation, presidential executive orders, bureaucratic rulings, and court decisions that established nondiscrimination rights." The minority rights revolution was generally not equated with multiculturalism, though the parallels to policies elsewhere that were so designated is quite clear. A distinctive feature of these efforts, Skrentny (2002: 4) went on to note, was that they "targeted groups of Americans understood as disadvantaged but not defined by socioeconomic class."

Two particular policies stand out as being of singular importance: affirmative action and bilingual education. At least from the perspective of state intent – however difficult it is to specify state intentionality – these policies resemble those enacted in Australia insofar as the focus is on individual members of disadvantaged groups, and not on the groups themselves. Thus, the legislative purpose of affirmative action was to assist minority individuals to obtain university admission, employment slots, and business ownership opportunities through a variety of administrative devices. In other words, its purpose was defined as assisting individual upward social mobility. Likewise, the Bilingual Education Act of 1968 was conceived as assisting individual immigrants – chiefly Latinos and Asians – in making the transition from their native languages to English language proficiency. Lawmakers did not see the act as designed to protect or preserve native languages over time. Perhaps the only significant exception to this focus on minority individual rights was the gerrymandering of electoral districts to enhance the likelihood of increasing minority membership in Congress.

Turning to a nonsettler nation, during the second half of the past century Britain became a site of both ethnonationalist movements and, coincident with the collapse of empire, the mass immigration of residents from various Commonwealth nations. Regarding the former, three movements arose with differing goals and approaches to pursuing those objectives: (1) the irredentism and violence of the republicans in Northern Ireland; (2) the peaceful pursuit of greater political autonomy and perhaps independence by Scottish nationalists; and (3) the equally peaceful culturalist preservation efforts of Welsh ethnonationalists.

Regarding the latter, the initial reaction of exclusionary British politicians and citizens was that the arrival of blacks (the then blanket term for virtually all non-European immigrants) would lead to, in Enoch Powell's hyperbolic phrase, "rivers of blood." The response of the British government to ethnonationalism varied depending on the particular movement and in part on whether the Tories or Labour were in power. Dealings with the IRA (Irish Republican Army) ranged from the use of massive force to seeking a negotiated settlement, while the Scottish and Welsh nationalists were variously ignored, challenged, and accommodated (with "New Labour" they were accommodated via the policy of "devolution"). Meanwhile, the response to the new immigrants was twofold. First, highly restrictive immigration policies were enacted to stem the flow of new arrivals. Second, there was a concerted effort – grounded in the Race Relations Act and administratively promoted by the Commission for Racial Inequality and Race Relations Councils – to reduce racism and intergroup tensions (Favell 1998; Solomos 2003).

None of this was viewed explicitly in terms of advancing a multicultural agenda but, as in the USA, Britain increasingly exhibited a multicultural sensibility. In part, this was because many of the initiatives advancing multiculturalism took place in educational institutions, which had been an important site for the percolation of a multiculturalist agenda (Modood 2005a: 171). Despite the persistence of racism, the social exclusion of immigrants, and ethnic-based inequalities in socioeconomic well-being, the lead author of the Runnymede Trust study on multicultural Britain concluded that it was possible to conceive of a "relaxed and self-confident multicultural Britain with which all its citizens can identify" (Parekh 2000a: x). Indeed, the rationale for the report, *The Future of Multi-Ethnic Britain*, was to identify the chief obstacles to achieving this state and to lay out a wide range of policy initiatives concerning such topics as policing and the criminal justice system, education, the media and entertainment, health and welfare, employment, political representation, and religious pluralism. What is clear from this report is that the advocates of multiculturalism thought it possible and desirable to promote and sustain diversity while forging a shared sense of what it means to be British, at the same time being cognizant of resistance to such efforts (Modood 2005a; Parekh 2005a).

As these examples indicate, whether as official state policies or as implicit approaches to ethnic diversity, multiculturalism in practice has meant that at the same time that differences were to be not only tolerated but valorized, there was also an expectation that such an approach would serve the interests of the state insofar as it simultaneously constitutes what Jeffrey Alexander (2001) calls a "mode of incorporation." As the experiences of these and some other advanced industrial nations indicate, the logic of such an approach is predicated on the assumption that multiculturalism threatens neither the core values of liberal democratic societies nor the incorporation of ethnically marginalized groups – both "multinational" and "polyethnic" ethnics, to use Kymlicka's (1995: 17) terminology.

Charting modes of inclusion

If there is a lesson to be learned from existing practice-related formulations of multiculturalism, it is that they are designed to serve a dual purpose. On the one hand, they are a response to the demands on the part of marginalized ethnic groups for collective rather than merely individualistic solutions to exclusion, inequality, and recognition (Fraser 1996). In other words, they are responses to the claims-making efforts of mobilized groups for recognition and/or redistribution (Young 1990; Parekh 2000b; Kymlicka 2001: 152–76; Sciortino 2003). On the other hand, at least from the perspective of decision makers, policy formulators, and most of the political advocates of some version of group rights, the other objective is to bring previously marginalized groups into the societal mainstream.

Moreover, as Alexander and Smelser (1999: 14–15) observe about the USA, but which is in fact more generally applicable, "Although the radical multicultural position advocated by many spokespersons for minority groups seems to contradict [the sense of] connectivity, the actual political and social movements advocating multiculturalism consistently employ a civil-society discourse." In other words, multiculturalism in a liberal democracy constitutes a "mode of incorporation" that is characterized by a particular type of civil participation.

It should be noted that this is not the way multiculturalism is construed by many commentators. Critics of multiculturalism seldom consider the possibility that it constitutes a mode of democratic inclusion. Such critics are varied and can be found across the political spectrum, though those on the political right are more inclined to be hostile to multiculturalism both as an ideal and as social policy. The arguments of those opposed to multiculturalism fall into several broad categories. The first argument is that multiculturalism is divisive and as such threatens national unity. This was the thesis advanced by historian Arthur Schlesinger, Jr., advocate for the "vital center," in his highly influential *The Disuniting of America* (1992). Counterparts to this thesis have been advanced for other developed nations, such as Reginald Bibby's critique of Canadian multiculturalism in *Mosaic Madness* (1990). The inverse of this argument is that multiculturalism serves to ghettoize marginalized populations rather than assisting them to enter the mainstream (Bissoondath 2002; Malik 2002; Ford 2005).

Another critique of multiculturalism emanates from the political left. Although often intertwined, this critique contains two complaints. First is the charge that the differentialist focus of multiculturalism results in the erosion of the possibility of progressive alliances and coalitions. A particularly influential argument along these lines is Todd Gitlin's (1995) contention that multiculturalism has contributed to the "twilight of common dreams." This argument parallels that of Schlesinger insofar as the concern is that multiculturalism divides rather than unites – in this case dividing not the nation but the progressive political left. The second aspect of the leftist complaint against multiculturalism is that one of the unintended consequences of the promotion of a politics of recognition (Taylor 1992) is that in the process a politics of redistribution is ignored or placed on the back burner (Fraser 1995). More ominously, as Tariq Modood (2005b) has noted, some critics have concluded that terrorist attacks such as 9/11 in the United States and 7/7 in Britain are an indication of the failures of multiculturalism – and in some instances the charge has gone even further by claiming that multiculturalism itself is in part to blame for such attacks.

It is necessary to move beyond these and related polemics and to similarly move past the philosophical controversies surrounding multiculturalism in its varied forms (see, for example, Habermas 1998; Benhabib 2002;
Tully 2002; Gutmann 2003), ranging from, to use the distinction employed
by Kwame Anthony Appiah (2005: 73–9), "hard pluralism" (e.g., Iris
Marion Young and John Gray) to "soft pluralism" (e.g., Will Kymlicka and
Joseph Raz), if a convincing sociological conceptual framework for multiculturalism is to emerge. In our estimation, two such efforts at mapping
the terrain offer particularly useful guideposts: Jeffrey Alexander's (2001)
essay on modes of incorporation and Douglas Hartmann and Joseph
Gerteis's (2005) article on "mapping multiculturalism' (which builds on
Alexander's work). We turn to these two efforts in order to clarify the
connections between multiculturalism, inclusion, and citizenship.

Alexander's thesis, which is intended to offer a theoretical rejoinder
both to multiculturalism's conservative critics and to radical multiculturalists (here his exemplar is Young's *Justice and the Politics of Difference*,
1990), is structured around the centrality he accords to the civil sphere,
which is portrayed by his concept of "fragmented civil societies." "An
impartial civil sphere," he contends, "does not necessarily rest upon the
kind of undifferentiated, homogeneous, melted social values that conservatives recommend and radicals deplore." His definition of the civil sphere
locates it squarely within the parameters of a modern liberal democratic
society, as is evident in his emphasis on the individual over the group, and
on the reciprocal notions of respect and trust. Thus, Alexander (2001:
339–40) writes that this sphere:

> is organized around a particular kind of solidarity, one whose members are
> symbolically represented as independent and self-motivating persons indi-
> vidually responsible for their actions, yet also as actors who feel themselves,
> at the same time, bound by collective obligations to all the other individuals
> who compose this sphere. The existence of such a civil sphere suggests tre-
> mendous respect for individual capacities and rationality and also a highly
> idealistic and trusting understanding of the goodwill of others. For how can
> we grant a wide scope for freedom of action and expression to unknown
> others – as the democratic notion of civil society implies – if we do not, in
> principle, trust in their rationality and goodwill?

In this scenario, incorporation entails the permitting of out-group
members to move into the civil sphere. This occurs in one of two ways:
either because the core group members become convinced that the out-
group members share a "common humanity" and are thus "worthy of
respect" or because they have been required by wielders of power to act
as if this was the case (reminiscent of Merton's idea of prejudiced nondis-
criminators). Alexander (2001: 242) writes:

Incorporation points to the possibility of closing the gap between stigma-
tized categories of persons – persons whose particular identities have
been relegated to the invisibility of private life – and the utopian
promises that in principle regulate civil life, principles that imply
equality, solidarity, and respect among members of society.

He identifies three incorporation regimes, which he treats as ideal types:
assimilation, ethnic hyphenation, and multiculturalism. The first two have
had lengthy histories in the United States and elsewhere, while everywhere
multiculturalism is a historically novel mode of inclusion. By assimilation,
Alexander (2001: 243) means that individuals are admitted into the civil
sphere only when and insofar as they are willing and able to shed their
ethnic cultural heritages – in his language, replacing their "polluted pri-
mordial identities" with the "civilizing" identity of the core group. In this
scenario, there is no intercultural dialogue between the center and the
periphery. Instead, the out-group remains forever the alien "other," while
its members opt to engage in a strategy of exit in order to obtain an admission ticket to the center. Assimilation thus defined requires that the ticket
can only be purchased once the deracination of those traits associated with
the marginalized ethnic group has been accomplished.

In contrast, the ethnic hyphenation model allows for greater fluidity
insofar as it permits, to varied degrees, the maintenance of certain "pri-
mordial" features at the same time as the individual ethnic is also taking
on the cultural characteristics of the core. This type is the least developed
of the three in Alexander's formulation. Although he does not use the term,
what he has in mind is that in this model the members of the core exhibit
greater tolerance of an individual from an out-group who manifests both
out-group and core-group traits. This is an instance of hybridization, but
one that is quite different from cosmopolitanism, which treats as equals
the different cultural components that come to compose a "common collective identity" (Alexander 2001: 245). The difference is a consequence
of the fact that in the ethnic hyphenation model the hierarchy of cultural
values is maintained, with the center constituting the benchmark by which
all out-groups are evaluated. Alexander does not say so explicitly, but the
implication of this model is that, like the former, it involves individuals
exiting their group of origin. What distinguishes this from assimilation is
that these individuals are permitted to bring some of their cultural baggage
with them as they enter into the civil sphere.

Multiculturalism arose as a response to – indeed a rejection of – both
of these modes of incorporation. Alexander (2001: 246) views it as a new
mode of inclusion, one that "remains in its infancy." What differentiates
it from the other two models is that rather than individuals extirpating
themselves from their particularistic ethnic identities, those identities are

revalorized and permitted to enter the civil sphere. In the process, the separation between the private and public realms becomes increasingly blurred. Although he does not put it this way, what Alexander's argument suggests is that it is not only individuals who enter the civil sphere, but minority groups, too. The result is a more complex, fragmented, and heterogeneous civil society that makes possible the expansion of democratic participation. The result is a new relationship between the universal and the particular, which in the other two modes were seen as antithetical. In a multicultural society, "incorporation is not celebrated as inclusion but as the achievement of diversity. When universal solidarity is deepened in this way, particularity and difference become guiding themes of the day" (Alexander 2001: 246). This then makes possible a politics of difference in place of the goal in traditional politics of a unified and homogeneous core.

In their effort to map multiculturalism theoretically, Douglas Hartmann and Joseph Gerteis (2005) build on Alexander's framework, but elaborate it to identify four rather than three varieties of incorporation. They do so by considering both the social and cultural bases of societal cohesion. To use Durkheimian language, they do so by distinguishing between social integration and moral regulation. With these two dimensions in place, they constructed a two-by-two grid containing four distinct types of incorporation: assimilation, cosmopolitanism, fragmented pluralism, and interactive pluralism. From their perspective, the last three can all appropriately be considered as types of multiculturalism. Although Hartmann and Gerteis intend their model to be useful in distinguishing competing theoretical perspectives on multiculturalism rather than existing incorporation regimes, we would suggest that it sheds light on the latter, too.

Social integration – or association – occurs either via the singular interactions of autonomous individuals or through the activities of mediating groups. Moral regulation occurs as a result of the existence either of substantive moral bonds or of procedural norms. The former constitutes a "thick" form of regulation, while the latter is a "thin" form (Gregg 2003). Factored into this framework is the need to consider the respective strengths of both internal group boundaries and external boundaries that out-groups confront.

With this in mind, their view of assimilation parallels that of Alexander. This mode of incorporation stresses the individual rather than the mediating group. At the same time, it involves a thick form of regulation based on "mutual responsibilities" that connect individuals to the center while detaching them from the group. This type is possible as long as internal group boundaries are sufficiently weak to permit individuals to exit, and the boundaries of the society as a whole (read: the nation, or what Parsons would call the "societal community") are strong enough to keep members bounded and bonded to shared values. As with Alexander, Hartmann and Gerteis contend that this assimilative incorporation regime demands the absence of particularism from the civil sphere, but is generally prepared to permit it in the realm of private life. They are speaking about theories and not real-world examples of their types. However, based on their description, it would be reasonable to conclude that France is perhaps the exemplar of this particular type of society – its republican ideal being especially resistant to multiculturalism (Kivisto 2002: 170–84). That being said, as Catherine Withol de Wenden (2004: 79) has argued, "As far as France is concerned, like most democracies, the rise of claims of difference means that the republican model of integration has no other choice but to negotiate with multiculturalism" (see also Kastoryano 2002).

Cosmopolitan multiculturalism is akin to Alexander's interstitial category, ethnic hyphenation. A cosmopolitan multiculturalism is one that values diversity. As with assimilation, the individual rather than the mediating group serves as the basis of association, and therefore in this version of multiculturalism neither group rights or the constraining impact of groups over individuals is endorsed. Instead, the operative terms characterizing such a society are fluidity and hybridity as individuals exercise their ethnic options, picking and choosing which aspects of their ethnic cultures to embrace and which to discard. This occurs in a dialectical process whereby newcomers and existing core members of the civil sphere exhibit a willingness to change as a result of interacting with others. This is a society where ethnic attachments are thin and manifestations of ethnicity are typically symbolic rather than instrumental. Again, if one were to point to an existing society that most closely resembles this type, the United States or Britain could justifiably be selected.

By contrast, fragmented pluralism is depicted as being furthest removed from the assimilation model. Here the center does not hold as mediating groups take on a salience not evident in the other models. Incorporation means inclusion into group membership, or as Hartmann and Gerteis (2005: 231) put it, fragmented assimilation is "assimilation *into* group difference." This type is far removed from – and thus serves as a challenge to – Bhikhu Parekh's (2000b: 219) claim that, "Like any other society, a multicultural society needs a broadly shared culture to sustain it."

At the theoretical level, they (concurring with Alexander) depict Iris Marion Young's work as perhaps an exemplar of this perspective. They also point to Afrocentrism. However, their empirical example derived from the idea of "segmented assimilation" is problematic. They depict segmented assimilation as amounting to entry into distinctive sectors of society that both in terms of related patterns of cultural values and social interaction function in isolation from other sectors. In the first place, we think this constitutes a misreading of what Portes and others associated with the idea of an adversarial culture of the streets contend, for such scholars claim that such a culture exists in dialectical relationship and tension with the culture of "decent people." Likewise, for scholars of the new immigrants, while the civil society they enter is fragmented, there are nonetheless linkages that prevent the society's sectors from being totally isolated from each other. In short, there is no existing society among the world's liberal democratic regimes that fits this model. Indeed, to the extent that multiculturalism is a product of elite decision making – political and/or cultural elites – it is inconceivable that any elites would actively endorse or promote such societal balkanization.

The third type of multiculturalism is dubbed "interactive pluralism." Hartmann and Gerteis (2005: 231–5) consider this type to be what both Alexander and Taylor mean when they speak about multiculturalism. One might add that it also appears to be the form most closely resembling the perspective advanced by Will Kymlicka and Bhikhu Parekh (differences between these two theorists notwithstanding). Here mediating groups play a central role in defining associative patterns, but in such a society not only do group members interact with nonmembers, but the groups themselves enter into dialogue and interaction with other groups. Not only is such a society characterized by the politics of recognition, but groups, like individuals, open themselves to being influenced and changed by the very process of intergroup interaction. Interactive pluralism shares with assimilation a premium placed on substantive moral bonds as a basis of societal cohesion. It differs insofar as those bonds – indeed, the character of the core culture itself – are subject to redefinition through what Hartmann and Gerteis (2005: 232) refer to as a "democratic hermeneutics in which understanding the 'other' involves a new understanding of the self." The two nations that come closest to this version of multiculturalism are Canada and, to a somewhat lesser extent, Australia.

The virtue of these typological exercises is that they make clear, by providing some measure of analytic precision, that there is a repertoire of modes of inclusion available to the world's liberal democracies. They do not deny the possibility that states might opt for modes of exclusion, but insofar as they choose to bring former outsiders into the civil sphere, they have options about how inclusion is to occur. The options are circumscribed in part by the nature of the demands for inclusion made by outsiders. They are also shaped by larger contextual factors. Both typologies make clear the fact that assimilation remains an alternative to multiculturalism. Beyond that, Hartmann and Gerteis contend, and we concur, that multiculturalism can take more than one form. To the extent that multiculturalism characterizes any particular nation, its specific form will have implications for the ways that inclusion and justice are linked.

THE LESSON TO BE DRAWN FROM
EXISTING THEORY AND PRAXIS

As this chapter indicates, the trend throughout the world's liberal democracies has been – albeit fitfully and with periods of retrenchment – toward greater inclusiveness. Barriers to citizenship predicated on class, race, and gender have been progressively dismantled. This has not occurred in a teleological manner, but has been the result of contestation and pragmatic politics on the parts of societal elites, who have concluded that being more inclusive has often worked in their interests, and on the part of those demanding inclusion, who have been willing to forego some of their demands in the short term for a seat at the table that will permit them to continue to negotiate their proper place in the social order in the long term.

Meanwhile, the increased mobility of peoples, along with the increased political mobilization of ethnonational and indigenous groups, has led to the infusion of large numbers of newcomers into these nations – both the historic immigrant-receiving nations and those that a century ago were migrant-exporting nations. This has led to the need to address new modes of incorporation, particularly modes of incorporation that focus not solely on the individual, but also on the group. The rise of multiculturalism has been both a mode of claims making on the part of previously marginalized or disenfranchised groups and a mode of incorporation by receiving nations, be it a product of explicit state policy or not.

As we have attempted to indicate in this chapter, multiculturalism in both theory and praxis is not monochromatic, but takes various forms. The discussion of the four large liberal democracies that exhibit the greatest openness to multiculturalism suggests that, whether or not multiculturalism as a sensibility or aspiration is backed up by the explicit endorsement of the state, a multicultural mode of incorporation is not going to be easily extirpated. This is not to suggest that both intellectual and everyday challenges have disappeared. They clearly have not, and in fact have perhaps become more insistent in the wake of the terrorist attacks in New York, Madrid, London, Bali, and elsewhere. Nonetheless, in a multiplicity of ways that take cultural, political, and social form, multiculturalism has become increasingly embedded in these nations. The theoretical discussion was intended to clear some of the conceptual brush from the debates that have raged since the 1990s by employing two interconnected theoretical formulations that are in tandem designed to offer clarity to the philosophical debates, by providing a sociological analytic to the discourse, and, as we have stressed, in so doing, offer a way to better assess what is occurring in existing societies.

We are quite convinced that the claim that multiculturalism is on the wane is not borne out. In addition, we concur with Jeffrey Alexander (2006: 457) that, "Multiculturalism is a project of hope, not despair." If understood in terms of a theoretical framework sketched out herein, multiculturalism as a mode of civic incorporation is likely to become more important in the future. This will become more evident in Chapter 5, when the significance of dual nationality is addressed.

3

Erosion

Citizenship in the modern nation-state confers an identity on individuals by binding them to and defining them as members of a political community. It thus constitutes a mode of belonging that involves casting one's lot with a collectivity, defined from the perspective of individuals as a willingness to engage with others in a joint or shared enterprise, while from the perspective of the community it is defined in terms of a set of expectations that its members will be prepared to act on in concert with others (Taylor 2002). In other words, citizenship defines a set of obligations on the part of the community's members. However, depending on one's theoretical perspective, the nature and range of those obligations will change. Likewise, citizenship brings with it a set of expectations regarding rights accruing to all individuals by virtue of them being members of a polity (Twine 1994).

Thus, citizenship means more than simply being the holder of a passport. A passport is one of the manifest signs of nationality (Torpey 2000). Although nationality and citizenship have been intimately related in the era of modern citizenship, they need to be analytically distinguished. Nationality means full membership in a state and the corresponding tie to that state's legal system, and with it the individual's subjection to state power. The interstate function of nationality is to clearly define a people within a delineated territory and to protect citizens of the state against the outside, at times hostile, world (Tilly 1985; Béland 2005). The domestic function of nationality is to define the rights and duties of members. According to the principle of *domaine reservée* (exclusive competence), each state decides within the limits of sovereign self-determination which criteria it requires for access to nationality. One general condition for membership is that nationals have some kind of close ties to the respective state – a genuine link.

DIMENSIONS OF CITIZENSHIP

Within this framework of nationality, modern citizenship is comprised of three mutually qualifying dimensions: (1) the notion of collective self-determination and democracy; (2) the legally guaranteed status of equal political freedom and other associated rights; and (3) affiliation with the political community. Thomas Janoski's (1998: 9) definition rather nicely captures these features of citizenship in the contemporary nation-state: "*Citizenship is passive and active membership of individuals in a nation-state with certain universalistic rights and obligations at a specified level of equality*" [italics in original]. One might merely add at this point that the idea of a specified level of equality tends to be articulated in the political arena either in very general terms or not at all.

The republican tradition in particular is concerned with activities that contribute to the public good and thus is prepared to ask a considerable amount from the citizenry, while counterpoised to it and with an emphasis on the individual, the liberal tradition seeks a more minimalist set of duties on the part of citizens. Meanwhile, recent communitarian thinkers view their project as redressing what they perceive to be the excessive individualism promoted by contemporary liberalism, seeking to find a modus vivendi between the republican and liberal positions. National traditions vary and insofar as they do, conceptualizations of obligation will likewise vary across nations (for example, some nations do and some do not require military service or an alternative service and similarly do or do not legally require voting). Moreover, within nations one can often detect tensions between these perspectives, and thus there can be considerable debate about the proper understanding of duty to the nation. The United States, for example, is often depicted as a nation that embraces the liberal tradition, and has presumably done so since the founding figures of the republic adopted the philosophical stance of John Locke and applied it to the founding documents of the new nation. However, as historian Bernard Bailyn (1967) has argued, there is plenty of evidence to conclude that from the beginning both liberal and republican perspectives have had great resonance within the nation, leading to long-standing, historically rooted differences of opinion on the parts of political leaders and ordinary people about the obligations of citizens.

At the same time, citizenship can be seen in terms of a bargaining process in which members of a political community expect and at times demand that certain rights accrue to them. This idea that rights inhere in the very notion of what it means to be a citizen can be seen as representing a norm of reciprocity wherein a delicate balancing act is performed that links rights and obligations. Again, as with obligations, different political theories offer competing perspectives regarding the types and range of rights deemed warranted. Liberalism is typically seen as concerned with maximizing individual rights, while republicanism is often depicted as offering a more restricted understanding of the rights due to citizens.

It is out of this discourse on rights and obligations that one line of contemporary discourse on citizenship emerges, a discourse that involves what we refer to as the "erosion of citizenship." Actually, as will become evident in this chapter, it is more correct to refer in the plural – to discourses rather than to a singular discourse. Those who claim to see a decline in the efficacy and salience of citizenship inevitably address issues concerned with the rights of citizens and with the obligations of citizens – though, as will become evident, many analysts focus primarily or entirely on either rights or duties, and not on both.

In terms of rights, a lively debate is underway about the assault on social citizenship brought about by the rise of neoliberal political regimes since the 1970s. Appropriately, this particular debate is usually framed in terms of T. H. Marshall's (1964) paradigm of the evolution of citizenship. It is to his famous thesis that we first turn, followed by a discussion of a select number of seminal contemporary scholars' efforts to account for what they see as the erosion of the type of citizen that Marshall had seen as a product of the modern welfare state.

Not a particularly conspicuous feature of Marshall's thesis, but there nonetheless, is a view of the citizen in contemporary liberal democracies as essentially passive (Turner 2001). This touches on the obligation side of the coin. The citizen in modern democracies has a right to participate in political decision making. Does the citizen also have an obligation to do so? Generally, and often without reflecting on Marshall, a number of contemporary theorists have raised concerns about what they perceive to be the steady decline of involvement in public life by ordinary people. This particular topic has been of major concern to those scholars interested in the fate of civil society. We turn later in the chapter to some of the key exponents of this type of concern, concluding with an attempt to draw conclusions about the pessimistic claims of the erosion thesis.

T. H. MARSHALL AND THE EXPANSION OF CITIZENSHIP RIGHTS

T. H. Marshall's (1964 [1950]) seminal essay "Citizenship and Social Class" is generally viewed as marking the beginning of contemporary theoretical developments on citizenship. There are two reasons for this assessment. First, it addressed a heretofore relatively neglected topic in social theory. Second, it did so by offering in broad strokes a breezy account of the development of citizenship over three centuries that spoke at the same time to the immediate concerns of its readers. That it continues to inform discussions of citizenship more than a half-century later is testimony to the elegance and perspicuity of Marshall's formulation.

At the same time, the essay is very much a product of its place (Britain: indeed, much has been written about the "Englishness" of Marshall's views [see, for example, Rees 1996: 14–18]) and time (the immediate period after World War II). Marshall's own political views have been variously described as liberal or social democratic. Which of these two characterizations is more appropriate need not concern us here. What is relevant in terms of placing Marshall into context is that he presented his essay – first given as the Alfred Marshall Lecture at the University of Cambridge in 1949) – at precisely the moment when Clement Attlee's Labour government was in the midst of enacting its vision of the welfare state. His thinking on citizenship took shape at the same time that the National Health Service was being created, the red-brick universities were expanding higher education opportunities, pensions and welfare provision offered something resembling cradle to grave protections, and at the same time as the government was beginning to nationalize basic industries.

Those on the reformist left viewed such developments as necessary to control the power of an unbridled capitalism and to contain the inequalities that it generated. The thinking of those most involved in forging a state role for social provision were often deeply influenced by the Fabian Society, even if they did not view themselves as parliamentary socialists. This was certainly the case for government bureaucrat and LSE Director William Beveridge, whose 1941 report to Parliament laid out a blueprint for a version of the welfare state. Rather than being an activist in the Labour Party, he was attached to the Liberal Party (Harris 1998).

Marshall, referring to the economist Alfred Marshall, for whom the lecture he was delivering was named, begins by noting that in his predecessor's work there is a latent thesis that treats citizenship as being predicated on the idea that, "there is a kind of basic human equality associated with the concept of full membership of [sic] a community" (Marshall 1964: 70). At the same time, there is recognition that a capitalist economy produces structured inequalities that are made manifest in the social class system. Thus, the individual is at the same time considered to be the equal of all others in the society *qua* citizen, but unequal in terms of social class location. T. H. Marshall takes this tension between equality of political status and inequality of economic condition as the starting point of his analysis of the postwar state of Britain. Unlike those Marxists who see the equality of citizenship as a sham (as evident in the pejorative term "bourgeois democracy"), an indication of an inherent contradiction in the capitalist order that needs to be overcome via a revolutionary transformation to socialism, Marshall the reformist views it as a characteristic feature of modern industrial societies. His task is to indicate how the formal rights of the citizen can be consistent with class-based inequalities, writing that, "I shall suggest that our society today assumes that the two are still compatible, so much so that citizenship has itself become, in certain respects, the architect of legitimate social inequality" (Marshall 1964: 70).

Three facets of modern citizenship

The core contention of Marshall's thesis is that citizenship in modern societies has developed in a manner that reveals three facets or component parts, which he describes as civil, political, and social. These parts are distinct not only analytically, as something akin to what Weber meant by ideal types, but also historically, with each revealing a distinctive historical trajectory that spans three centuries. It is worth quoting Marshall at length to understand how he distinguished the three:

> The civil element is composed of the rights necessary for individual freedom – liberty of person, freedom of speech, thought, and faith, the right to own property and to conclude valid contracts, and the right to justice. The last is of a different order from the others, because it is the right to defend and assert all one's rights on terms of equality with others and by due process of law. This shows that the institutions most directly associated with civil rights are the courts of justice. By the political element I mean the right to participate in the exercise of political power, as a member of a body invested with political authority or as an elector of the members of such a body. The corresponding institutions are parliament and councils of local government. By the social element I mean the whole range from the right to a modicum of economic welfare and security to the right to share to the full in the social heritage and to live the life of a civilized being according to standards prevailing in the society. The institutions most closely associated with it are the educational system and the social services. (Marshall 1964: 71–2)

Marshall contends that in premodern conceptions of citizenship, these three elements were inseparable, in contrast to the modern version. The reason he offers for this difference is that whereas in the past key social institutions were relatively undifferentiated, in the modern world they operate in relatively autonomous spheres. It is for this reason that in the above quotation he identifies the institutional spheres relevant to each element. In his estimation, it is not "doing too much violence to historical accuracy" to contend that over a three-century period, an historical sequencing of the development of each element occurred: the emergence of civil rights occurred chiefly in the eighteenth century, political rights in the nineteenth, and social rights in the twentieth (Marshall 1964: 74).

One of the curious features of his discussion is the general lack of attention to issues of agency. On the whole, he does not address the matter of who pushed for the promotion of these various rights at particular historical moments and who resisted. Thus, although there is a recognition that the main problem about nineteenth-century political rights was that they were not universally granted, there is no discussion of the role that the ascendant bourgeois class played both in the expansion of political rights and in its efforts to curtail the expansion of rights they possessed to the disenfranchised working class. Likewise, the role of an organized working class – in, for example, the Chartist movement discussed in the preceding chapter – is overlooked. Missing also, as several commentators have argued, is an appreciation of struggle and contestation (Giddens 1982; Barbalet 1988; Turner 2001). One could argue that this leaves the impression that the social forces at play amounted to something like functionalism's system requisites. However, what is clear is that for Marshall state action is of paramount importance, with the pressures of various constituencies impinging on the state being of only secondary importance to his thesis. In short, there is something of a teleological character to the thesis. There is also a unilateral character that, while perhaps reflecting in broad contours the British case, does not necessarily reflect the situation in other nations. Germany in the nineteenth century, for example, saw the introduction of social rights in order to stave off the demands for political rights by the working class.

Class abatement

In Marshall's account, the advent of social citizenship is coincident with the rise of the welfare state. Social citizenship furthers the process of social integration already advanced by civil and political rights, but it does something else insofar as it goes beyond the provision of the formal equality of the citizen to promote equality outside of the political realm. Whereas the other two forms of citizenship did not challenge competitive capitalism, social citizenship does so by promoting policies aimed at "class abatement." Although Marshall backs away from his earlier claim "that in the twentieth century citizenship and the capitalist class system have been at war," he does see citizenship as containing the capacity to modify the class structure and counteract some of the most deleterious consequences of inequality (Marshall 1964: 96).

However, class abatement does not mean the end to social classes or to inequality. In terms of classes, it means that class distinctions are no longer as salient today as they were in the past. Here Marshall is clearly speaking about British society's rigid class structure and its concomitant intense class-consciousness. The goal of the welfare state is "not a classless society, but one in which class differences are legitimate in terms of social justice" (Marshall 1964: 106). In terms of inequality, it means that the inequalities predicated on the privilege of background will be reduced, but in their place a new – and legitimate – type of inequality will emerge based on merit. The goal is not equality of outcomes, but rather equality of opportunity. He singles out for consideration the role of the educational system in providing equal opportunities for all in their pursuit of occupational success.

The inevitable outcome is the reproduction of a hierarchical world of work, and in this way it can be said, "citizenship operates as an instrument of social stratification" (Marshall 1964: 110). However, to the extent that the welfare state performs its function well, that stratification will be based on differences regarding the individual's personal attributes and achievements and not on her class origins.

In judging whether or not it does perform well, Marshall points to three key indicators. The first is the extent to which it manages to compress both ends of the income distribution scale. In other words, the welfare state seeks to reduce the levels of extreme wealth and extreme poverty. The second task is one of social integration. This is achieved to the extent that citizens experience a shared worldview based on a common sense of national identity. The third, predicated on the first two, entails "the enrichment of the universal status of citizenship" vis-à-vis other aspects of personal identity (Marshall 1964: 116). While Marshall clearly had in mind citizenship trumping class identity, this enrichment can also be seen as elevating the status of citizenship over other markers of identity such as gender and race. Like most of his academic generation, Marshall was, to put it charitably, insensitive to the issue of gender. Regarding race, the migration of people of color from former British colonies had not really taken off (the year before his lecture, passengers on the *Empire Windrush* that arrived at Tilbury Docks included nearly 500 Jamaicans, symbolically signaling the beginning of a multicultural Britain). Later in his life Marshall addressed the issue of immigration, but only in passing, framed by a social class perspective and the issue of social service provision (Marshall 1975: 210; see also Rees 1996: 17).

Such provision was predicated on the expansion of rights, in particular the expansion of the rights associated with social citizenship. With this expansion has come a shifting balance between rights and duties. While the former have grown and are clearly perceived to be the proper fruits of citizenship, the latter are not simply limited, but also somewhat imprecise. Citizens in Britain had a duty to pay taxes, to attend school, and to perform military service (conscription has since been eliminated as one of the duties associated with citizenship). However, these are compulsory, and thus do not require "an act of will" or a "keen sentiment of loyalty" (Marshall 1964: 117). There is a duty to work, but this duty's relationship to improving the commonweal tends to be ambiguous. Marshall (1964: 117) writes that: "The other duties are vague, and are included in the general obligation to live the life of a good citizen, giving service as one can to promote the welfare of the community. But the community is so large that the obligation appears remote and unreal." Although in times of crisis it is possible to appeal to "the Dunkirk spirit," Marshall assumes that in normal times the ordinary citizen of the modern welfare state will be relatively passive. This is clearly evident in the current terrorist threat posed by Islamic *jihadists*. If in the short-term aftermaths of the attacks of 9/11 in New York City and 7/7 in London such a spirit could be detected, in both instances it was short-lived.

More than a half-century after Marshall published his lecture, a veritable cottage industry of commentary on it has developed (particularly insightful examples include Turner 1986; Barbalet 1988; Roche 1992; and Bulmer and Rees 1996). We make no effort here to explore the full range of responses, both favorable and critical, to his thesis. Suffice it to say that part of the staying power of the essay is due to its literary suppleness, which allows for multiple fruitful readings that open up a variety of angles of vision on a host of issues related to modern citizenship in liberal democracies.

Our interest here is to look at two discourses that arose in the latter part of the twentieth century. They address, in various ways, not the expansion but the erosion of citizenship. One discourse can be read as a challenge to Marshall's assumption that the welfare state once in place could be seen as a fixed and durable part of the sociopolitical landscape. Critics from both the left and the right have questioned this assumption, and with it the idea that the state was to be the guarantor of social rights. This is a discourse about the erosion of rights. The second discourse can be seen as building on Marshall's thesis rather than directly challenging it. It focuses on the duties and obligations of citizens rather than on rights. Whereas Marshall took the passivity of citizens as a relatively unproblematic given, this discourse raises concerns about the future of democracy in situations where citizens withdraw from public life into the realm of the private. We take up the first topic in this chapter and turn to the second in the following chapter.

CRITIQUES OF THE WELFARE STATE

All of the liberal democracies are welfare states, with public policies in place that are intended, to use Marshall's words, to promote "class abatement."

In such regimes, the state assumes a role that it had not played in the earlier laissez-faire stage of capitalist development. It ought to be construed, as its advocates clearly saw it, as an alternative not only to laissez-faire but also to a socialist alternative. Welfare states can be appropriately viewed, not simply as a challenge to the inequalities generated by capitalism, but as a bulwark of capitalism.

Marshall is correct in stating both that the origins of the welfare state can be seen in the nineteenth century and that its real blossoming occurred in the twentieth. Thus, to take the case of the United States, the birth of the welfare state, as Theda Skocpol (1992) has convincingly illustrated, can be located in the aftermath of the Civil War, when federal legislation was passed that provided pensions for soldiers and their widows and orphans. However, this did not serve as a basis for a permanent welfare state, for as the recipients of this program died off, as was intended, there was a built-in sunset provision. In fact, it was not until the world crisis of capitalism that occurred during the Great Depression that the political will to create the architecture for what was seen as a permanent welfare state was erected – replete with unemployment benefits, pensions in the form of Social Security, public housing, legislation that enhanced the position of organized labor, and so forth.

In the case of Britain, there were early initiatives in the late nineteenth century and again after World War I that can be seen as representing the birth of the welfare state, but, as in the USA, it was in response to the twin crises of the Depression and World War II that a welfare state was created in an effort to combat what Beveridge's *Report on Social Insurance and Allied Services* (1942) referred to as the Five Giants: Want, Disease, Ignorance, Squalor, and Idleness. Germany differed from the Anglo-American experience only insofar as it developed a more comprehensive welfare state in the nineteenth century. It did so under Bismarck's direction after the 1871 unification of the nation, arising out of concern about the growing influence of socialism and with an explicit effort to stave it off.

Not surprisingly, given the different political coalitions that served to shape various liberal democratic nations' respective welfare systems, there is considerable variation in both form and content. Some are more egalitarian than others. Some are more comprehensive than others. Some elicit wider levels of public support than others. Some place a premium on universal entitlement programs while others place greater emphasis on targeted, or means-tested, programs (Korpi 1983; Rueschemeyer et al. 1992). Some welfare states have historically relied on mixed economies consisting of a combination of privately owned and nationalized industries, while others have not. These differences are reflected in Gosta Esping-Anderson's (1990) "distinct regime theory," which distinguishes traditional, liberal, and social democratic welfare state models.

Yet despite these differences, "class abatement" occurs to the extent that it does by a reliance on two types of income redistribution: progressive taxation policies and the provision of access to education, healthcare, pensions, unemployment compensation, and the like. The latter represent, in Marshall's language, "social rights," goods and services to which, as a citizen, one is entitled. Social rights are thicker or thinner depending on the nation. The free cradle-to-grave health coverage and free university education to qualified students in the Scandinavian countries are examples of thicker social rights, while the heavy reliance on private sector insurance and high tuition charges in American universities are the product of a society that has on offer a considerably thinner version of social rights.

Critics of the welfare state can be found across the political spectrum. Those in the center, who endorse in a fundamental sense the idea of a welfare state, fault it in terms of specific performance measures and perhaps the levels or types of benefits provided, but do not challenge the appropriateness of such a system. However, critiques emanate from both the left and the right that call into question not only the efficacy, but also the legitimacy of the welfare state. We turn briefly to an examination of these two critiques, one of which has had profound political consequences during the last quarter of the twentieth century and into the twenty-first.

The critique from the left

From the left, whether speaking in the post-Soviet era of the dwindling number of proponents of orthodox revolutionary Marxism or of the more significant number of democratic socialist theorists, there is general consensus that, in the words of one prominent spokesperson for the latter position, Claus Offe (1984: 147):

> The welfare state has served as the major peace formula of advanced capitalist democracies for the period following the Second World War. . . . [It] seeks to balance the asymmetrical power between labor and capital, and thus to overcome the condition of disruptive struggle and contradictions that was the most prominent feature of the pre-welfare state, or liberal, capitalism. In sum, the welfare state has been celebrated throughout the post-war period as the political solution to societal contradictions.

If that description defined the welfare state's functional significance, it also framed the nature of the critique, which at its most basic tends to contain four elements: (1) it is bureaucratically cumbersome and ineffectual in redressing market-generated inequalities; (2) it is administratively repressive and undemocratic, reducing people to the status of dependent clients;

(3) it encourages passivity on the part of citizens; and (4) it serves to legiti-mize the existing state of affairs by fostering an ideology that glosses the persistence of capitalist exploitation.

Offe's critique and related ones by theorists such as Jürgen Habermas and James O'Connor are actually more sophisticated than these four points would indicate, for what they contend is that there are inherent contradictions between a capitalist economy and the welfare state that cannot be overcome or reconciled. The result is that the welfare state con-fronts persistent crisis tendencies. O'Connor (2003) focused on the fiscal crisis of the state, while Habermas (1975) concentrated on motivational and legitimation crises. Offe (1984, 1985) builds on both to offer a more comprehensive account of the contradictions of the welfare state.

His argument is that for the welfare state to function in its regulatory capacity, as a promoter of accumulation (through, for example, infrastruc-ture development and maintenance), and in the delivery of services, it requires fiscal inputs (in the form of taxes) from the economic system and mass loyalty on the part of the citizenry (Offe 1984: 52–61). Out of this complex, contradictions arise that take economic, political, and ideological form. At the economic level, the problematic nature of the relationship between the capitalist economy and the state is contained in the reality that the latter both facilitates capital accumulation when it invests in the promotion of economic development, but it simultaneously retards accu-mulation insofar as it siphons off capital to make possible social service delivery. The viability of the state's ability to operate a welfare bureaucracy depends on a robust economy that provides favorable incentives to invest-ment. Yet in various capacities as regulator (e.g., setting minimum wage policies, establishing the rules of the game for collective bargaining, man-dating workplace health and safety standards, and protecting the environ-ment) it can create disincentives to investment. It can also be seen as an impediment to capitalist growth insofar as it withdraws larger and larger segments of the workforce from the market economy and puts them into public sector employment, working in social service agencies, healthcare, education, transportation, and the like (Offe 1984: 125–9).

As political pressures for the expansion of the rights associated with social citizenship intensify, the tendency in the advanced welfare states is for them to expand to meet those demands. The right (see below) is not alone in noting that the expansion of entitlements can result in motiva-tional problems that have a direct impact on the economy. If people can rely on government payments as an income source, a disinclination to accept dirty, dangerous, and low-paying work can result. If people come to expect that they are entitled to relatively generous government-funded pension schemes and health benefits, they will be more inclined to retire from work as early as possible. As people live longer in these societies, this increasingly means that those who have withdrawn their labor from the market may reasonably expect to live for three or four decades as a retiree. Pension schemes were not formulated with an understanding that people might spend nearly as much or even more of their adult lives outside of the labor market as inside it. These and similar entitlements have placed increasingly heavy financial burdens on the state (and, it should be noted, on those corporations that provide substantial pension plans to retirees). Should the state seek to meet that burden by increasing revenues, it can result in undermining investment, thus generating an economic crisis. On the other hand, if the state's response is to cut benefits, public dissatisfaction with such measures can produce a legitimation crisis.

However, these entitlements do not tell the full story of the crisis tendencies of the welfare state. The rise of the "new" social movements in the 1960s, sometimes depicted as postmaterialist – anti-war, student, environmental, anti-nuclear, peace, feminist, and so forth – were directed at the state more than at the capitalist economy, challenging what Alain Touraine (1971) termed the "totally administered society". One of these issues in particular added a new dimension to the fiscal problems of the welfare state: the environmental movement. By introducing onto the political agenda the argument that there were ecologically defined limits to economic growth, the environmental movement called on the state to reign in ecologically harmful capitalist development, to mandate that firms invest in technologies designed to protect the environment, to be directly involved in the clean-up of existing environmental hazards, and to be in various ways proactive in defense of the environment. To the extent that welfare states responded favorably to the demands of this movement, it exacerbated the conflict between state and economy.

What is clear from this analysis is that Offe and other democratic socialists call attention to a significant lacuna in Marshall's analysis, which involves his inattentiveness to the accumulation requisites of capitalism and the limitations that are thus imposed on the resource base and on the capacity of the welfare state to function with relative autonomy. It is useful to place this critique into historical context. Marshall's thesis was presented at the beginning of what turned out to be a quarter of a century that has been frequently characterized as the golden age of the historic compromise between capital and labor. It marked the period in the twentieth century when the industrial liberal democracies experienced unprecedented growth and rising incomes. This was, as John Kenneth Galbraith (1955) described it, the era of "the affluent society."

In contrast, the analyses of Offe, Habermas, O'Connor, and others took shape during an era of economic transformation that threatened the relatively smooth functioning of the welfare state. Rising unemployment, high inflation, declines in real income, the OPEC (Organization of Petroleum

Exporting Countries) oil crisis, and the systematic campaign of deindustrialization initiated by capitalist firms signaled that the liberal democracies had entered into a new era. Offe and Habermas during this time
referred to the new epoch as the period of "late capitalism," a term that
is perhaps vested with a bit of wishful thinking insofar as it can be read
as implying the final stage of capitalism's fateful history. Offe's (1985)
subsequent characterization of the new stage of capitalist development as
"disorganized capitalism" is a more accurate characterization, one that
resonates with subsequent discussions of a post-Fordist economy (see also
Lash and Urry 1987 on disorganized capitalism). Much of this transformation hinges on the increasing mobility of capital. Its footlooseness has
meant that in two ways it threatens the financial integrity of the welfare
state: by searching for cheaper sources of labor in a global market and by
using numerous strategies to avoid paying taxes, both legal and illegal
(Sassen 1996).

This results in welfare states being increasingly hard pressed to find the
resources necessary to guarantee the provision of those entitlements associated with the social rights of citizens. Unlike orthodox Marxism, which
predicts that the welfare state is inevitably doomed by capitalism's inherent
contradictions (which are such that the system's crisis tendencies will even-
tually lead to its collapse, with the options being barbarism or socialism),
the democratic socialist reaction is considerably less apocalyptic. Rejecting
the idea that revolutionary struggle can lead into a classless radiant future,
democratic socialism offers a reformist alternative, one that continues
to rely on the role of state power in holding in check the power of capitalism and in redressing the inequalities it generates. In this regard, it is in
full agreement with Marshall. However, in the new economic order there
is good reason for concern that social rights cannot be maintained at
current levels, and thus the future spells the persistent threat of their
constriction.

It is here that one can detect an implicit criticism of Marshall for his
assumption that citizens in the welfare state are essentially passive. The
interest in the new social movements by reformist socialists is a product
of their understanding of the role of a mobilized citizenry in preserving
and enhancing social rights – as well as civil and political rights. Touraine
(1981) in particular has argued that these collective social actors, when
they have a capacity to muster sufficient organizational, financial, and
ideological resources and develop appropriate strategic decisions, have a
transformative potential that allows for the possibility that they might
change the course of social development that has been advanced by the
dominant class.

As we turn to the critique of the welfare state from the right, it will
become clear that it represents a far more radical and thoroughgoing

challenge to the Marshallian conception of citizenship, calling into question the very notion of social rights. Yet at the outset it ought to be noted that there is at some level considerable agreement between left and right about the shortcomings and political pitfalls of the welfare state. Offe (1984: 149) saw this connection insofar as he agreed with the right's argument that the welfare state exacerbates rather than reduces social conflict by imposing disincentives to investment and stimulating the disincentive to work. Likewise, Esping-Anderson (1982: 8) concurs with the right's claim that the welfare state undercuts motivation, investment, efficiency, and authority; it, in effect, "eats the very hand that feeds it."

The critique from the right

From the conservative perspective, the welfare state is a reflection of a problem shared by all the advanced industrial liberal democracies. Samuel Huntington (1976) identified it as the "democratic distemper," while Michel Crozier (1975) defined it similarly as the excess of democracy. Daniel Bell's (1976) analysis of the "cultural contradictions of capitalism" located the problem in terms of a historical juncture where the "axial principles" of the economy and culture are at odds. While the former places an emphasis on rationality and something resembling a secular version of the Protestant work ethnic, the latter promotes self-realization and hedonism. Niklas Luhmann (1995) posed the problem in systems terms by arguing that in response to demands placed upon it, the state needs to say "no" far more often than it says "yes." In different forms, what all of these theorists are getting at is the problematic character of the rising sense of entitlement on the part of citizens, who define their identities as citizens increasingly in terms of a set of comprehensive and expanding social rights. These expectations are deemed problematic because, simply put, the welfare state cannot in the long run deliver while at the same time maintaining an economic climate conducive to growth.

Not all of the figures cited above are opposed to the idea of social rights as an aspect of citizenship. Bell, for example, describes himself as a socialist in economic matters, a political liberal, and a cultural conservative. His goal is to find a modus vivendi that relies on compromises designed to work to the benefit of all three sectors of society. However, a far more influential view – and one with real political consequences during the past quarter-century – is what has become known as neoliberalism, though earlier it was more typically called neoconservatism. Neoliberalism is an ideology that articulates as its goal the return to something approximating the liberal laissez-faire economy found during the rise of capitalist industrial societies in the nineteenth century.

As Maurice Roche (1992: 71–89) has amply and admirably chronicled, this type of thinking comes in more and less radical positions, though for our purposes we need not be preoccupied with the variations, except to make the following point. As can be seen above, not only are social rights – or at least their scope and range – deemed to be problematic, but so is the expansion of political rights. As Keith Faulks (2000: 62) has pointed out, influential radical free market conservatives such as Friedrich von Hayek are suspicious of and only grudgingly accept democratic action, with Robert Nozick going even further by insisting, in Faulks's words, that "any attempt to seek social justice through the practice of democratic citizenship is an infringement of civil rights."

The key to understanding neoliberalism in general involves two interrelated claims. First, the welfare state is part of the problem and not part of the solution. Far from remedying inequality, it serves to perpetuate it in two ways: by fostering dependency and by dampening investment incentives, thereby serving as a brake on growth. This part of the argument dovetails with that of the left. This leads to the second claim, one not shared by the left, which amounts to a repudiation of the Keynesian economic policies that had accorded to the state a significant role in stimulating the economy and protecting society from the full impact of both inflation and recession. The argument is that the dismantling (or at least the significant restriction in the size and influence) of the welfare state would free the market from both financial and regulatory constraints that impede growth.

If permitted to function without such constraints, growth would be such that all members of society would benefit. The wealthy would become wealthier, but this would not be a zero-sum game where it would occur at the expense of those in the middle or at the bottom of society, for the consequence of expanded opportunities for wealth creation would be a trickle-down effect whereby all benefit. Wealth creation replaces income redistribution. This perspective has appropriately been characterized as "market fundamentalism," an economic version of the view that a rising tide raises all boats.

The regimes of Margaret Thatcher in the United Kingdom and Ronald Reagan in the United States represent the two most concerted attempts to implement a neoliberal agenda. While in both instances one could find vestiges of Social Darwinian thinking (ideologues George Gilder and Charles Murray, for example, were widely read and often cited by key figures within the Reagan administration), the central premise of market fundamentalism is that there was a solution to poverty, and it resided in the unfettered market rather than the welfare state. Operating within this framework, both governments sought to enact policies that were intended to rein in their respective welfare states. One part of their campaign involved tax cuts. The cuts were highly regressive, with the assumption being that benefits to the wealthy would stimulate rapid economic growth. They also cut into the financial capacity of the welfare state to deliver services. Linked to starving the welfare state were policy shifts that eliminated or cut benefit programs. Similarly, under the guise of regulatory relief, government-operated programs designed to promote workplace safety, a clean environment, and so forth were rolled back.

Such policies are an expression of a perspective that turns Marshall's thesis on its head (Green 1999). Inequality, far from being a problem, is perceived to be beneficial to society and does not necessarily spell the impoverishment of a segment of the population at the bottom or insecurity for those in the middle. The state, far from being capable of effecting class abatement, is depicted as the cause of endemic intergenerational poverty. The market, far from being incapable of creating wealth other than at the expense of some sectors of the society, is in fact the solution to the problems created by inequality, for the market not only causes inequality, but also the conditions by which inequality is no longer a genuine societal problem.

For market fundamentalists – and perhaps Nobel laureate Milton Friedman is the best example – the magic of the market is connected to a general antipathy to the state. For this reason, not only have neoliberals sought to roll back the welfare state, but they have also attempted to introduce the market into arenas of social life heretofore treated as functioning outside of the market (Savas 1999). This occurred under the guise of privatization. For example, plans were floated to shift police and fire services from the public sector to private companies that would bid on jobs competitively. While in only a small number of isolated cases did localities actually decide to contract out for these basic public services, it became far more common in the United States to turn prisons over to private for-profit companies, with the claim being made that such prisons would be more cost effective (Rosenau 2000).

The most significant instance of introducing the market into the public realm occurred in public education. Although the challenge to public schools began earlier, it intensified considerably with the passage of the "No Child Left Behind Act." Why did inner-city schoolchildren perform so poorly on standardized tests and, based on other performance measures, "underachieve?" The neoliberal response to this question was to argue that the problem was that schools have no incentive to do well, and moreover that entrenched labor unions and burdensome educational bureaucracies compounded the inertia of the system. Dismissed from consideration is the possibility of inequitable funding of public education due to the over-reliance on local property taxes – or, in other words, that the cause of differential school performance might be predicated on class inequities. Thus, instead of revamping the funding of public education in order to overcome inequalities across communities by creating a truly level playing field, the solution put forth by neoliberals was to make schools compete for students, generally under plans that called for school choice. Thus, under voucher schemes students and their parents could shop around for the school of their preference.

Poorly performing schools would be forced to take measures to improve their educational services or, as with any business, they would have to shut their doors. Add into the mix the emergence of schools run by private companies, such as Chris Whittle's Edison Schools, and the intrusion of the market into public education is complete. Especially significant about Whittle's for-profit enterprise is the introduction of corporate advertising into school buildings, both in hallway posters and via Channel One, the television news programs his company produces, for it reinforces the notion that students and their parents are ultimately customers and that it is the job of schools to compete for their "market share."

This is a telling illustration of the neoliberal challenge to the notion of the welfare state as guarantor of social rights, for it highlights the desire to collapse the role of citizen into that of consumer. Insofar as this occurs, an erosion of social citizenship results (Hoffman 2004: 79–96). While the United States, with the weakest welfare state of all the advanced industrial nations, and Britain, in the wake of Margaret Thatcher, have gone further than other states in enacting policies that erode social rights, the fiscal crises of all of the other advanced industrial nations have put pressure on states to initiate retrenchment plans that curb or curtail the benefits heretofore guaranteed to citizens. Germany, for example, has been more resistant to this trend than some other major nations, but here, too, with the election of the Christian Democratic Angela Merkel, there is pressure to strengthen the market at the expense of the state.

If the idea of citizenship entails a view of the self as connected to a larger collectivity, such is not the case for the consumer, who from Adam Smith forward is depicted as a solitary individual seeking to obtain the highest quality goods and services at the lowest possible price. When the citizen is reduced to the role of consumer, she is no longer expected to take into account the well-being of the commonweal, being merely expected to behave in the marketplace in ways that are intended to enhance her position in it. Self-interest (or, as Ayn Rand would have it, the "virtue of selfishness") trumps actions motivated by the needs of the nation, the local community, or the disadvantaged.

One important conclusion that can be drawn from the neoliberal "experiment" points to the fallacy of Marshall's optimistic conviction that, once in place, the three types of citizenship would become institutionalized and would not be subject to reversal. Clearly, this is not the case because social citizenship in numerous advanced industrial nations has – one can argue about just how far – been rolled back during the past two decades, while during the same period inequality has risen.

THE TRIUMPH OF THE MARKET OVER CITIZENSHIP?

Colin Crouch, Klaus Eder, and Damian Tambini (2001: 11) have argued that in recent years "the triumph of the market over citizenship has become the most important feature of social politics." While this has been especially evident in liberal regimes – in particular in the United States, beginning with the Reagan presidency and continuing through the first Bush and Clinton administrations to the second Bush presidency, and in the United Kingdom since the Thatcher years and continuing into the New Labour era of Tony Blair – it can be seen to a more limited extent in the social democratic regimes as well, though the latter have proven to have more resilience and resistance to the market than the former. The general thesis is that the trend during the latter part of the past century up to the present has been away from the social democratic model and toward what some have come to call the Anglo-American model.

The "enabling state"

This is clearly the case made by University of California social policy analyst Neil Gilbert (2004) in his study of the transformation of the welfare state. Gilbert begins by calling into question Esping-Anderson's (1990) distinct regime theory, seeing the differences between existing welfare states as becoming less significant over time. This is because a shift has occurred as a result of neoliberalism whereby the logic of the social democratic welfare model has eroded while that of the more market-oriented Anglo-American model is ascendant, not only in the nations that first nurtured it, but elsewhere in the developed world as well. Gilbert doesn't note this, and it takes us beyond the scope of this book, but in fact, the market model has also expanded in significance in the developing world, due chiefly to the mandates imposed on poorer nations by such institutions as the World Bank and the International Monetary Fund.

Gilbert (2004: 44) contrasts the social democratic model with the "enabling state" promoted by neoliberalism. The former is characterized by "an emphasis on *universal* access to *publicly* provided benefits that offer strong *protection* of labor as *social rights* of citizenship" [italics in the original]. The latter, instead, promotes a market-oriented approach to the provision of benefits, with a clear preference for the privatization of social service delivery. Instead of universal access, the emphasis is on selective targeting of service eligibility. Moreover, in place of generous benefits for nonwork – unemployment and disability insurance schemes, for instance – there is an emphasis on promoting work. Thus, Gilbert would agree with Anton Hemerijck's (2001: 134) observation that, "In short, inactivity – paid nonwork – seems to have become a mainstay of the advanced European [read social democratic] welfare state." It is precisely this approach that has been challenged by the enabling state's framework.

This is nowhere more evident than in the Clinton administration's endorsement of the enabling state approach with the policy shift from, as its sponsors posed it, welfare to workfare. Indeed, Gilbert (2004: 88) notes of the USA since the 1990s that "steering people back to work as soon as possible has become the guiding principle for the social protection of the unemployed." This is predicated on a rearticulation of the relationship between rights and responsibilities, with the former being de-emphasized and the latter emphasized. Linked to this is the fact that less attention is devoted to income maintenance and more to promoting social inclusion via involvement in the workforce (Gilbert 2004: 61). The logic of this shift is captured by Hemerijck (2001: 135): "Not poverty *per se* but a sense of being socially redundant and economically irrelevant will provoke an emergent underclass of inactives to turn their back on the values and institutions of the mainstream society."

The idea of the enabling state is to guard against long-term dependency on the part of those who are not part of the paid workforce. While an aspect of this exit from the market concerns the unemployed or underemployed poor and those who cannot participate in the labor force due to physical or mental health problems, a growing part of the population not involved in compensated work are retirees. One of the difficult demographic realities that confront all of the advanced industrial nations concerns aging populations. Indeed, for a number of nations at or below zero population growth, immigration has proven to be the only viable alternative to population decline, and with it economic constriction. It is not surprising that during the heyday of the post-World War II welfare state, the age at which workers retired declined appreciably. This was particularly evident among public sector employees – whose livelihoods relied most directly on an expansive welfare state – who were often able to retire after 20 years of service, meaning that retirement ages were often in the fifties. At the same time, life expectancies increased during this time, leading to a situation where many people actually lived more years as retirees than as wage or salaried workers. This has placed strains on public and private sector pension schemes as well as appreciably increasing health-care costs (Lowenstein 2005).

Thus, in a variety of ways the enabling state has sought – with limited success – to encourage people to care for themselves with the expectation of less and less state provision both when out of the labor force during one's "productive years," as well as during retirement. For example, in the UK, people are encouraged to go beyond the National Health Service by purchasing private health insurance and using private hospitals that exist outside the NHS. In the USA, private retirement accounts – in particular what are referred to as 401K's – are seen as representing a more important part of one's retirement income, with Social Security constituting a mere supplement. This, of course, applies only to those with incomes high enough to actually save and invest a portion of income – thus excluding the poor. In addition, those state-provided provisions regarding such things as the age at which retirement benefits (such as Social Security in the USA), kick in have increased, thereby reducing the costs to the state associated with welfare provision.

This represents the two-pronged approach to welfare provision by the enabling state. First, it entails cutting back on benefits. One way of doing this is to avoid universal entitlement programs in favor of selective or needs-based criteria. This has always been the preferred modus operandi of the US welfare system. Gilbert argues that a common rationale for universal entitlement programs that has been frequently advanced is that the means tests required for selective benefits lead to stigmatization. This was a key claim made by Richard Titmuss, an early exponent of the British welfare state. Gilbert (2004: 142) challenges this position, contending that there is little empirical evidence to support it. The second way of cutting back on benefits is by legislative decision to simply reduce the scope of state involvement in care.

It is not surprising that neoliberal policies aimed at cutting back on state involvement in insuring the welfare of the citizenry have simultaneously advanced ambitious tax-cutting initiatives. The two are interconnected for, without resources, the state is forced to reduce its scope of action. Thus, the calls for tax cuts, beginning in the Anglo-American world during the Reagan and Thatcher years, have persisted (if not intensified) since then, leading to states having fewer resources than they had earlier. Though varying in degree, similar strains can be felt by all of the advanced liberal democracies. Not all neoliberals would necessarily go as far as Grover Norquist, unvarnished ideologue and influential behind-the-scenes advisor to the Bush administration, and argue that the goal is to reduce the state to a size such that it could be drowned in a bathtub, but they differ from him only in degree.

In a BBC interview, Norquist (November 8, 2005) spoke about the move from welfare to workfare instituted during the Clinton era and subsequent reductions in the availability of state assistance during the Bush administration in terms of "liberating" people from welfare. This claim derives from the ideological *idée fixe* that welfare states encourage dependency, with people being reduced to clients rather than autonomous workers. What is interesting about this thesis is that it does not actually seek to make such people active and engaged citizens. Rather, it is intended to have them defined as autonomous workers who manage to economically provide for themselves and their families (Turner 2001). Such autonomy is not possible, it is argued, if government plays the role, as Margaret Thatcher was fond of disparaging it, of a "nanny state."

Gilbert (2004: 182) summarizes what this implies when he writes that, "the protective blanket of the welfare state has become widely perceived as smothering the vigorous virtues – initiative, diligence, commitment, fair play, enthusiasm – in the name of charity, patience, kindness, and sympathy." He does not go on to make the obvious point: namely, that what neoliberalism wants to advance are what have characteristically been viewed as masculine virtues – indeed, in some instances, the manly virtues of the privileged classes, sometimes learned on the playing fields of Eton or the secret societies of Ivy League universities – while simultaneously moving what are typically considered to be feminine virtues out of the public realm and (back) into the private sphere. Jane Addams can justifiably be seen as one of the principal intellectual architects of the twentieth-century welfare state. As she made clear in a 1907 essay on the "Utilization of Women in City Government," women were particularly well suited to perform roles in administering the welfare state, since to do so amounted to extrapolating the caring skills honed in the private sphere into the public realm (Addams 1960). From this perspective, it is quite clear that neoliberalism can be read as a reaction to the feminization of the state.

The second feature of the assault on the welfare state involved a critique of the capacity of government to deliver the benefits associated with social rights in an efficient and cost-effective manner. The presumed rationality of the private sector was trumpeted as an antidote to direct state provision. In this regard, neoliberalism is not, as some critics have argued, a throwback to the Social Darwinism of a century earlier, which in its most pristine and muscular form expressed no interest in offering social rights either in general or in particular to those defined as most in need of various forms of social provision (Sumner 1925). In contrast, neoliberalism has aggressively promoted the privatization of functions formerly seen as falling under the bailiwick of the state. Gilbert (2004: 99) observes that, "By the 1990s, business schools around the country were training social entrepreneurs to apply commercial skills to the management of social welfare organizations." Even such unlikely candidates for social service delivery as defense contractor Lockheed Martin sought to capture a piece of the social service market. This is a new twist on the 1960s depiction of the warfare/welfare state.

Never did those critics consider that the two elements of the state would become fused the way they have in recent years. As such, handing over the provision of social services to the private sector was part of a larger agenda of privatization. In some nations, with Britain being a particularly telling example, it meant returning nationalized industries such as mines and railroads from state ownership to corporate ownership. It could also mean turning over what had historically been viewed as institutions appropriately located outside of the market, such as schools, to for-profit enterprises. Public services such as trash collection, fire departments, and prisons were also subjected to privatization efforts. The assumption underlying these and related ventures is that services will be delivered more cost-effectively, thereby making possible lower public sector spending and thus lower tax rates.

There are many suspect economic assumptions involved in this effort to reduce the role of the state, not to mention the problems associated with the enhanced prospects of cronyism and corruption. At the very least, it is quite clear that there is no compelling empirical evidence to suggest that a shifting reliance on the private sector for delivering social services has proven to be a good economic decision from the perspective of the tax-paying public – not to mention the intentioned beneficiaries of various welfare programs.

For his part, Gilbert attempts to stake out a position somewhere between what Margaret Sommers (2001) refers to as neoliberalism's "romancing the market" and "reviling the state," and that stance from the left which views the morality of the market in totally negative terms, considering it as "red in tooth and claw" (Gilbert 2004: 183; see Schwartz 1999 for a cogent argument of the position that Gilbert seeks to dismiss). At the same time, he concludes that the enabling state has been remarkably successful in the United States, the focus of his study, and by implication in the rest of the Anglo-American world. He doesn't focus on the social democratic regimes, but assumes that the enabling state has made inroads there, as well. Where the enabling state has taken root, he is quite clear about the consequences:

> As it has evolved since the early 1990s, the enabling state generates no counterforce to the capitalist ethos, no larger sense of public purpose that might be served beyond increasing productivity, no clear ideal of public service, and dwindling support for the goals of social protection and security. In many respects, the course of the enabling state endorses antistatist attitudes, which lends weight to the movement toward a market-dominated society. (Gilbert 2004: 189)

The focus of Gilbert's analysis is the state and not the citizen. This means that, although his work is concerned with the way that social programs intended to promote equitable access to social rights function, he does not explicitly address the impact of recent neoliberal-inspired policy shifts on those to whom such policies have been directed. In particular, he fails to address the matter of the increased levels of inequality in neoliberal regimes.

Jeff Madrick (2003), in a critique of Gilbert's position, suggests, perhaps somewhat unfairly, that it differs little from the policy positions of the Cato Institute, a libertarian conservative think-tank. However, he is quite correct when writing that, "Gilbert, for his part, utterly ignores the rising inequality of incomes that have accompanied the enabling state. It is no small irony that in America in particular, the leading 'enabling state' in the world, incomes and wealth have become much more unequal over the last thirty years" (Madrick 2003: 73). Although Gilbert refers on numerous occasions to Marshall, he never hints that in Marshall's brief on behalf of the proper role of the state in effecting class abatement the state was committed to reducing existing levels of inequality (White and Donoghue 2003).

Social exclusion

In contrast, Ruth Lister (2004: 158–75) has made a case for linking poverty to human rights and in turn to citizenship. She notes at the outset of her discussion that neither the governments of the liberal democracies (with the exception, in principle if not in practice, of France) nor international institutions such as the World Bank have defined poverty per se as a human rights issue. However, poverty causes social exclusion: the lack of economic resources, combined with low levels of human capital and the sorts of social capital that would facilitate economic advancement, prevent the poor from achieving a genuine voice in the political arena. Lister (2004: 75) describes social exclusion as "a travelling concept" that originated in the work of Max Weber; but more recently social policy analysts in the nations of the European Union have embraced it. Although the term means slightly different things to different analysts in different geographical contexts, the bottom-line shared understanding is that if categories of people are in fact victims of social exclusion, they are incapable of exercising their rights as citizens in the same way as those who are fully included into the polity.

This points to the inherent dilemma of citizenship in a society based on social inequalities – be they based on class, race, gender, sexual identity, religion, physical or mental disability, other ascribed feature of identity, or, as is typical, the intersection of two or more of these factors (Turner 1986; Dean 2003). Citizenship in capitalist societies constitutes a mode of identity that offers the promise of being equal in an unequal world. From the perspective of the far left, this points to the inherent contradictions in societies that are simultaneously capitalist and democratic, with the result being that citizenship must be at bedrock something of a sham. The logic of citizenship in such societies is to offer legitimacy to the existing state of affairs by an essentially passive mass of citizens.

From the perspective of the elitist right, the idea of being equal in an unequal society amounts to a convenient gloss on the reality that only a small sector of the population is sufficiently knowledgeable and capable to make political decisions wisely and effectively. The followers of political philosopher Leo Strauss, who include many of the key figures associated with the neoconservative wing of the administration of George W. Bush, do not believe that the people are genuinely capable of self-rule (Drury 1999). Rather, in contemporary societies the veneer of democratic self-rule constitutes one of the abiding myths of national identity and such myths need to be not only preserved, but used in an ongoing way in order to insure the tacit support of the people. This represents the significance of symbolic politics in such regimes (Edelman 1985). Such a view of politics is predicated on the idea that there is a wide gulf between the small group of elites who understand how to rule and the large majority of the population that does not possess such knowledge. One of the central features of this political philosophy is that it provides a rationale for governmental secrecy and dissimulation. The idea of educating the citizenry in order to prepare them for democratic self-rule is treated as misguided. The idea that ordinary people, as long as the vast majority of them live in relative comfort, will defer to rulers is assumed. To the extent that this perspective can be seen as constituting a fairly apt description of contemporary politics, it suggests that the unspoken reality of citizenship is that there are in fact two categories of citizens: a small elite with what they see as an essentially republican view of citizenship and the large majority of what amounts to second-class citizens.

Of course, the position of Marshall (1964) and those countless theorists who succeeded him is one that has sought to offer an alternative to both of these views, which in their own distinctive ways denigrate citizenship. In contrast, the Marshallian tradition valorizes citizenship, and insofar as it does so can seriously consider the prospect of being equal in an unequal world. However, for this to be possible it requires a context characterized by genuine class abatement. Marshall's own use of this term contained a certain imprecision, but it was clear that it meant two things. First, it meant that inequality would not be overcome entirely, but instead a legitimate, functional form of inequality would replace an illegitimate, dysfunctional form. Second, although Marshall did not develop this line of argument in any detail, if citizenship was actually going to make equals of people in their role as citizen it would have to insure policies of redistribution that prevented unacceptable levels of economic and social inequality to exist. In other words, the assumption underpinning Marshall's thesis is that although inequality does not disappear, there is a level of inequality that is unacceptable because once a society moves beyond that level, the equality of citizens as citizens is jeopardized. Marshall did not provide guidelines that specified what level of inequality was deemed acceptable and what unacceptable. This is also true of subsequent commentators.

However, there is a shared conviction within this tradition of thought that the balancing of levels of inequality during the immediate decades after World War II, the heyday of the welfare state in the liberal democracies, had a salutary impact on citizenship. On the other hand, in those nations that have experienced the most vigorous and successful assaults on the welfare state, inequality in recent decades has risen to an unacceptable level. Nowhere has the rise of inequality been more significant than that nation which has embraced neoliberalism most single-mindedly, the United States, which has increasingly become a "winner-take-all" society (Frank and Cook 1995). What has happened in the USA during the last quarter of the twentieth century is that, to put it simply, the rich have gotten richer, the poor have gotten poorer, and the middle classes have experienced increased levels of insecurity.

By any measure, inequality has increased. On the one hand, as Godfrey Hodgson (2004: 90) puts it, "Wages, income, and wealth were all very unequal indeed, both by the standards of anything seen in America since the 1920s and by the standards of the other developed countries." This is particularly evident with wealth, where "the top 10 percent" of the population owns "83 percent of all financial assets" (Hodgson 2004: 91). On the other hand, the USA has the highest poverty rate of all the advanced industrial societies, and given the fact that class and race powerfully intersect, this means that the poorest sectors of society, the "truly disadvantaged" (Wilson 1987), have experienced not only high rates of unemployment and underemployment, but also declining wage levels and few if any financial assets beyond their incomes. Given the lack of universal health coverage, a substantial portion of the poor live without health insurance. The poorest members of the black community often live in hyper-segregated neighborhoods (Massey 1996), living apart from the societal mainstream. Their housing is often substandard and the schools and public amenities in their neighborhoods are inferior to those found in more affluent locales.

The concern of contemporary Marshall-inspired thinkers is that the growing tide of inequality leads to increased levels of social exclusion for the most marginalized and poorest sectors of the society. At the same time, even the middle class finds itself confronting challenges produced by inequality and the related concentration of economic power. Thus, the role of money in politics has made it increasingly difficult for people of relatively modest means to run for office, particularly at the national level. In addition, the concentration of media outlets in the hands of a few giant multinational corporations has resulted in a reduction of the range of opinions being voiced and a similar reduction in efforts aimed at in-depth, critical reporting. Rather than being a vehicle for the education of the citizenry, the media – and this is especially the case for television – have increasingly blurred the distinction between news and entertainment.

It is not surprising that pessimistic proponents of Marshall's view of citizenship have concluded that class abatement is threatened in neoliberal regimes and insofar as this is the case, it means that the poorest sectors of society experience increased levels of social exclusion. It is also not surprising that the most pessimistic of these commentators have also voiced concern about the deleterious impact of the erosion of social rights on the middle classes. This harks back to a position advanced decades ago by Lipset (1963; see also Glassman et al. 1993), who argues – rooting his thesis in Aristotle – that a healthy and viable democratic society necessitates a large and comfortable middle class with considerable ability to shape the political agenda of a society. Such a society necessitates class abatement, which means that it is essential to reduce the percentage of people in the lower classes as much as possible, while also limiting both the size and the power of the wealthiest sectors. With this in mind, we turn to the recent concern voiced about the presumed withdrawal of citizens – especially the middle class – from involvement in the civic and political realms.

4

Withdrawal

T. H. Marshall (1964: 118–19) pointed out that in the welfare state rights grow in significance, while obligations do not. For better or worse, as noted in the preceding chapter, he concluded that a relatively passive citizenry, at least in normal times, should be expected. This fact may not be troubling to elite democratic theorists, but advocates of republicanism and communitarianism consider it to be a matter of concern. Coincident with the theoretical challenges to social rights (and to some extent to political rights as well) is a discourse about the need to rethink obligations. More specifically, this chapter will address concerns that have been voiced in recent years about the tendency of citizens to withdraw from participating in the public sphere.

The idea of obligations raises the question of not only what those obligations might be, but how they are embedded in civic virtues. What is expected of the virtuous citizen? William Galston (1991: 221–4) has identified four types of civic virtue, which he defines as general, social, economic, and political. General virtues refer to a basic level of loyalty to the society and a willingness to abide by its laws. Social virtues point to the capacity to live an autonomous life among others, which calls for being simultaneously independent and open-minded in regard to those who differ from you or express ideas that differ from your own. Economic virtues include possessing a work ethic that includes not only a sense of diligence to the task at hand but also a willingness both to be adaptable to economic change and to have a capacity to delay gratification. Finally, political virtues necessitate an ability to respect the rights of other people, the knowledge necessary to evaluate the performance of political rulers, and a willingness to participate in political discourse.

With this in mind, to borrow from Angus Stewart's (1995: 63) distinction, there are two conceptions of citizenship: "state citizenship" and "democratic citizenship." If the legal status attached to membership and the rights accruing thereby refers to "state citizenship," the idea of citizens as active agents involved in the decision-making processes of a political community invokes the type of belonging that he calls "democratic citizenship." This chapter turns to assessments of the proper understanding of the democratic citizen, focusing on influential accounts that have expressed concern about what is viewed as a deleterious withdrawal on the part of growing numbers of citizens from the public sphere.

Those who see withdrawal as troubling do so because their understanding of democracy entails a conviction that it cannot persist without citizen participation in political life. This conviction is perhaps nowhere so succinctly and directly expressed as in Hanna Pitkin and Sara Shumer's (1982: 43) following assertion:

> The basic idea is simple: people can and should govern themselves. They do not need specially bred or anointed rulers, nor a special caste or class to run their affairs. Everyone has the capacity for autonomy, even quite ordinary people – the uneducated, the poor, housewives, laborers, peasants, the outsiders and castoffs of society. Each is capable not merely of self-control, of privately taking charge of his own life, but also of self-government, of sharing in the deliberate shaping of their common life. Exercising this capacity is prerequisite both to the freedom and full development of each, and to the freedom and justness of the community.

Although not alone, the disparate group of intellectuals associated with communitarian thought has in recent years played a singularly significant role in pressing the case that the withdrawal of citizens from civic life imperils democracy; they include the godfather of communitarianism, Amitai Etzioni (1993) and also sociologists Robert Bellah (to be discussed below) and Philip Selznick (1992), political theorist Michael Sandel (1998), theologian Stanley Hauerwas (1981), feminist political theorist Jean Bethke Elshtain (1996), and philosopher Alasdair MacIntyre (1984). While many others disclaim the communitarian label, they share in common with communitarians a view of contemporary life that suggests that the public's general sense of obligation to the common good has declined – some think to a precipitous and troubling extent.

The literature on this topic that has been produced during the past two decades is substantial. In at least two instances scholars sharing this general sense of unease with the presumed decline in civil responsibility have produced books that became bestsellers in the United States and elsewhere, with appeal far beyond an academic audience: Robert Bellah and his associates Richard Madsen, William M. Sullivan, Ann Swidler, and Steven M. Tipton's *Habits of the Heart: Individualism and Commitment in American*

Life (1985) and Robert Putnam's *Bowling Alone: The Collapse and Revival of American Community* (2000). Rather than attempting a broad survey of books concerned with the withdrawal of citizens from civic life, we will confine ourselves to an examination of these two books. We offer a brief synopsis of each book in order to lay out the issues and concerns of their respective authors, as well as the way that they articulate their sense of the scope and depth of the problem along with their proposed solutions. We do so because we think that, taken together, these two books encapsulate the central arguments of those scholars named earlier, as well as others who would self-identify as republicans or communitarians and have expressed concern about a presumed decline in civic participation.

INDIVIDUALISM AND ITS DISCONTENTS: TOCQUEVILLE REVISITED

Turning first to Bellah et al., it is useful to note that the phrase "habits of the heart" derives from a passage in Alexis de Tocqueville's *Democracy in America* (1969 [1853]). Indeed, *Habits* is very much the product of a self-conscious effort to reflect on and update the insights of that classic work at the sesquicentennial of its initial publication. Both books can be read as meditations on the implications of individualism for civic engagement. Tocqueville introduced the term "individualism" in Volume II of *Democracy*, explaining that, "it is a word recently coined to express a new idea" (Tocqueville 1969: 506). In his view, the democratic ethos of America produced a culture of individualism, which served to distinguish it from the old regimes of Europe, though he also saw America as emblematic of the future of Europe. His take on individualism was decidedly ambivalent. On the one hand, as the following passage indicates, he defined it in part by distinguishing it from egoism:

> Egoism is a passionate and exaggerated love of self that leads a man to think of all things in terms of himself and to prefer himself to all. Individualism is a calm and considered feeling which disposes each citizen to isolate himself from the mass of his fellows and withdraw into a circle of family and friends; with this little society formed to his taste, he gladly leaves the greater society to look after itself. (Tocqueville 1969: 506)

This message may appear incongruent with another theme in *Democracy*, namely that Americans are, in contrast to their European counterparts, great joiners. Before turning to this point, one observation is in order: individualism so construed in this formulation does not lead to a state of alienation or anomie since people turn not into solipsistic beings but rather they invest their energies in creating and maintaining relatively small circles of intimates. Individualism and egoism were postulated as distinct states. However, later in the volume, Tocqueville turned pessimistic by suggesting that while this is the case, it is also conceivable that over time individualism might attack "public virtues" as it "merges into egoism," at which point "each man is forever thrown back on himself alone, and there is danger that he may be shut up in the solitude of his own heart" (Tocqueville 1969: 507–8).

Whether or not individualism ultimately fuses with egoism, as Tocqueville's definition makes clear, it poses a problem for citizenship insofar as people turn their backs on participation in the public sphere, refusing to embrace a set of obligations that focus on the commonweal and not simply the interests of one's circle of intimates. As such, there is an inevitable tension between citizenship and individualism, and in an age of individualism this suggests that republican virtues are always at risk. Tocqueville identified the problem, but did not offer a particularly compelling solution. At points, he writes about the capacity to temper excessive individualism by the promotion of "self-interest rightly understood." Unfortunately, he fails to offer a cogent account of what this type of self-interest would look like, or how it ought to be differentiated from the more corrosive form of self-interest. What is clear is that individualism is seen as a given in the modern world, and what is at stake for a republican version of citizenship is to temper it in some fashion so that it does not undermine a sense of obligation on the part of citizens.

Habits of the heart

This is the central theme that Bellah and his associates picked up on 150 years later as they offered a critical analysis of the "habits of the heart" of Americans in the latter part of the twentieth century. They present a bleak diagnosis, contending that "individualism may have grown cancerous – that it may be destroying those social integuments that Tocqueville saw as moderating in influence its more destructive potentialities" (Bellah et al. 1985: viii). Moreover, they suggest that their predecessor's fear that individualism might merge with egoism may well have occurred, leaving "the individual suspended in glorious, but terrifying isolation" (Bellah et al. 1985: 6). In this claim, they echo the concern of an earlier social critic, Philip Slater, who in *The Pursuit of Loneliness* (1970) contended that Americans were increasingly living "alone together." However, as shall be seen below, they disagree with Slater about the solution – indeed, by the time they wrote their book, Slater's explicitly utopian quest for community, which he thought found its most significant expression in the communes created by the 1960s youth counterculture, had taken on the quality of a period piece.

The work of Bellah and colleagues is an exercise in cultural analysis and not a study in social psychology. What they seek to sketch out are the implications of the triumph of a culture of modern individualism at the expense of two older traditions in American history: the biblical and the republican. Both of these traditions, albeit in different ways, stressed the obligations that individuals had to their communities, and in this way both contributed to the notion of an engaged citizenry committed to the commonweal. Bellah and colleagues point to two types of individualism – utilitarian and expressive – that have contributed to the erosion of both biblical and republican discourses. Although they don't make the parallel, the former type looks very much like what political philosopher C. B. Macpherson (1964) called "possessive individualism," which he understood to be a product of capitalism's competitive marketplace. The latter in turn can be seen as an expression of the emergence of a therapeutic culture. In this regard, they do note that their understanding of expressive individualism is similar to Philip Rieff's (1966) "psychological man," who, he contends, is a manifestation of the "triumph of the therapeutic." Bellah and his associates (1985: 311) think Rieff is on to something, but overstated the case.

With these two modes of individualism, the authors are prepared to explain what at first glance appears to be a paradox. Individualism is ascendant while at the same time Americans remain active in the public sphere. Indeed, they contend, "Americans are more engaged in voluntary associations and civic organizations than the citizens of most other industrial nations" (Bellah et al. 1985: 163). Why do they remain engaged in civic life even if the rationales provided by the biblical and republican traditions exert less and less influence over the culture they inhabit? In answering this question, Bellah and his colleagues remained attentive to the accounts provided by the middle-class subjects they interviewed. What they discovered was that these individuals tended to explain their participation in a wide variety of community organizations in terms of what it did for them. Rather than stating that they were involved because of a sense of obligation, be it religiously or politically derived, they instead explained their civic involvements as activities that made them feel good by offering a sense of meaning and self-expression. While there is no doubt that one can discover that underpinning their activism are lingering vestiges of biblical and republican values, the authors, nonetheless, voice concern that the turn towards inwardness that they detect is a product of the combined impact of utilitarian and therapeutic individualism.

Commitments are viewed as "enhancements of the sense of individual well-being rather than as moral imperatives" (Bellah et al. 1985: 47). In an implicitly Durkheimian analysis, without so identifying it, they describe a state of anomie in which an externally based, socially defined moral meaning is lacking. The consequence is that the culture is increasingly devoid of a language of commitment that manages to connect individuals to communities of memory. This lack of a discourse of commitment in turn erodes the identification of individuals to institutions. Given the centrality that religious institutions have played in American civic life, it is not surprising that the authors pay particular attention to religious life, highlighting what Thomas Luckmann (1967) some decades earlier had predicted: the increasing privatization of religious life. It also illustrates the distinction that sociologist of religion Wade Clark Roof (1999) has made more recently between religiosity and spirituality. While the former entails commitment to and involvement in religious institutions, the latter is a far more private matter. In one of the most widely cited passages from *Habits*, the authors illustrate this privatization when they describe the religious faith of a woman they call Sheila Larson. She describes her faith as "Sheilaism," explaining it in the following way: "I believe in God. I'm not a religious fanatic. I can't remember the last time I went to church. My faith has carried me a long way. It's Sheilaism. Just my own little voice" (Bellah et al. 1985: 221).

Individualism is evident not only in such manifestations of privatized religion, free from institutional entanglements, but, paradoxically, in religious institutions as well. This is particularly evident in the dramatic growth of evangelical Christian mega-churches such as Willow Creek Community Church in suburban Chicago and Lakewood Church in Houston, both of which have over 10,000 people attending Sunday services (Leland 2005). The format of these media-savvy churches is to treat worship as entertainment and to advertise their "product" in terms of what it can do for individuals. There is very little emphasis placed on duties to the church or obligations to the world at large or to those in need – the poor, the ill, and the outcast. Instead, the focus is on how the church might encourage members to enter into what the Lakewood Church website calls "a victorious Christian life," a life outlined in a *New York Times* bestseller authored by the Senior Pastor Joel Osteen (who in an order of succession typical of such churches, took over from his father), titled *Your Best Life Now*. Far from the demanding otherworldly asceticism of predecessor fundamentalist religious bodies, the Willow Creeks and Lakewoods are steeped in an individualistic therapeutic culture that is quite at odds with orthodox Protestant theology. As such, their take on Christianity could not be further removed from what the martyred Protestant theologian Dietrich Bonhoeffer (1959) had in mind in *The Cost of Discipleship*. Indeed, he offers an apt characterization of these churches as purveyors of "cheap grace."

Defining the good society

Returning to Bellah and colleagues' thesis, the moral discourse on citizenship is seen as revolving around three separate conceptualizations of politics. The authors distinguish "the politics of community," "the politics of interest," and "the politics of nation" (Bellah et al. 1985: 200–1). The first is a consensual politics grounded at the local level, with the New England town meeting of the past being a paradigmatic expression. The problem with this form of politics is that it has appeared to work best in settings characterized by relatively small-sized communities that are basically homogeneous. Bellah and colleagues express concern about the capacity of this form of politics to function effectively in a large, highly complex, and heterogeneous nation-state.

The second refers to interest group pluralism, which entails competition among groups that pursue their own self-interest in a manner akin to behavior in the economic marketplace. Some theorists might argue that, as with the presumed working of the invisible hand in the competitive marketplace, so in the political arena the common good emerges out of intergroup competition. However, one can easily point to evidence that illustrates how self-interest decidedly works against the interests of the whole of society. While definitely part of the American political process, the politics of interest points to the obvious limitation of such an approach to the construction of a shared sense of communal identity.

The third conceptualization is concerned with those times that particular interests give way to the "national purpose." It tends to arise in times of crisis, with wars and national disasters being typical triggers (the "Dunkirk spirit," in Marshall's formulation). It is also often a symbolic form of politics. This could clearly be seen in the immediate aftermath of 9/11, when individuals across the United States, in rather spontaneous expressions of patriotism, began to fly flags from their motor vehicles. Such a politics tends to link the individual in an unmediated manner to national political leaders – but in a manner wherein the leaders make decisions and the citizenry is primarily passive.

Unlike Rousseau's vision of the social contract, with its emphasis on the necessity of avoiding mediating institutions in the citizen's relationship to the state, Bellah and colleagues concur with Tocqueville's belief that mediating institutions between the individual and state are essential for a democratic politics to prevail. In their view, such institutions serve two vital functions: "as moderating the isolating tendencies of private ambition on the one hand and limiting the despotic proclivities of government on the other." They go on to note that, "Vigorous citizenship depends on the existence of well-established groups and institutions, including everything from families to political parties, on the one hand, and new organizations, movements, and coalitions responsive to particular historical situations, on the other" (Bellah et al. 1985: 212).

It is in *The Good Society* (1991), the sequel to *Habits of the Heart*, that Bellah and associates shift from an emphasis on cultural discourse to a focus on these essential groups and institutions. Indeed, the first chapter is entitled "We Live through Institutions." Expressing some ambivalence about the communitarian label that some placed on *Habits*, the authors are nonetheless clear that increased citizen participation is necessary at the local and national levels (there are hints that they also see the need for such participation at the global level). They are equally clear that a political culture that places a premium on the autonomous individual, and that valorizes the market so much that it seeks to extend its logic into all facets of social life, and/or that relies too heavily on the procedural state, serves to undermine an informed and engaged citizenry (Bellah et al. 1991: 6).

This book is an explicit exercise in public philosophy in the tradition of Walter Lippmann, Herbert Croly, and John Dewey. In brief, their argument is that radical individualism, and an acquisitive market economy that privileges private property over the public good, are the main factors contributing to the erosion of citizen involvement. Added to this, they are also concerned about the negative effects on participation caused by a highly bureaucratic welfare state that replaces democratic decision making with administrative decision making (theirs being a leftist critique that parallels the critiques surveyed in the preceding chapter). However, they are critical of those who would roll back the welfare state in an effort to establish a minimalist state that is solely concerned with protecting the society from its enemies, external and internal – the so-called "watchdog theory of the state". In the authors' view, "only an institutionally strengthened politics can renew real democracy," and it would appear that a vibrant politics necessitates something other than a minimalist state (Bellah et al. 1991: 133).

A revival of citizen involvement calls for a transformation of the public sphere. Political parties are viewed as a key component of this revival, and their strengthening is treated as vital. Parties must gain greater control over campaign financing, at the expense of individual candidates, if the impact of powerful special interests is to be successfully reduced. At the same time, parties need to create policy institutes and other vehicles for the development and articulation of carefully crafted public policy agendas. The role of the media must be transformed if genuine political debate is to be possible. One specific proposal offered by the authors is to ban all political advertisements on radio and television. In this way, the ground would be paved to replace the sound-bite campaign with one characterized by substantive political debate. Another proposal calls for, on the one hand, greater localism (federalism, in their terms), and, on the other, a greater reliance on supranational organizations in the pursuit of global economic justice, security, and the promotion of human rights. Bellah and colleagues also call for a shift in the character of public debate that focuses less on private interests and more on the public good. Finally, they note that the revival they seek cannot occur without an educated citizenry, and they charge all of the major societal institutions with the task of creating an informed citizenry as part of a larger project in moral education (Bellah et al. 1991: 142–4).

We leave aside the issue of the likelihood that the sorts of transformations they call for are at this historical moment politically viable (in the USA for certain, but elsewhere as well). It is useful to note that what is seen at root to be a problem brought about by the cultural ascendance of modern individualism has a solution that is not simply in the hearts and minds of the citizenry – though this is part of the solution they envision – but also requires a social structural solution. Lacking in this analysis is a critical assessment of the structural roots of modern individualism. As with other cultural traditions in America, the authors depict individualism as being grounded in American history, but never make clear in precisely what ways it is grounded or indeed how it came to be. Since theirs is in fundamental ways a Durkheimian-inspired cultural analysis, one might look to his understanding of the division of labor in industrial societies for an explanation. However, no explicit effort is made in this regard to link their account to Durkheim.

Moreover, both works can be seen as a type of social criticism commonly found in the social sciences, characterized by its averseness to an explicitly Marxist analysis that would place capitalism center stage (of course, one need not be a Marxist to so locate capitalism). Like the children's book *Where's Waldo*, the exegete can expend considerable time looking for capitalism in both *Habits* and *The Good Society*. To be sure, there are traces throughout both texts. Thus, there is a section in the latter work on "The Tyranny of the Market," in which Bellah et al. (1991: 92–3) refer approvingly to economist Robert Heilbroner's critical analysis of the increasing commodification of everyday life.

However, missing from the discussion is any effort to consider the inherent tension between the "possessive individualism" engendered by the capitalist market and the citizen concerned with finding a way to harmonize individual desires and needs with the promotion of the common good. Also missing is any consideration of the possibility that what has occurred over time is that the peculiar *mentalité* of the capitalist market has spread well beyond the economic sphere to shape the way people think about the rest of society, including the polity. In such a society it is possible to conceive of citizens being defined, not by participation in political decision making, but, as noted in the preceding chapter, as consumers. This is in part what social historian Lizabeth Cohen (2003) had in mind when she wrote about the emergence of a "consumers' republic" (recall that in the aftermath of 9/11, George W. Bush's injunction to Americans was twofold: remain vigilant and go shopping). The social criticism of Bellah et al. ought not to be seen as repudiating this possibility. Rather, it should be viewed as a criticism that, by concentrating on the cultural, is insufficiently attentive to social structural – particularly economic – factors.

ENTER PUTNAM

Bellah and colleagues did not question whether or not Americans continued to be a nation of joiners a century and a half after Tocqueville's observations. They assumed, without exploring empirically, that people continued to be engaged in the realm of civil society. This assumption was questioned in 1995, when Harvard political scientist Robert Putnam published an essay with the provocative title, "Bowling Alone: America's Declining Social Capital." Putnam, himself an amateur bowler in his youth, begins with the observation that although more Americans are bowling than ever before, they are increasingly "bowling alone." To be more precise, since people tend to go bowling with friends and family, they are not literally bowling alone. What they are not doing at the rates that Americans did a half-century ago is to bowl in organized leagues. This became a metaphor for the withdrawal from active engagement in civic life. It is also precisely what Tocqueville predicted would be the consequence of modern individualism.

The decline of social capital

However, Putnam's analysis diverges from the Tocqueville/Bellah thesis insofar as it does not identify individualism as the primary causal factor contributing to a decline in civic involvement. Instead, he seeks to offer a historically grounded social structural explanation. Rather than a cultural approach, Putnam presents an institutional analysis of varying degrees and levels of civic engagement. This approach was evident in his earlier research on democracy in modern Italy that culminated in *Making Democracy Work: Civic Traditions in Modern Italy* (Putnam 1993). In that work, Putnam concerned himself with identifying the features that distinguished the civic vibrancy of the north of Italy from the anemic commitment to public life in the south. His argument hinges on the idea of social capital. Indeed, he is, along with James Coleman (1988–9, 1994) and Pierre Bourdieu (1986), primarily responsible for introducing the idea of social capital into the social sciences (Portes 1998; Lin 2001; Field 2003). Putnam's take on social capital differs significantly from these two theorists in one fundamental way. Both Coleman and Bourdieu viewed social capital in terms of the social networks that serve as potential resources for individuals – resources that can be used in particular contexts to enhance their respective positions. As such, they treated it as a parallel concept to financial and human capital. Putnam differs by viewing social capital not primarily as a resource differentially available to individuals but, rather, as a factor that contributes to cooperation and trust, both prerequisites for civic participation. Without totally dismissing the idea of social capital as a private good, his emphasis is clearly on the public good. In short, it is seen as a crucial variable shaping different levels of community involvement (Edwards and Foley 1998).

His version of this concept suggests that it "refers to features of social organizations, such as trust, norms and networks that can improve the efficiency of society by facilitating coordinated actions" (Putnam 1993: 167). What this meant in the north of Italy was that a historically rooted sense of mutuality between governmental institutions and the civic realm facilitated the perpetuation of a situation wherein people were enticed to take an active role in public life. Key to the civic-mindedness of this region is the strength of secondary associations such as trade unions, mutual aid societies, churches, and the like. Concurring with Mark Granovetter's (1973) "the strength of weak ties" thesis, Putnam contends that in contrast to the strong ties of intimate interpersonal relationships, the weak (and often cross-cutting) ties involved in membership in secondary associations facilitates those things necessary for active citizen participation in civic life: trust, mutuality, and appropriate norms of reciprocity. The preconditions for civic-mindedness are historically rooted, dating back as far as the medieval guilds (Putnam 1993: 127–9). The same factors that contribute to civic involvement also serve to explain why the north of Italy is the most economically dynamic and modern industrial region of the nation.

Putnam's account of the south of Italy can be instructively compared with the characterization of that region offered several decades earlier by Edward Banfield (1958). Using the term "amoral familism," Banfield sought to provide an explanation for the lack of civic involvement in southern Italy. In his account, the premodern folkways of "a backward society" served to explain why attachments to the public realm were so weak. It was not a product of individualism, a distinct product of modernity, but rather the result of the overarching capacity of one particular societal institution – the family – to weaken the efficacy of all other institutions. In other words, to use Lewis Coser's (1974) terminology, the southern Italian family was a "greedy institution" that did not permit cross-cutting or competing allegiances to other institutions. Rather, it demanded a total commitment to family loyalties at the expense of attachments to civic institutions. This being the case, support for governmental institutions would be weak, as would trust outside the sphere of intimates. Putnam's assessment focuses primarily on the nature of social capital in the north of Italy and its lack in the south, but his argument can be seen as parallel-ing Banfield's insofar as the focus is on the role of social institutions in either facilitating or inhibiting civic engagement.

The "bowling alone" thesis

When Putnam turned his attention to the United States, the concept of social capital again framed his critical analysis of what he construed to be the steady decline in community involvement during the past several decades. The lack of civic participation is treated as the product of the erosion of social networks that link people to their communities, or, in other words, to the decline in social capital. In *Bowling Alone* (2000) he attempted to accomplish two things. First, he sought to offer empirical evidence that civic involvement is in fact declining, and, secondly, he attempted to identify the reasons for the decline. Based on the data he supplies, it would appear that there has been a dramatic decline in com-munity participation during the last quarter of the twentieth century. This is clearly the case with political participation. Not only do fewer Americans vote today than they did in the past, but in terms of other measures of political involvement, ranging from holding office in a club or organization to signing a petition, Putman (2000: 45) reports an overall decrease over a two-decade period of 25 percent.

Turning to civic organizations, Putnam notes that many organizations – including fraternal service organizations such as the Rotary Club and the mainstream civil rights organization, the NAACP – have experienced a substantial decline in membership. While he does note that some organiza-tions, such as Greenpeace, have grown during the same time period, he contends that these organizations are different insofar as they make no time claims on their members. Instead, they are essentially mail-order member-ships where "members" do no more than pay a membership fee, allowing a professional staff to conduct the business of the organization. A more revealing measure of decline in civic participation for Putnam is the reduc-tion in the number of hours Americans commit to organizational life. He reports that whereas Americans spent 3.7 hours per month working for community organizations in 1965, by 1995 the figure was 2.3 hours per month. Moreover, during this same time period, the percentage of Americans actively participating in such organizations declined from 7 to 3 percent (Putnam 2000: 62).

High levels of religious involvement have long served to differentiate the United States from other advanced industrial nations, particularly the nations of Western Europe. Nonetheless, here too Putnam sifts through the findings of major studies concerned with trends in institutional membership and regular attendance and concludes that since the 1960s there has been an approximately 10 percent decline in church membership and a far more precipitous decline in participation in various religious activities (ranging somewhere between 25 percent and 50 percent). Like Bellah and colleagues, Putnam attributes much of this erosion to the privatization of religion (Putnam 2000: 74–6). He detects a similar pattern in philanthropic giving and volunteer work (Putnam 2000: 116–33).

Turning to potential countervailing trends, Putnam first examines workplace connections, pondering whether the fact that Americans are working longer hours might mean that they have transferred their civic involvements to that locus. With admittedly limited evidence available, he is unconvinced by this prospect (Putnam 2000: 90). More significant is the growth in membership experienced by a variety of groups – both self-help such as Alcoholics Anonymous and Weight Watchers, and the local chapters of advocacy groups such as the National Alliance for the Mentally Ill and Mothers Against Drunk Driving. Although Putnam does not discount these trends out of hand, he dismisses the idea that they reflect anything resembling a revival of civic participation.

At some level, he appears to harbor a (remarkably romantic) view that the main street businessman member of the local Rotary Club is the ideal typical example of the truly engaged citizen. In this regard, Garry Wills (2000: 15) has described Putnam's perspective on the past as having a "roseate Norman Rockwell glow." Thus, Putnam faults contemporary organizations for their highly volatile memberships and their heavy reliance on paid professional staff, neither of which suggests to him true staying power on behalf of the rank-and-file members. Finally, he is equally suspicious of the claims made by Internet enthusiasts about the capacity of computer-mediated communication to enhance and indeed to expand the prospects of organized public life (Putnam 2000: 148–80), though given the nascent character of "digital formations" it is perhaps premature to be quite so dismissive about the varied ways in which computer networks are shaping patterns of social relations (Latham and Sassen 2005).

Putnam's discounting of the possibility that new forms of organizational life and virtual communities might serve as a counterfoil to the declines of more traditional civic involvement is at times strained. Thus, one complaint about newer organizations is that their membership rolls change rather dramatically. Implicitly, he appears to be arguing, following our earlier point, that the individual who joins the local Rotary and routinely attends its luncheon meetings over many years serves as the model of civic virtue, rather than the person who moves from organization to organization, treating them as ad hoc locations for addressing particular issues of vital and immanent concern. Putnam never seriously entertains the possibility that these "main street" organizations have decreased in size in recent decades simply because they have lost their *raison d'être*, with remaining members increasingly engaged in Merton's (1968) sense of ritualistic behavior, going through the motions without a clear sense of organizational ends.

Likewise, the fact that organizations rely on professional staffs does not necessarily signal a reduction in the work or a devaluation of the contributions of volunteers. Amnesty International is a case in point. Although the professional staff is responsible for much organizing and certainly for the investigative work of the organization, Amnesty could not function were it not for the efforts of local chapters composed of volunteers engaged in such activities as letter writing on behalf of prisoners of conscience and educational campaigns about human rights issues.

Moreover, as Putnam himself contends, American history ought not to be viewed as a narrative about the progressive loss of community, but rather as a matter of waves. Part of the problem with his analysis of the present is that he uses the 1950s and 1960s as the benchmarks by which to judge levels of civic participation without adequately exploring the extent to which this presumed golden age of civic involvement was unique in American history.

For these reasons we think it reasonable to conclude, as Bryan Turner (2001: 199) has, that although civic engagement has declined in recent history, nonetheless, "Individual involvement in voluntary associations, clubs and leisure groups is probably more robust than the Putnam thesis about the decline of social capital would suggest." Turner's assessment is given additional credence by the scholars assembled by Putnam himself in *Democracies in Flux: The Evolution of Social Capital in Contemporary Society* (2002). Thus, Robert Wuthnow (2002: 75) concludes that "there has been some decline in social capital in the United States over the past two or three decades; however, evidence does not indicate that social capital has declined drastically or to radically low levels, nor does it show that social capital of all kinds has declined." Similar patterns, along with the expected differences associated with differing historical national experiences, can be discerned in other chapters in the book that trace the recent fate of social capital in Britain, Germany, France, Spain, Sweden, Australia, and Japan (see for example Hall 2002 on Britain).

Underlying Putnam's thesis is a straightforward, and problematic, causal argument: high levels of social capital lead to high levels of civic involvement, which in turn lead to a vibrant democratic polity. Carl Boggs (2001:

285) correctly contends that, "at no point does Putnam establish any connection between the social and political realms that would permit such
far-fetched claims about the impact of SC." Indeed, Boggs observes that
voluntary organizations have managed to coexist with authoritarian political systems, and thus ought not to be viewed uncritically as bulwarks of
democracy. Moreover, he argues that by ignoring the ideological content
of organizations, Putnam underestimates the significance of the darker side
of social capital as manifested in street gangs, religious cults, and an array
of reactionary political movements that in combination represent a challenge to a pluralist democracy (Boggs 2001: 286).

As many commentators have noted, and Putnam himself realizes, our
understanding of many of the issues associated with civic engagement is
limited by the quality of the empirical data we have available. More problematic, we think, is Putnam's account of the causes contributing to the
erosion of civic engagement. He identifies four major potential causal
factors: (1) time and financial pressures; (2) suburbanization, commuting,
and urban sprawl; (3) television; and (4) generational succession. Contrary
to scholars such as Arlie Hochschild (1997), who have written about the
"time bind" of dual-career middle-class American families who are working
longer hours than in the past, Putnam does not think that this change
contributes significantly to decline. Rather, he concludes that time and
money pressures contribute "no more than 10 percent of the total decline"
(Putnam 2000: 283). What he fails to consider is evidence that there is a
bifurcation between educated professionals, who are in fact working longer
hours, and those less educated members of the workforce who are not
(Gerson and Jacobs 2004). What makes this particularly significant is that
the more affluent and higher-educated sectors of society have historically
been more involved in civic activities than other sectors have been. It is
precisely these individuals who confront the time bind most intensely, a
factor that Putnam ignores by not adequately considering the significance
of social class.

Putnam attaches only 10 percent of the blame to the spatial factors he
associates with the geography of suburban communities and the fact that
commutes are often longer than they once were due to sprawl. This leaves
two primary culprits: television and generational change. In his estimation,
television contributes to 25 percent of the erosion, while generational
change is responsible for "perhaps half of the overall decline" (Putnam
2000: 283).

Television viewing is depicted as a manifestation of the privatization of
social life, a technologically induced aspect of the Tocquevellian theme
concerning the tendency to restrict social relations to the sphere of social
intimates. Putnam is clear that television per se is not the culprit. Thus,
viewers of PBS's *NewsHour* and the BBC's *World Report* are utilizing

"television's capacity to keep people informed about events in the larger world. However, a minority of television viewers actually watch this sort of programming. In contrast, large audiences watch the formulaic entertainment programs – the situation comedies, dramas, and, more recently, the proliferation of "reality" programs (an example of what Baudrillard calls "hyperreality" and Debord refers to as "spectacle") – that constitute the bread and butter of the major networks' schedule of programs. Putnam contends that there is a correlation between watching many hours of entertainment television and a lack of civic engagement. However, he fails to make a convincing case that correlation speaks to cause.

Generational succession refers to the differences in civic engagement on the part of the generation that came of age during World War II, the Baby Boomer generation, and Generation-X. The first is viewed as a particularly civic-minded generation (and thus is, according to former television newsreader Tom Brokaw [1998], "the greatest generation"), while the latter two are not. Though Putnam hesitates to draw the conclusion that the crisis condition of war may have played a decisive role in shaping the public involvement of the World War II generation, such a conclusion is difficult to avoid. In this regard, it is important to remember that World War II united the nation, whereas the Vietnam War, which was the decisive world event during the formative period of Baby Boomers, divided the nation and contributed to a legitimation crisis of the state. Watergate, of course, compounded that crisis. Thus, the watershed historical events shaping each of these two generations were very different.

Meanwhile, Generation-X lacked a similar potentially transformative event that its members needed to respond to in ways that would impact their futures. Instead, the collapse of communism and the end of the Cold War were simply external events that did not require commitment or decision on the part of this generation's members. The very name given to this generation attests to the idea that something is missing and that their collective identity suffers as a result. They are portrayed as being devoid of something that their parents' and grandparents' generations had: a defining historical moment.

While there is no doubt much to be said for Putnam's generational succession argument, there are also elements of it that lead to a rather circular conclusion, one that suggests that the reason that the World War II generation was more civic-minded than the generations of its children and grandchildren was because it was more civic-minded. It is worth noting that Putnam does not ask why this generation was so unsuccessful in educating its offspring for civic responsibility, or indeed if and how they attempted to do so. To the extent that Putnam hesitates to define generations in terms of specific historical events, he needs to provide an account of larger structural factors that serve to distinguish these three generations.

This he does not do, because, as David Schultz (2002: 91) puts it, "Putnam's approach situates the individual as the ontological center of democracy." He does not explore the differential impact of groups on democracy. Nor does he consider the role of inequality. Portes (1998: 19) is not alone in pointing out the class bias of the thesis. Linked to this failure (as with Bellah et al.), and missing from his account, is an inquiry into the potential impact of capitalism. In this regard, Putnam's analysis, too, is part of a line of liberal social criticism concerned with the erosion of public life that, as critics argue, can be viewed as tending to conflate intermediate and causal variables (Edwards et al. 2001). It is not that Putnam dismisses the potential role played by capitalism out of hand. However, what he has to say is revealing. He writes that, "Many grand masters of nineteenth-century social theory, from Georg Simmel to Karl Marx, argued that market capitalism had created a 'cold society,' lacking the interpersonal warmth necessary for friendship and devaluing human ties to the status of mere commodities" (p. 282).

The problem he finds with this line of thought is that "it explains too much," insofar as market capitalism has been a characteristic feature of the United States for two centuries, during which time civic involvement has in cyclical fashion waxed and waned (Putnam 2000: 282). He agrees that one type of what he refers to as "economic determinism" (his choice of words is revealing in that a focus on the impact of the economic system seems to be equated with a crude mechanistic version of Marxist thought) is having an impact on the erosion of social capital: multinational corporations and globalization. However, he qualifies his position by writing that its impact is chiefly experienced at the level of philanthropic and civic activities, questioning why it might affect "our readiness to attend a church social, or to have friends over for poker, or even to vote for president" (Putnam 2000: 283). This statement reflects a mixing of civic involvement with an activity – playing poker with friends – that by his definition qualifies as "bowling alone." To use the language he employs, we remain a nation of *schmoozers* (people who spend many hours in informal conversation and communion). The concern is that we are presumably no longer also a nation of *machers* (people who make things happen) (Putnam 2000: 93).

A more fundamental problem with Putnam's general unwillingness to consider capitalism's potential role in the decline of civic engagement is that he views capitalism as ahistorical. Foley and Edwards (1997: 551) refer to this as "the suppression of the economic dimension of contemporary social conflict." We would contend that, more specifically, it is a suppression of a genuine consideration of the role of capitalism in the "downsizing of democracy" (Crenson and Ginsberg 2004). In a footnote to the passage referring to Simmel and Marx, Putnam cites Daniel Bell's *The Cultural Contradictions of Capitalism* (1976) but does not explore his thesis. This book was a sequel to Bell's influential *The Coming of Post-Industrial Society* (1973), where he contended that increasingly the economy, polity, and culture operate on the basis of distinct and at times antithetical "axial principles." For the economy, it is instrumental rationality, which requires the control by a class of managerial and technical experts. The polity simultaneously is guided by principles that promote equality and the expansion of citizen involvement. Bell's particular focus is on culture in the sequel. His thesis is that the culture shaken from the mooring of the Protestant ethic takes on an antinomian, hedonistic character, one that Bell (1976: 54), with the youth counterculture of the 1960s clearly in mind, depicts as a transition "from the Protestant ethic to the psychedelic bazaar." From his perspective, the conflicts and tensions inherent in a postindustrial economy derive from the different and competing sets of normative expectations engendered by these axial principles.

Bell is anything but an economic determinist. Indeed, despite the book's concern with the "cultural contradictions of capitalism," he skirts the issue of the actual role that capitalism may have played in generating these contradictions. Instead, his thesis has something of a functionalist flavor in which the different institutional sectors of society operate with relative autonomy. Add to this the fact that his emphasis on industrial society rather than capitalism in much of his discussion has a Durkheimian ring rather than a Marxist one (indeed, like Bellah, Bell's socialist youth progressively yielded to a more mainstream sociological theorizing). Thus, he does not contend that democratic sensibilities arise from capitalism, but rather from the political sphere itself. Likewise, the cultural arena appears to generate its own axial principle *sui generis*.

Despite its problematic features, Bell was attentive to significant changes in capitalist industrial society, in particular: (1) the shift from competitive small firms to corporate capitalism; (2) the transformation of laissez-faire capitalism into an increasingly planned economy in which the polity becomes the "cockpit;" and (3) the move from a goods-producing society to the information society predicated on and organized around knowledge. Simply put, Putnam glosses over these changes.

More radical interpretations of the precise nature of the historical development of capitalism are simply ignored. Yet a consideration of these interpretations might reveal the necessity of according capitalism a critical role in the changes Putnam has chronicled. One especially relevant argument is the "disorganized capitalism" thesis, which, as noted earlier, was developed independently by Scott Lash and John Urry (1987), on the one hand, and Claus Offe (1984), on the other. They contend that, beginning in the 1960s, around the time Bell was articulating his postindustrial thesis and the time that Putnam views as the start of the decline in civic involvement, capitalism entered a third historical stage of development.

They describe the earliest period as liberal capitalism, characterized by laissez-faire policies. The second phase, shaped by Fordist production methods (embodied in the assembly line) and the management practices associated with Frederick Winslow Taylor, was the era of organized capitalism.

They argue that this stage has given way to disorganized capitalism in what many commentators have called the post-Fordist era. Contrary to Bell's conviction that postindustrial society would require an increasingly interventionist state, which meant both the implementation of Keynesian economic policies and the administration of a welfare state designed to insure societal stability, Lash and Urry viewed the third stage as entailing a retreat from the social contract between capital and labor that had been erected in the post-World War II era. The Reagan and Thatcher regimes signaled a new relationship between the economy and society. Their neo-liberal policies involved a frontal assault on the welfare state that was seen as crucial to the Marshallian version of social citizenship. Such policies have since spread, with varying degrees of success, to other advanced industrial nations, including those with considerably more substantive welfare states.

The result, as Alain Touraine (2001: 9) has portrayed it, is a situation in which "the market has replaced the state as the principal regulatory force" not only in the economy but also throughout the rest of society. Touraine (1971), it might be recalled, articulated a leftist version of the postindustrial thesis, one that, in contradistinction to Bell's, focused on the new system's capacity for domination and for restricting freedom. Rather than sectors of society operating on the basis of their own discrete axial principles, he treated the economic system as shaping the cultural logic of the entire society. Others on the left share this view, including thinkers who in other respects are quite different from one another (Habermas 1975; Harvey 1989; Jameson 1991).

Perhaps the person who comes closest to raising issues germane to Putnam's thesis is Richard Sennett. In *The Corrosion of Character* (1998) he traces the implications of white-collar work in the era of the new capitalism, in which a premium is placed on fluid workplaces and flexible workers. This is a world where corporations competing in the global marketplace are increasingly unwilling to commit to their workers over the course of their careers. No longer are corporate giants such as IBM and GM willing to invest in workers, providing them with life-long job security, generous health benefits, and comfortable pensions. Rather, the order of the day is to downsize, ship work offshore, and employ workers on a temporary contractual basis, often treating them as self-employed and thus not entitled to fringe benefits. Sennett questions the impact of this new economic order on human character, particularly on the possibility of creating and sustaining an integral self linked to the capacity to trust and to enter into relationships predicated on loyalty and shared norms of reciprocity. In a society where the previous social contract (Rubin 1995) that shaped the relationships between business and labor has been called into question, Sennett contends (2006: 83–130) that workers, both blue- and white-collar, confront the "specter of uselessness."

Sennett, of course, is writing about a phenomenon that has in recent decades begun to change the nature of work for the professional middle class. A similar phenomenon hit the working class earlier. Note the timing here, too, for what became known as deindustrialization, which Barry Bluestone and Bennett Harrison (1982: 6) defined as "the widespread disinvestment in the manufacturing sector," took root at precisely the time that Putnam suggests civic participation began its decline. As tens of thousands of manufacturing jobs disappeared, due to their export to Third World nations or because of automation, union membership declined precipitously.

Putnam (2000: 81) discusses the decline in union membership since the 1950s, when a third of the workforce was unionized, to the end of the twentieth century when the figure had dropped to 14.1 percent. With his penchant for quantifying the impact of various causal variables, Putnam contends that the shift from an industrial to a service economy accounts for only one-fourth of the decline, and if other structural factors are added to this, only half of the decline can be explained. He identifies the primary reason for the decline as a result of the reduction in demand for unions on the part of workers. In other words, the primary reason that there are "fewer union members is because fewer workers want to join" (Putnam 2000: 82). His explanation for this erosion of demand is that workers today are as much a product of the "cult of the individual" as are the professional and managerial classes.

This account and explanation takes the form of an assertion rather than a conclusion based on empirical evidence. Putnam fails to seriously consider the possibility that employers played a significant, perhaps the most significant role, in undercutting the strength and size of unions. Yet it is clear that corporate capitalism, with the support of neoliberal administrations (somewhat more tacit in the case of the Clinton administration), has mounted an aggressive campaign against unions. As the labor movement's base in the manufacturing sector eroded, major corporations in retail – led by the giant Wal-Mart – have relentlessly pursued anti-unionization campaigns. Indeed, Wal-Mart's notorious opposition to unions is widely known, and given that they are at present the nation's largest employer, paying lower wages than their competitors, they are seen as leading what some have termed the "race to the bottom." Labor unions have been forced into a defensive posture whereby they are more likely to be discussing concessions to employers than demands for improved wages, benefits, and working conditions (Lichtenstein 2003; Milkman and Voss 2004).

Putnam does not consider whether differences in social capital vary according to class location, and up to the present no one has offered any empirical findings that would help to determine whether working-class Americans and middle-class Americans possess different stocks of social capital that in turn contribute to differing levels of civic engagement. However, in a different but parallel national context, precisely such a conclusion has been made by Yaojun Li, Mike Savage, and Andrew Pickles (2003), in their examination of changes in levels of social capital in England and Wales between 1972 and 1999. The authors conclude that, with some fluctuations, middle-class social capital and civic engagement have remained quite constant during this period, while the working class has experienced a marked decline.

That Putnam does not consider the class-based character of capitalism can account in part for a curious feature of his work that has not escaped reviewers: for all the concern about the decline of citizenship participation, the book is curiously optimistic (Chaves 2000; Hunter 2000). His is in many respects a quintessential American moral tale, one that suggests that if ordinary Americans would simply turn off their television sets and join a metaphorical bowling league, civic life could be revived, which in turn would revitalize democracy. This leads to a concluding point that returns full circle to Marshall. The discourse on the erosion of citizen involvement is largely silent about citizenship's role in class abatement – in its capacity to mitigate the scope and the deleterious consequences of the inequalities produced by capitalism. Ariel Armony has made this case in a cross-national study that concludes that Putnam's thesis concerning the relationship between social capital and civic engagement is a "dubious link." Summarizing his conclusion, Armony (2004: 178–9) writes that:

> After showing that the civil society thesis does not explain institutional quality – specifically when we try to predict the effectiveness of the rule of law at the institutional level – I test an alternative hypothesis: economic inequality, a key structural condition, accounts for the production of social capital and in turn explains the quality of democratic institutions across nations. . . . My findings show that participation in voluntary organizations does not predict institutional quality, and social trust does emerge as a strong predictor of democratic institutions that work effectively. But, as further analysis reveals, trust is dependent upon socioeconomic conditions that work adequately for some and not for others.

This finding, of course, links the topic discussed in the preceding chapter to the topic treated here, suggesting that the erosion of democratic rights and the withdrawal of civic engagement are intimately connected.

The Third Way and Social Democracy

If Putnam is silent about the impact of the ascendancy of neoliberalism precisely during the time that he sees an erosion of a vibrant participatory democracy occurring, such is not the case with Anthony Giddens's (1998) effort to stake out what he describes as "the third way," which he depicts as an alternative to neoliberalism and to the socialism of the "old" Left. He seeks to locate his position beyond the binaries of the old left/right dichotomy, contending that he seeks a "renewal of social democracy" from the vantage of the "radical center," an idea that some critics have argued amounts to an oxymoron (Mouffe 1998). Giddens has been viewed as the intellectual architect of Tony Blair's "New Labour" platform, serving not as a policy advisor but as the creator of the conceptual edifice that undergirds Blair's attempted transformation of the Labour Party (Boynton 1997; *The Economist* 1999). That Blair's New Labour project is in many respects in tatters, in no small part due to his involvement in the war in Iraq, need not concern us here since there is evidence to suggest that from the start his administration did not entirely subscribe to what Giddens had in mind. Rather, what we are interested in exploring is Giddens's more general response to the rise of neoliberalism.

What precisely is "the third way" and what are its implications for citizenship? Although citizenship per se is not an explicitly defined topic in his thesis, Giddens shares a concern that the role of citizenship has been devalued, and that the question of rights and obligations needs to be rethought. He shares with the declensionist thinkers discussed above that, "Civic decline is real and visible in many sectors of contemporary societies, not just an invention of conservative politicians" (Giddens 1998: 78).

He begins his brief on behalf of the third way with the claim that after the fall of Soviet-style communism, the option of a command versus a market economy ceased to exist. Simply put, we have moved into an era where capitalism is the only viable option (Giddens 1998: 24). The question then revolves around the fate of social democracy in a situation where it can no longer be linked to socialism – which Giddens views first and foremost as a system in which the state plays a critical role in economic management (Giddens 1998: 7). But it is not simply Soviet-style command economies that Giddens criticizes. He appears to be little enamored of the mixed economies of what was seen in an earlier time period as "the middle way," namely the democratic socialist Scandinavian countries (Childs 1936). In this discussion, Giddens appears prepared to concede much to neoliberal economic policies. If state-owned industries are anathema in the new order, then one assumes that privatization of, for example, public transportation systems is acceptable, and perhaps even desirable, in the third way.

In Giddens's view (1998: 7–11), the classical model of social democracy is anachronistic. He disagrees with this model's encouragement of a state that dominated economic life and civil society. He is not sure that the cradle-to-grave welfare state – the so-called "nanny state" in the parlance of neoliberal critics – is the route to the future, and he is concerned about the low level of ecological consciousness that characterized this perspective. By privileging the bureaucratic state, the classical model fostered a situation in which citizen participation levels declined as citizens increasingly came to view themselves as instrumental consumers of social rights.

This being said, the third way is posed as a revisionist social democratic platform that is intended to challenge key features of neoliberalism (of course, Giddens has in mind the Thatcherite legacy, which constituted the most radical neoliberal agenda promoted in any of the advanced industrial nations). In his view, neoliberalism demands a minimalist state, its social welfare function replaced in many regards by a free-standing and strong civil society. At the same time, it promotes both what he refers to as "market fundamentalism" and a very traditionalist moral authoritarianism. It accepts inequality as inevitable and perhaps even desirable, while like its classical social democratic counterpart, exhibits a low ecological consciousness (Giddens 1998: 11–14). Its understanding of obligations tends to revolve around the notion of personal responsibility, which is the flip side of the assault on the idea of social rights.

According to Giddens, a central shortcoming of market fundamentalism is that it creates unacceptable levels of inequality. The third way, like its earlier social democratic counterpart, supports egalitarian principles. Giddens (2000b: 89) writes in a Fabian Society publication, "An emphasis on equality, it should be made clear, still presumes redistribution of wealth and income." As such, the third way supports a limited version of meritocracy, one that is prepared to impose limits on the levels of inequality that meritocracy inevitably yields. However, it is not clear how he thinks redistribution ought to be achieved. In an article in the *New Statesman*, he exhibits a lack of enthusiasm for progressive taxation policies as a major tool for combating inequality, and in fact seems rather supportive of supply-side policies (Giddens 1999: 27).

Still, he offers the third way as an antidote to neoliberalism. In making his case, he begins by pointing to an inherent contradiction in neoliberalism that has implications for the vibrant civil society it claims to promote. Neoliberalism advances the claims of both market fundamentalism and the conservatism that it sees residing in traditional communities. As Giddens points out – something Marx was equally aware of a century and a half earlier – capitalism is the great destroyer of tradition and community. Thus, to the extent that neoliberalism facilitates the functioning of an increasingly unregulated market capitalism, it places at risk both traditional values and the community structures that make civil society viable.

Critics have argued that the third way does not actually constitute an alternative to neoliberalism so much as it represents a tepid middle-of-the-road approach that, while perhaps blunting the excesses of neoliberalism, is in some fundamental ways complicit with its goals of weakening the state and strengthening the dominance of the market (Faux 1999; Callinicos 2001). If the Blair and Clinton administrations come closest to a third way politics, critics would appear to have a good case in arguing that it amounts to neoliberalism "lite." Touraine (2001: 91), for example, sees it as too centrist and focused too much on market deregulation and economic growth and too little on redistributive politics; he contends, perhaps somewhat tongue-in-cheek, that he would prefer a two-and-a-half way.

However, again, our focus is on the theoretical argument and not on actual political practices that operate with differing levels of commitment to the idea. Giddens contends that the third way is actually concerned with effecting a revival of social democracy and as such constitutes in reality a new politics of the left (though at times Giddens can be confusing on this score, particularly when he writes about moving beyond old received notions of right and left). In a recent attempt to update the idea of the third way, Giddens (2003) has issued a "progressive manifesto" in which he argues that rather than being a middle way, the third way is intended to transcend both the Old Left and neoliberalism. At the same time, it is seen as advancing a progressive agenda that is rooted in the politics of the left and not the right.

The third way makes its claim to be social democratic by first addressing the significance of civil society, particularly vis-à-vis the state. It does so by contending that civil society – that institutional realm of social interaction based on a sense of cooperation, loyalty, trust, and civility – requires a state committed to advancing and expanding democracy, performing duties well beyond the minimalist requirements of neoliberalism. Indeed, Giddens expresses concern about a situation wherein a powerful civil society confronts a weak state, for in his view an effective state is a necessity – à la Marshall – in reducing the inequalities generated by a market economy and alleviating the problems they generate. He is quite clear on this point, writing, "If left to its own devices, markets produce too much inequality and too much insecurity. The task of government is to reduce these, and to provide resources that will allow individuals to cope with those that remain" (Giddens 2002: 35). Civil society cannot be expected to accomplish this task. Its purpose is different, serving first and foremost as a public sphere or forum wherein citizens can enter as equals to debate the major issues of the day and to participate in constructing a shared vision of community.

Thus, Giddens envisions a symbiotic relationship between the state and civil society, and likewise between the state and a market economy. A strong civil society is necessary for both democracy and a successful market economy (Giddens 2000b: 29). In effect, what he calls for is a keenly calibrated balance amongst these three sectors of society. If the Old Left's endorsement of the welfare state privileged the state over the other two sectors, and the market fundamentalism of neoliberalism privileged the economy, Giddens is definitely not suggesting that civil society ought to trump the polity and the economy. He does not believe that the voluntary associations of civil society alone are capable of making democracy work (Cohen 1999). Indeed, he notes that if civil society is too powerful, particularly vis-à-vis the state, it can lead to serious problems. Pointing to the example of Northern Ireland, what is of particular concern is the destructive potential of sectarian communal allegiances (Giddens 2002: 37). Rather, he argues that the three realms must operate in tandem in the promotion of a pragmatic democratic politics.

Giddens's central thesis is twofold. First, the problem with contemporary liberal democracies is not, as conservatives such as Huntington, Crozier, Luhmann, and others would have it, that there is too much democracy, but rather that there is too little. In other words, third way politics seeks to deepen and expand democracy. He is not concerned with the democratic distemper, but with democratic anemia. This means that it is necessary not only to seek policies that make the polity more democratic, but also to penetrate into other spheres of life. He writes, for instance, of the need to democratize the family. Somewhat curiously, he does not explicitly address the need to make economic decision making more democratic. However, he is clear about one thing: a vibrant civil society is necessary for the working of, to borrow the term from Benjamin Barber (1984), "strong democracy." Second, the problem with inequalities of various sorts is that they lead to social exclusion, which limits the ability of some to participate fully as equals in the practice of democracy. Thus, the third way is committed to reducing levels of inequality. In contrast to the state-centered approach of Old Labour, with its advocacy of the welfare state, the politics of the radical center calls for the creation of a "social investment" state, one that is intended to equip individuals with the human capital necessary to be autonomous citizens rather than dependent clients. As he put it, "In place of the welfare state we should put the *social investment state*, operating in the context of a positive welfare society" (Giddens 1998: 117). More recently, Giddens (2003: 13) has suggested that the earlier version of the third way, which focused on the enabling state, must be complemented by the "ensuring state," one that is not simply designed to prepare people to be autonomous, but is also prepared to recognize that it "has obligations of *care and protection* for citizens, and that some of these obligations should be provided as *guarantees*."

In arguing that a third way politics seeks to link rights and obligations in a way that the older version of social democracy did not insofar as it focused primarily on rights, or neoliberalism does not due to its focus on duties, Giddens seeks to be sensitive to those factors that limit rights and impede the fulfillment of responsibilities. As Thomas Janoski (1998: 45) has pointed out, Giddens is not entirely clear about what he means by rights or how he construes the interconnection between rights and obligations. However, he is clear that citizen mobilization is necessary if the sort of civil involvement called for by Bellah et al., Putnam, and others is to occur. To his credit, unlike Putnam, he sees this as a political project and not as a matter of attitude realignment. In advancing his argument, Giddens takes us full circle. Alan Ryan (1999) has noted that a parallel to Giddens's position can be found in the ethical liberals of a century ago, such as T. H. Green and Leonard Hobhouse (Giddens 2000b: 86).

It is also the case that Giddens's position has a distinctly republican flavor, with its emphasis on duties tied to rights. His views dovetail with those of republican political theorists such as Norberto Bobbio and Maurizio Viroli. Thus, he would likely concur with them when they write:

> The ideals of republicanism are alternatives to the right's cultural models. Whereas political movements and parties of the right invoke the idea of liberty as the absence of impediments to individual action, supporters of republicanism proclaim that true political freedom is emancipation from forms of domination or, in other words, emancipation from dependency on the arbitrary will of other individuals. (Bobbio and Viroli 2003: 2)

We would add that Giddens's work can appropriately be viewed as a recasting of the Marshallian thesis and a fusing of that thesis with the themes of the earlier-discussed declensionists. At the same time, Giddens moves the discussion forward. He does so, first, by being cognizant of the impact of globalization (Giddens 1998: 129–53; Giddens 2000b). In this regard, writing in that decade-long interregnum between the collapse of communism and the events surrounding 9/11 and its aftermath, he describes the prospects of a newly conceived democratic state, one without enemies (a notion Carl Schmidt could not imagine). His brief discussion is tantalizing but theoretically underdeveloped. Second, he sees the need to rethink the boundaries and with it received notions of inclusion and exclusion. Indeed, he insists that the third way is intent on promoting inclusionary policies. Of particular significance is what this means for women, racial and ethnic minorities, and immigrants – topics neglected by the figures we have so far examined. In introducing this topic, he describes with little elaboration the prospects of forging cosmopolitanism in a pluralist democracy. Moreover, given his contributions elsewhere to discussions of globalization (Giddens 2000a), he opens up a dialogue about citizenship as a mode of belonging that might transcend the nation-state. It is precisely these concerns that we turn to in the following chapter.

5

Expansion

The discourses on inclusion, erosion, and withdrawal share in common a presumption that citizenship is to be understood in terms of the nation-state. There is good reason for such a presumption given that nation-states in the modern era have claimed a monopoly on defining the specific parameters of citizenship regimes and establishing the ground rules for inclusion and exclusion (Tilly 1990). Thus, it is not surprising that in various forms the debates over these three topics have a fairly extensive history in all of the world's liberal democracies.

However, a new discourse has recently emerged that we have chosen to describe as "expansion." What makes it distinctive is that it challenges the container concept of citizenship, whereby the nation-state is viewed as the ultimate arbiter of questions concerning membership, and the content of citizen rights and duties (Faist 2001a, 2004, 2007; Münch 2001). This discourse arises in the context of the growing interdependency of nations – economically for certain, but also politically and culturally. Located in terms of what scholars variously refer to as transnationalism (Faist 2000b, 2000c, 2004; Kivisto 2001) and globalization (Lechner and Boli 2005), new modes and loci of belonging that transcend existing political borders have begun to arise. It should be noted that the novelty of this discourse is such that it is a relatively new topic in the social sciences (Turner 2006) and at the level of public policy. In those nations that have entered into parliamentary discussions about the viability of expansion, the topic has percolated into public discourse, while in other places where such initiatives have not taken place it has not become a topic of public interest.

Seyla Benhabib (2004: 1) describes contemporary developments in the following way:

The modern nation-state system has regulated membership in terms of one principal category: national citizenship. We have entered an era when state sovereignty has been frayed and the institution of national citizenship has been disaggregated or unbundled into diverse elements. New modalities of membership have emerged, with the result that the boundaries of the political community, as defined by the nation-state system, are no longer adequate to regulate membership.

Although the rapidly growing literature on the expansion of citizenship is rich and complex, we think that the discussions can be divided into two central themes about the way citizenship is coming to be redefined. The first shift concerns the impact of the rapid proliferation of dual citizenship (Faist 2007; Faist and Kivisto forthcoming), while the second entails the emergence of various modes of what has come to be referred to as postnational citizenship. In terms of the latter, there are two distinct foci. One looks at "nested citizenship," which implies a set of two or more memberships located in concentric circles. The only significant instance of this development at present exists in the case of the European Union, where national identities do not disappear, but become embedded in the larger, overarching trans-state entity (Faist 2000a; Faist and Ette forthcoming). The second focus is on what has variously been described as global, world, or cosmopolitan citizenship (Lechner and Boli 2005).

As will become obvious in the structure of this chapter, dual citizenship requires far more sustained attention than postnational citizenship. This is quite simply due to the fact that as an empirical phenomenon during at least the last quarter of the past century, the number of dual citizens worldwide has grown dramatically and as a consequence it requires sustained attention. It should be noted that dual citizenship does not challenge the nation-state per se, but rather calls into question any one state's right to claim a monopoly on the membership of its citizenry. On the other hand, although nested citizenship is also an empirical phenomenon that requires scrutiny, it is solely confined to Europe, for there is no truly parallel regional counterpart to the European Union in any other part of the world. Thus, this is a more circumscribed topic. When, at the conclusion, we briefly touch upon the debates about citizens of the world, we increasingly enter the realm of speculation, addressing issues that can only be understood in terms of the *longue durée*. We turn to our major focus herein: dual citizenship.

DUAL CITIZENSHIP

Dual citizenship increased dramatically in the latter decades of the twentieth century and this trend has continued unabated in the present century.

An ever-increasing number of nation-states, for a range of reasons, have
come to accept, or at least tolerate, dual citizenship. On the face of it, this
is a surprising trend because in the not-too-distant past it was widely
assumed that citizenship and political loyalty to sovereign states were
thought to be indivisible. This new development casts doubt on the assumption that overlapping membership violates the principle of popular sovereignty and that multiple ties and loyalties on the part of citizens in
border-crossing social spaces contradicts or poses a serious challenge to
state sovereignty (Faist 2004).

To appreciate this fact, we will explore dual citizenship by first examin-
ing its history, with an eye to identifying factors that have contributed to
its rapid expansion. Second, we shall provide a survey of nation-specific
responses to the challenge of dual citizenship, focusing not only on the
developed nations that have been the sole concern of the preceding chapters, but of developing nations, as well. The reason for this is that the policy
initiatives of developing nations related to citizenship are having a direct
and significant impact on the developed nations because of world migration
from the nations of the South and East to those of the North and West
(Faist 2000b; Papastergiadis 2000). This discussion will offer us some clues
about future trends.

The history of dual citizenship

What are the major reasons that dual citizenship in the past has been
viewed negatively, as something that should be both prohibited and avoided?
One primary reason has been a concern that issues of diplomatic protection
of dual nationals could result in conflict between nations. Peter Spiro
(2002: 22) contends that, contrary to what might be assumed, this negative
attitude toward dual citizenship resulted not from cases of "disloyalty and
deceit, divided allegiances and torn psyches." Rather, countries were much
less concerned about the dual nationals themselves, and much more about
how they could treat their dual nationals. In a time before international
human rights agreements, nations did whatever they wished to their own
citizens, but were limited in terms of what they could do to citizens of
other countries. Conflicts between nations over citizens of both states
could result in war. For example, the war of 1812 between Britain and the
USA was in part instigated over a disagreement concerning the treatment
of individuals claimed as nationals by both countries.

Such issues were problematic for the USA in particular during the founding period of the republic due to the fact that many European nations did
not acknowledge the naturalization of their citizens in the new nation.
As Spiro (2002: 23) observes, "At times the issue even inflamed the public

imagination, as when Britain put several naturalized Irish-Americans on trial for treason as British citizens." The USA also confronted a number of cases wherein naturalized citizens returned permanently to their countries of origin, but demanded that the USA afford them diplomatic protection. This historical backdrop notwithstanding, despite the early emphasis on international relations, much of the subsequent rhetoric against dual nationality has focused on the individual's presumed divided loyalties – which were commonly seen as being tantamount to political bigamy.

A second and related concern about dual citizenship involved the matter of military service. Referring again to the war of 1812, one of the precipitating factors that led to war was the decision of British military officers to press naturalized Americans of British descent into their military. Other nations attempted to similarly induct naturalized Americans from their particular nations when those nationals ventured back to their respective homelands. This included France, Spain, Prussia, and various other German states (Koslowski 2003: 158). In the German case, issues surrounding military service became increasingly knotty by the middle of the nineteenth century. In 1849, the US Ambassador to the Northern German Federation, George Bancroft, made a vigorous case against the idea of dual citizenship, arguing that countries should "as soon tolerate a man with two wives as a man with two countries; as soon bear with polygamy as that state of double allegiance which common sense so repudiates that it has not even coined a word to express it" (quoted in Koslowski 2003: 158).

What Bancroft was reacting to was the fact that according to German law at the time German citizenship could not be lost. Thus, even as German emigrants become naturalized citizens of their new homeland, they also remained German citizens. Germany was not unique in this regard. US opposition to dual citizenship led to a series of diplomatic initiatives with Germany and other states, spearheaded by Bancroft. In 1868 a treaty was entered into between the USA and Germany that provided for the right of a German national to expatriate after five years' residence in the USA (Koslowski 2003: 158–9). Clearly, by the second half of the nineteenth century, the idea that dual citizenship was a situation to be avoided gained adherents among political leaders in both immigrant-exporting and -receiving nations. Thus, similar agreements, known as the Bancroft Treaties, were entered into between the USA and 26 other nations, including Austria-Hungary, Belgium, Britain, Denmark, Norway, and Sweden. These treaties served chiefly to establish a situation in which one nationality would be gained at the expense of the other; dual citizenship was construed as an undesirable and in general an impermissible outcome.

The Bancroft Treaties were emblematic of an increasingly shared position among political elites about the need to prevent dual citizenship whenever possible. Nevertheless, while not always welcomed, dual citizenship has long existed owing to differing criteria being employed by various nations in granting citizenship. To make sense of these differences, it is important to realize that specific states responded in various ways to the following four criteria. The first criterion is *jus soli*, or birthplace, which means that citizenship is extended to all individuals born within a nation's borders – generally including territories or protectorates under the jurisdiction of the state in question. The second criterion is *jus sanguinis*, which refers to citizenship determined by lineage, which typically has meant that it is determined by parentage, but sometimes has meant that it can be acquired on the basis of a more distant familial relationship. Third, marital status can serve as a criterion. Marriage to a citizen of a different nation can affect one's own national affiliation in two ways. In some instances, marriage can result in the loss of citizenship, while in other instances it can mean the acquisition of a new citizenship (in any particular case, either one or the other or both can occur). Fourth, residential location can be a criterion. Living in a country of which one is not a citizen for a specified length of time in some cases alters one's citizenship ties to both the nation of origin and the nation of residence (Hansen and Weil 2002: 2).

The interaction of these four criteria can and has resulted in legitimacy being accorded to dual citizenship. For example, *jus soli* and *jus sanguinis* criteria in tandem can readily result in dual nationality as the result of population movements from one state to another. If a child of parents who are nationals of a country granting citizenship on the basis of ancestry is born in a nation operating with *jus soli*, then that child automatically has two citizenships from birth. While this scenario is not a new one, the number of children attaining two nationalities from birth in this way rises with population mobility (Hansen and Weil 2002: 2). In practice, many countries use a combination of these two criteria, and in fact none use *jus soli* exclusively. Immigrant-receiving nations tend to favor *jus soli*, as this best reflects the needs of both the nation and the settlers themselves. On the other hand, emigrant-sending nations – including most European nations historically – tend to favor *jus sanguinis*. What this illustrates is the fact that although the desire to unify citizenship attainment policy across nations in order to cut down on the incidence of dual nationality has been strong, each nation has its own interests in mind in creating its own distinctive policies related to citizenship (Martin 2003: 9).

In an effort to avoid according dual citizenship to the offspring of couples with differing citizenships, it was customary for citizenship laws in the nineteenth century and first part of the twentieth to dictate that a woman marrying a citizen of another country lose her original citizenship and attain that of her husband. Therefore, any children born to them would be citizens of a single nation. However, such explicitly gender-biased laws have increasingly been challenged. Feminist demands have led to the revision of such laws to allow women to retain their former citizenship ties; hence, children born out of such unions have dual nationality (Spiro 2002: 20). In fact, if a child was born of two nationals of different *jus sanguinis* nations in a third *jus soli* nation of which neither parent was a citizen, the offspring could potentially have three citizenships. Many nations have attempted to prevent such a situation from arising, from the passing down of nationalities from parent to child, by requiring dual (or multiple) national children to choose a single nationality upon reaching adulthood. Germany, for example, in its passage in 1999 of what is arguably the most liberal citizenship law in Europe, mandated such a requirement. Nonetheless, as David Martin (2003: 10) has noted, even where such legal provisions exist, they are typically not vigorously enforced.

Stephen Legomsky (2003: 81) succinctly summarizes the factors at play in creating the preconditions for dual citizenship despite opposition to it in principle. He describes three maxims that interact in a variety of ways to yield dual or plural citizenship: (1) "each state decides who its own nationals are"; (2) "a state typically provides alternative multiple routes to nationality"; and (3) "the rules vary from state to state."

Within this framework, one can point to a variety of reasons that dual nationality is increasingly accepted – if not necessarily legally sanctioned. In the first place, one can point to globalizing forces. As noted above, most of the world was quite averse to the idea of dual citizenship until about three decades ago, when a profound shift of opinion became evident. Martin (2003: 4) contends that the move toward growing (if sometimes grudging) acceptance of this shift has resulted from "the expanding interconnection of the world community." While dual nationality has always existed due to a lack of uniformity of nationality laws from nation to nation, the dramatic increase in international mobility, marriage, and commerce has elevated the number of dual citizens, and with it the growing call for accepting dual citizenship. A substantial number of people today live in countries of which they are not citizens, desiring to naturalize, but also desiring to continue to be citizens of their countries of origin, with which they continue to maintain ties (Martin 2003: 5).

Legomsky (2003: 82) points to the centrality of increased levels of migration to the proliferation of dual citizenship, which has been spurred by "technological advances in information, communication, and transportation, combined with sizeable economic disparities among nations, widespread armed conflicts, systematic violations of fundamental human rights, and other worldwide forces." Looking specifically at Western Europe, which had in the nineteenth century exported more people than it imported and during that time had preferred to define nationality along ancestry lines, Weil (2001) notes that after World War II, these nations were forced to rethink such policies. The result was the dramatic increase in the number of dual nationals within their borders.

A second factor contributing to the growth of dual nationality is the fact that concerns over diplomatic protection no longer have the same relevance that they did in the nineteenth century. While it may be too much to contend, as some have, that the historic concern over conflicts of diplomatic protection have become virtually obsolete, it is the case that in an era of international sensitivity to human rights, whether or not individuals are a nation's own citizens makes less difference than it did in the past in terms of the country's treatment of them due to the growing significance of an international human rights regime. As Spiro (2002: 25) points out, if Germany is treating a German citizen badly, members of the international community will protest even though they have no nationality ties to the individual.

The women's movement represents the third factor. This is particularly the case in nations where nationality is transmitted by ancestry. Although it has traditionally been the rule that children born in wedlock take their father's nationality and those born outside of marriage take that of their mother, thus in both instances discouraging dual nationality, the push for women's equality during the past century has resulted in an increase in the number of nations that legitimize the passing on of both nationalities to offspring (Koslowski 2003: 161). One result, perhaps unintended, has been that efforts to promote gender equality have made it more difficult for women to take their spouse's nationality.

As noted above, many older nationality laws granted foreign women automatic citizenship upon marrying a citizen of that country (and many also automatically stripped a women's citizenship upon marrying a foreigner). The general trend during the twentieth century was to repeal such laws, beginning in the 1930s in some nations and continuing until the last decade of the past century in other nations. Spouses of both genders now often have to be a resident of a country for a specified number of years and undergo the same naturalization processes. Weil (2001: 28) has noted that a stimulus for this change is the desire to avoid "false marriages" that are designed to expedite the acquisition of citizenship.

The fourth factor contributing to the expansion of dual citizenship involves the shifting interests of immigrant-sending countries. During the nineteenth and early twentieth centuries, political and cultural (including religious) elites tended to be opposed to emigration; this situation has changed dramatically during the past several decades. In part, the reversal from opposition to general support of the idea of dual citizenship has arisen as a result of demands made on the part of overseas nationals to their native homelands. However, state elites would not likely have been prompted to support the desires of their expatriates, particularly when the latter are motivated by the fact that immigrants who naturalize enjoy more rights and benefits than do foreign residents. Realizing that the retention of homeland nationality is largely an identity issue, they came to see that if they could maintain ties with a constituency abroad, it might be to the state's benefit. For one thing, dual nationals with a favorable orientation toward their homeland might in various ways use their political influence (voting, lobbying, and the like) in their new nation to promote policies favoring the homeland. In other words, nations of emigration have a vested interest in promoting political transnationalism (Guarnizo et al. 2003).

Another, and perhaps more significant, reason that countries of emigration want to encourage enduring ties with their foreign nationals is economic in nature. If allowed to remain citizens even after naturalizing elsewhere, emigrants will be more likely to continue traveling back to the country of origin and maintain close ties with individuals and institutions there, which as Martin (2003: 7) points out, "might foster continued [economic investment] or charitable donations in the country of origin, thus boosting the national economy." On the one hand, developing nations seek to encourage immigrant entrepreneurs to create and sustain economic networks with the homeland. As Portes et al. (2002: 294) contend, although the percentage of immigrants who are entrepreneurs is quite small, nonetheless the "transnational firms" they create "can be viewed as bridges helping to keep ties alive with the home countries and even strengthening them over time." In addition, remittances have become a major factor contributing to the GDP (gross domestic product) in many developing nations.

Fifth, the dissolution of empires and nations has led to the expansion of dual citizenship. When colonial empires crumbled after World War II and former colonies became independent nations, many former empires allowed their own citizens who had settled in the colonies to exercise full citizenship in these newly formed nations while simultaneously preserving their citizenships in the metropole – either by formal treaty or more informally. For example, with the demise of Spain as a colonial power, it entered into treaties with Chile, Peru, Paraguay, Nicaragua, Guatemala, Bolivia, Ecuador, Costa Rica, Honduras, the Dominican Republic, and Argentina. In a different era and context, when the Soviet Union disintegrated, 25 million people of Russian ancestry found themselves residing in non-Russian states. To allow these people to be part of the new Russia, dual citizenship was legitimated (Koslowski 2003: 161).

Miriam Feldblum (2000: 478) summarizes the factors that have led to a progressive loosening of restrictions on dual citizenship, particularly since the 1980s, as follows: "increased migrations, gender equity reforms in nationality transmission and retention, reforms in nationality criteria, informal policy practices to ignore the ban on dual nationality, and actual legislation to lift the traditional ban on dual nationality." Koslowski (2003: 160) adds to these internal causes the following external forces when he contends that the "trend toward increasing toleration of dual nationality is enabled by international security factors such as post-war European integration, North Atlantic security structures, the end of the Cold War, and the decline of conscription." At the same time, it is useful to observe that despite these internal and external forces contributing to a profound shift in the way states and publics view dual citizenship, many of the old laws, nonetheless, remain unchanged (de la Pradelle 2002: 194).

Excursus on international laws and conventions

The Bancroft Treaties noted earlier became something of a model insofar as they ratified the generally agreed-upon opposition to dual citizenship on the part of governments. The Convention on the Status of Naturalized Citizens, entered into by many Western nations in 1906, declared that naturalized individuals who left the country in which they naturalized and returned permanently to their original homeland lost their naturalized citizenship (Aleinikoff and Klusmeyer 2001: 73–4).

Of particular significance was the 1930 Hague Convention Concerning Certain Questions Relating to the Conflict of Nationality. In part a consequence of conflicts arising over military service in World War I, the convention's preamble states that, "it is in the interest of the international community to secure that all members should have a nationality and should have one nationality only" (quoted in Koslowski 2003: 159). Although the USA supported this ideal, in the end it did not sign the convention because it failed to provide that a woman's nationality should be considered independently of her husband's and that her citizenship should not be automatically revoked upon marrying a foreign national. The convention was intended to deal with the issue of the diplomatic protection of dual nationals. In principle, a state cannot afford protection to a dual national against the other country whose citizenship the individual holds. Since this guideline was established, there have been many exceptions on the grounds of universal human rights, and in many cases arbitration between the nations involved has been employed to resolve disputes. Frequently, the nation with which the individual has stronger ties is permitted to intervene on that individual's behalf (Hailbronner 2003: 22–3).

The Hague Convention was intended to promote single nationality. However, in declaring that each state had the right to determine who were and who were not its citizens, and in offering no uniform guidelines for such determinations, it actually did very little to curb the incidence of dual citizenship (Aleinikoff and Klusmeyer 2001: 72). Thus, it is not surprising that over the next several decades the issues posed by the Hague Convention were revisited again and again. The effort to reduce the number of dual citizens and to sort out military obligations in the case of dual citizenship were addressed both by the United Nations and by the Council of Europe as the emergence of the European Union raised questions about the impact of greater labor mobility within Western European nations and the opening of borders to new immigrants from outside of the EU. However, at the same time, the move to reduce gender discrimination in citizenship laws, such as the 1979 UN Convention on the Elimination of All Forms of Discrimination against Women, inevitably meant that there was a greater openness to dual nationality. At the same time, there was a concern about people who were stateless. The Hague Convention argued that every person should have one nationality, but some displaced persons lost their citizenship of origin and were not readily granted citizenship by the nations that offered them asylum. This, for example, was a problem confronting Western Europe after World War II when political refugees fled Warsaw Pact nations.

By the end of the twentieth century, the primacy accorded to preventing dual nationality had eroded considerably. Thus, Aleinikoff and Klusmeyer (2001: 73) note that the European Convention on Nationality of 1997 no longer sought to reduce or eliminate dual nationality, which had been the chief goal of its 1963 convention. Rather than being primarily concerned about split national allegiances and security, this convention was much more focused on achieving "greater unity between its members," the "legitimate interests" of individuals, averting statelessness and discrimination, and determining "the rights and duties of multiple nationals" (Council of Europe 1997: 5). In addition to the EU signatories of this conven-tion, several non-EU members were also signatories, including Albania, Bulgaria, the Czech Republic, Hungary, Moldova, Poland, Russia, Slovakia, and the former Yugoslav Republic of Macedonia (Koslowski 2003: 170).

WHICH NATIONS PERMIT AND WHICH PROHIBIT DUAL CITIZENSHIP?

In *Citizenship Made Simple* (Kimmel and Lubiner 2003), a user's guide for immigrants to the USA, the reader is provided with a list of nations that permit their citizens to naturalize in the USA while continuing to maintain their homeland citizenship. The list is instructive. It includes Albania, Antigua, Barbados, Belize, Benin, Bulgaria, Burkina Faso, Cambodia, Canada, Cape Verde, Central African Republic, Columbia, Costa Rica, Côte d'Ivoire, Croatia, Cyprus, Dominica, Dominican Republic, Ecuador, El Salvador, France, Ghana, Greece, Grenada, Guatemala, Hong Kong, Hungary, Iran, Ireland, Israel, Jamaica, Latvia, Lesotho, Liechtenstein,

Macao, Maldives, Mexico, Morocco, Namibia, Nevis, New Zealand, Nigeria, Panama, Peru, Poland, Romania, St. Christopher, St. Kitts, St. Lucia, Slovenia, Sri Lanka, Switzerland, Syria, Togo, Tunisia, Turkey, Tuvalu, and the United Kingdom.

A cursory glance reveals an interesting mixture of developing and developed nations. Moreover, this list is growing. Additional nations have been added to it since the appearance of the book. For example, India, the second most populous country in the world, has recently legalized dual citizenship. While it is clear that developing nations have political and economic reasons for permitting dual nationality, why do so many developed nations also permit dual citizenship? Why do the developed nations in this list do so, while others do not? Why, for instance, does Canada permit dual nationality while the USA does not? Why does France, while Germany does not? In this section we will examine a select number of developed nations, including all of the major ones, in order to better comprehend the similarities and differences in responding to dual citizenship.

United States

Although the USA is officially a nation that prohibits dual nationality, in fact it tolerates it. This is reflected by the fact that the nation has not prosecuted anyone for dual citizenship for several decades. One might describe the approach as one based on ambivalence. One can find a similar attitude in the past. For example, legislation passed in 1878 did not formally bar dual nationality, but it declared that in the case of a conflict of loyalties the "claim of foreign allegiance should be promptly and finally disavowed" (Bar-Yaacov 1961: 100). However, this changed over time to an apparently more decisive opposition to dual nationality, at least on the part of individuals seeking naturalization. Thus, in 1906 a law was enacted that compelled foreigners naturalizing in the USA to "renounce for ever all allegiance and fidelity to any foreign prince, potentate, State, or sovereignty" (quoted in Bar-Yaacov 1961: 101). In the 1940 Nationality Act, dual citizens who rendered military service to another state of which they were also citizens were stripped of their US citizenship. In the Immigration and Nationality Act of 1952, any US citizen over the age of 22 who was a dual citizen by birth and had resided within the other nationality's borders for at least three years could lose her US citizenship under certain circumstances. Such loss was permitted if the individual voted in elections in the other nation, served in its military, or was employed by the government (Bar-Yaacov 1961: 19). This explicit effort to prevent dual nationality persisted until the 1960s, after which time a greater tolerance of dual citizenship emerged.

Naturalizing citizens at present take an oath of renunciation of their existing homeland nationality that is not unlike the oath noted above from 1906. However, significant changes have occurred during the past century. In the first place, as a result of the Supreme Court decision, *Afroyim v. Rusk*, US citizenship cannot be rescinded without the individual's express expression of interest in being divested of that nationality (Renshon 2001: 272–3). In addition, naturalization in another country does not automatically annul US citizenship (Spiro 2002: 20). Michael Jones-Correra (2001) contends that the government's current approach to dual citizenship amounts to a "don't ask, don't tell" policy. Sanford Levinson distinguishes between individuals seeking to become naturalized US citizens and US citizens seeking to naturalize in another nation. He contends that current law favors the latter, writing that, "American law tolerates political bigamy so long as the second political marriage follows, rather than precedes, the acquiring of United States citizenship" (quoted in Schuck 2002: 72).

In summary, when naturalizing as US citizens, citizens of other nations are supposed to renounce these previous citizenships in an oath, but in practice this is not always carried out. This is due, in part, to the fact that not all countries permit expatriation, and hence fewer US noncitizen residents would be qualified for naturalization. The US government does not publicize the fact that it does nothing to insure that naturalized citizens have, in fact, severed their ties with their nation of origin, and this probably deters some people unaware of this fact who otherwise would naturalize (Spiro 2002: 21–7). Whether or not the oath is administered in the naturalization proceedings, the USA simply does not actively search out and strip the citizenship of naturalized citizens who opt to maintain other nationalities (Schuck 2002: 68).

Meanwhile, for Americans naturalizing elsewhere, Stanley Renshon (2001: 235) summarizes the situation as follows:

> no American citizen can lose his or her citizenship by undertaking the responsibilities of citizenship in one or more countries. This is true even if those responsibilities include obtaining a second or even a third citizenship, swearing allegiance to a foreign state, voting in another country's elections, serving in the armed forces (even in combat positions, and even if the state is a "hostile" one), running for office, and if successful serving.

The USA allows citizens, including dual citizens, who reside overseas to vote both in US elections and in non-US ones. Although residents living abroad do not have their own Senators or members of the House of Representatives, in the case of the Democratic National Committee they do have their own representatives. Americans living outside of the USA can participate in a wide range of ways in the nation of residence without fear of expatriation, including voting, serving in the military, and serving in political office. Finally, dual nationals from birth are not required to choose one nationality over the other upon reaching the age of majority or some other established date, presumably under the assumption that only the citizenship of the country of residence will typically be actively employed (Spiro 2002: 25).

Peter Spiro (ibid.) identifies three reasons for the fact that the USA today tolerates dual citizenship. First, nationality law never required dual nationals from birth to renounce one nationality at adulthood, mainly because most dual national Americans by birth hold another citizenship merely as a "technical matter." In order to insure this, dual nationals who were in any way "politically active" in another country were at risk of expatriation. For the vast majority of dual nationals this simply was not an issue. Second, as noted above, although requiring naturalizing citizens to take the oath of renunciation of other nationalities, the USA has never actually required them to follow through and officially terminate their other citizenship, mainly because for much of US history, emigrant countries have not allowed their citizens to expatriate. Finally, the Supreme Court has since "severely restricted the federal government's power to deprive individuals of their citizenship on the basis of ties to other nations."

Other historic settler nations

How similar and how different is the US evolution of dual citizenship policies from that of other liberal democracies? In particular, is there evidence of a convergence of policies among the historic settler nations? To answer this question, we review Canadian and Australian policies.

According to Donald Galloway (2000: 87), dual citizenship does not figure largely in Canadian law, and the idea of the dual citizen has not historically raised political passions. In the aftermath of World War II and the subsequent increase in immigration, particularly of displaced persons from Eastern Europe, a legislative debate ensued that raised the question of what Canadian citizenship meant. At that time, it was decided that naturalizing immigrants would not be required to relinquish all other citizenship ties; rather, it was deemed permissible that they could formally maintain previous national identities (Galloway 2000: 99). This was motivated in no small part by the fact that many of the political refugees entering the country did not have the permission of the communist states they had fled to depart or repudiate their citizenships. Thus, the Canadian position presumed that the newcomers were dual citizens only in a formal sense. Interestingly, in 1947 – one year after this decision – the Canadian Citizenship

Act declared that Canadians who purposefully attained another citizenship could be divested of their Canadian citizenship (Galloway 2000: 99).

This latter policy was overturned three decades later, when Canada adopted a very liberal stance toward dual citizenship (Koslowski 2003: 162), and as a consequence found its naturalization rate rise in comparison to the USA (Bloemraad 2006: 3). Thus, at the present time, individuals naturalizing in Canada are not required to renounce other citizenships, while Canadians are free to take on other nationalities without risk of losing their Canadian one. Galloway (2000: 99) contends that the reasons for this shift in position are difficult to ascertain since "the matter was not even raised in the Parliamentary debates." However, more recently, in the mid-1990s, as anti-immigrant sentiment grew, the issue of dual nationality was publicly debated, and the Parliamentary Standing Committee on Citizenship at that time made recommendations against the nation's permissive stance toward dual citizenship (Galloway 2000: 100). That being said, there was insufficient political desire to amend existing laws and thus the 1977 legislation still stands, and it is for this reason that Aleinikoff and Klusmeyer (2001: 76) have defined Canadian policy as "open."

The Australian case differs, in part because of the differing relationships these two nations have had to their British colonial past. For much of its history, Australia has lacked a clear definition of citizenship, and for most of its relatively short history as an independent nation it has been very discriminatory in terms of conferring citizenship rights. According to Gianni Zappala and Stephen Castles (2000: 37–8), the nation has not had a document clearly delineating citizens' rights, and only in 1948 did the concept of Australian citizenship emerge out of the previous British concept of subjecthood. Even after this time, the notion of citizenship still had a strong connotation of British heritage rather than being defined by rights and duties. Moreover, it gave clear preference to the "Anglo-Celtic" peoples. Thus, British immigrants to Australia – even those who had not naturalized – were automatically given virtually all the rights of Australian citizens, while other immigrants were subjected to stringent naturalization requirements and even after becoming citizens did not enjoy many of the rights of their Anglo-Celtic counterparts (Zappala and Castles 2000: 38). Non-British immigrants were required to renounce their previous nationalities, while their British counterparts were not.

After World War II, Australia implemented a new immigration policy intended to produce demographic and economic growth. The original intention was to bring in new immigrants from Northwestern Europe. However, that produced numbers considerably smaller than needed. In contrast, many migrants arrived from Eastern and Southern Europe and the demand for entry was growing from various nations in Asia and Africa.

In response, Australia changed its stance on the source of immigrants dramatically and rapidly. First they began to accept previously undesirable European immigrants, and then this growing inclusiveness expanded to include nonwhites – thereby ending the historic policy of "white Australia" (Kivisto 2002: 107–9). It implemented an assimilationist policy, intending to Anglicize its increasingly diverse population. This gave way to a policy of official multiculturalism, based in part on the Canadian model. At the beginning of the twenty-first century about 42 percent of Australia's population is comprised of immigrants or the offspring of immigrants from over 100 nations (Zappala and Castles 2000: 34).

Related to these changes in immigration policy was a revision of citizenship laws, pushed by the Labor Party. Throughout the 1990s discriminatory aspects of the nation's citizenship laws were repealed, linked to the multiculturalist emphasis on valorizing the cultural practices and languages of the nation's diverse population. However, since 1996, a backlash has increasingly put multiculturalism on the defensive. Dual citizenship must be placed within this context. Although the 1948 Australian Citizenship Act's discouragement of dual citizenship remains the law of the land, for some time dual citizenship has been tolerated, with no official enforcement of the renunciation requirement. While the Labor Party was in power, efforts were made to legally permit dual citizenship. These were stilled when the electorate tilted rightward. At the moment, the nation's citizenship policies are the object of considerable debate, especially because Australia's constitution does not clearly define what it means to be an Australian citizen.

Parenthetically, it should be noted that New Zealand has a more liberal and inclusive view of dual citizenship. That nation's citizenship laws allow for dual citizenship, although the state reserves the right to deny it if it "is not conducive to the public good" (Renshon 2001: 237). Thus, it might be said that, like the USA, other former British colonies have increasingly shifted to permitting dual citizenship in some instances and tolerating it in others.

Western Europe

In this section we will focus on the three largest nations of Western Europe – the United Kingdom, France, and Germany – and then will provide brief commentaries on other nations in the region. In the case of the UK, Aleinikoff and Klusmeyer (2001: 76) define it as "open." Generally, British nationality legislation has focused on the extension of nationality, rather than its restriction. This is different from the USA, which defines citizenship in terms of a set of rights and obligations. In contrast, the UK has typically treated nationality in terms of "subjecthood," which emphasizes duties and obligations to the state, but does not specify rights. This shaped British nationality policies during the era of colonialism. Residents of British colonies were considered to be British nationals (as specified by the Imperial Conference of 1911 and the British Nationality and Status of Aliens Act of 1914). However, this subject status did not generally result in uniform rights between the mother country and the colonies (Bar-Yaacov 1961: 20). At the same time, with the passage of the Nationality Acts of 1918 and 1922, Britain, like the USA, conferred citizenship upon all individuals born in the United Kingdom.

As early as 1870, the UK addressed the matter of dual citizenship insofar as it permitted individuals born with two or more citizenships to renounce their British citizenship upon reaching adulthood. At the same time, British citizens who obtained citizenship elsewhere voluntarily lost their British citizenship, while naturalizing citizens were required to terminate their previous citizenships (Bar-Yaacov 1961: 97–108). In a series of further revisions of citizenship up to World War II, the clear intention was to reduce as far as possible dual citizenship, thereby endorsing The Hague Convention stance.

The 1948 British Nationality Act changed this. It dictated that British nationals would only lose their citizenship if they explicitly requested expatriation and if this request was approved by the Home Secretary (Hansen 2002: 185). This is the procedure still in effect today. The shift in policy came about largely so that citizens of the UK could become citizens of former colonies such as Canada, Australia, and New Zealand once they had "established their own citizenship laws" without losing their British nationality (Koslowski 2003: 161).

Currently there are virtually no restrictions on dual nationality. British citizens can freely obtain other nationalities while retaining their British citizenship, and naturalizing citizens do not have to relinquish other citizenship ties. Ultimately, the UK's attitude toward its nationals' other citizenships is one of indifference; other citizenship ties are simply deemed to be irrelevant. There is one exception: diplomatic protection is not afforded to British nationals residing in countries in which they also have citizenship; in these cases, the individuals must look to their nation of residence for protection. At the same time, the UK refuses to notify other inquiring nations as to whether their nationals have obtained British citizenship without the consent of those individuals (Hansen 2002: 180–2). Randall Hansen (2002: 185–7) identifies two reasons why the UK has in the recent past embraced a policy that permits and at times encourages dual citizenship. First, the UK has treated citizenship in pragmatic, rather than philosophical, terms. Second, dual citizenship is considered to assist in the integration of foreign residents.

Turning to France, Aleinikoff and Klusmeyer (2001: 76) deem it, too, to be "open" with regard to dual citizenship. This is interesting insofar as the French have an ideological antipathy to dual citizenship that is rooted in the nation's ideals of equality, liberty, and fraternity. Each citizen, it is argued, ought in principle to have all the rights, duties, and benefits that any other citizen possesses. The concern is that there can be instances where dual citizens might realize more than their single-nationality counterparts (de la Pradelle 2002: 196). In the Civil Code of 1804, French nationals who naturalized elsewhere lost their French citizenship, which also included such things as the confiscation of property if naturalization had not been approved by the French government beforehand (Bar-Yaacov 1961: 118–19). The Code revoked the citizenship of expatriates who acted in ways out of line with French citizenship, including not only those naturalizing elsewhere, but also those who had abandoned their "intention to return" (de la Pradelle 2002: 198, 201).

As with the UK, a change in official views of dual nationality began to emerge after World War II. The Nationality Code of 1945 declared that French nationality would not be automatically lost if a French citizen obtained another nationality. Rather, the French government would have to take specific action to expatriate individuals, an action that occurred rarely (de al Pradelle 2002: 202). In 1954 a revision of the law mandated that male citizens under the age of 50 who had acquired an additional nationality could not be divested of French citizenship unless the government approved the expatriation. Interestingly, the rationale for this revision had less to do with extending rights than with refusing to relinquish obligations. The law was intended to prevent men from escaping their military duties. However, the law came to be applied more generally, resulting in the implicit promotion of dual citizenship.

The Law of 9 January 1973 provided that French nationals who attained another citizenship would not lose their French citizenship unless the country of naturalization signed the 1963 Council of Europe Convention, in which case renunciation is required. Three conditions must be met in order to lose French citizenship: the individual must live permanently outside of France; he must not be obligated to perform any military service in France; and she must formally renounce her French citizenship after attaining another nationality (de la Pradelle 2002: 202).

In practice, like the British case, the French are at present largely unconcerned about the existence of French dual nationals. France does not require an individual who is naturalizing to renounce other citizenships. On the other hand, it does permit its citizens to retain their citizenship status when naturalizing elsewhere (Aleinikoff and Klusmeyer 2001: 66).

In contrast to the civic nationalism of France, Germany is often portrayed as the exemplar of ethnic nationalism. Interestingly, the 1913

Reichs- und Staatsangehorigkeitsgesetz (RuStAG) did not explicitly forbid dual citizenship, though it is commonly believed that it did. According to Heike Hagedorn (2003: 185), when the law was established, dual citizenship "was apparently not considered to be an important issue." It was not until 1977 that a law was passed that prescribed that naturalizing individuals must renounce their previous nationality, with several exceptions. The 1991 Alien Act was the first German legislation targeting dual nationality. It requires individuals seeking German citizenship to renounce previous citizenships unless their nation of origin does not permit expatriation or "makes it difficult for them to take on a new nationality" (Hagedorn 2003: 185). Other exceptions in the act included elderly people; political refugees; cases in which "the release from citizenship causes disproportionate difficulties and the refusal of naturalization would be an unreasonable hardship"; cases in which losing a former nationality would result in severe economic consequences; situations in which the country of origin will only grant release of citizenship following the appropriate military service; and cases of dual nationality with another EU member state which permits naturalizing Germans to retain German citizenship. Importantly, none of these exceptions describe individual rights to dual nationality; rather, these serve as guidelines that are employed by the German government in deciding individual cases (Wiedemann 2003: 336–7).

When Germany passed a new citizenship law in 1999, it was intended to repudiate the ethnonational character of previous law. According to Koslowski (2003: 162; see also Martin 2003: 10–11), "As of January 1, 2000, dual nationality is permitted for children born in Germany of foreign parents, but they must choose between German nationality and the other nationality by the time they become 23 years old." This introduced the idea of *jus soli* into German law. Although Germany's laws do not explicitly permit dual citizenship, in practice it is allowed. In particular, it "has tolerated dual nationality among ethnic Germans from Eastern Europe and Russia, children of mixed marriages, and draft age foreigners, if the home country requires military service in order to be released from its nationality" (Koslowski 2003: 162). As a result of these policies, experts have estimated that by the end of the last century there were probably more than 2 million German dual nationals (ibid.).

Given the size of the Turkish population in Germany, much of the issue of dual citizenship is framed in terms of this particular ethnic community. There are at present approximately 2 million Turkish citizens living in Germany. Despite the fact that Germany does not legally permit dual citizenship for adults, there are many Turkish-German dual nationals because Turkey permits individuals who renounce Turkish nationality (as many do to obtain German citizenship) to apply to be reinstated as a Turkish citizen, a law that appears to have been created with the German situation in mind. The new German law also permits dual nationality in cases where the home country of a naturalizing citizen will not expatriate her.

In addition, German nationals who want to naturalize elsewhere while retaining their German citizenship are permitted to do so provided that they are able to prove persisting ties with Germany (de Groot 2003: 207; Koslowski 2003: 162–6). In this way, if the government so desires, it may permit dual nationality with preferred states such as the USA while denying it with others, such as Turkey. It has also provided new circumstances in which renunciation is not required of naturalizing individuals. Old people, those who suffer political persecution, and those who would suffer economically or otherwise as a result of losing their former citizenship ties are allowed to retain another nationality. In practice, Germany often accepts dual nationals from Greece, Iran, Croatia, Afghanistan, Morocco, Tunisia, Eritrea, Lebanon, Bosnia-Herzegovina, and Syria (Hagedorn 2003: 190–1; Kreuzer 2003: 350). The net result of this situation is that, despite formal legal opposition to dual nationality, in fact Germany permits rather widespread dual nationality. This being the case, Germany is in practice quite similar to Britain and France.

A similar convergence of attitudes and official responses to dual nationality can be found in other Western European nations. For example, as of 1990 Switzerland no longer required an oath of renunciation on the part of naturalizing citizens (Koslowski 2003: 162). Prior to 1992, Italians who voluntarily attained other nationalities were subject to the loss of Italian citizenship unless the individual retained Italy as the nation of primary residence. Now, however, Italy is much more open to dual citizenship, allowing its nationals to attain other citizenships without giving up their Italian one (de Groot 2003: 209). Spain permits its nationals to attain additional nationalities while keeping their Spanish citizenship, but only with certain countries and not for naturalized Spanish citizens. These countries include all of Latin America, Andorra, Philippines, Equatorial Guinea, and Portugal. More recently, the country has begun to consider expanding this list to include EU member states (de Groot 2003: 209). Portugal no longer requires an oath of renunciation to naturalizing citizens (Aleinikoff and Klusmeyer 2001: 67).

How many dual citizens are there?

Given the growing openness to dual nationality, it is clear that the number of dual citizens in the developed nations has grown significantly in recent decades. However, just how many dual citizens reside in these nations is far from clear. Spiro (2002: 21) summarizes the situation in the USA as follows:

"No national or international statistical surveys of the incidence of dual nationality have been conducted to date, but the trend . . . has clearly been upward." The same can be said of the other industrial nations.

The number of individuals marrying outside of their own nationality as well as moving about from one nation to another is increasing, hence increasing the number of dual citizens (Schuck 2002: 66). Worldwide there are tens of millions of people who find themselves in situations where, laws permitting, they could be eligible for dual citizenship (Aleinikoff and Klusmeyer 2001: 79). Add to this the fact that worldwide the number of nations permitting dual nationality is growing. Renshon (2001: 234–6) refers to previous studies that concluded, for example, that in 1996 there were 40 nations granting dual nationality. Two years later another estimate placed the figure at 55. Renshon (2001: 236) himself finds that at the turn of the century there were 93 nations that allowed dual citizenship, albeit in most instances with some restrictions.

Turning to specific countries, it is estimated that there are between 4 and 5 million American citizens residing permanently in other countries, many of whom already have or likely will obtain dual citizenship in the nation of residence (Spiro 2002: 21). Meanwhile, the number of dual nationals residing in the USA is due in part simply to increased naturalization in the USA. To illustrate this fact, Spiro (2002: 21) notes that, "More individuals naturalized in 1997 than in the entire decade of the 1970s." Aleinikoff and Klusmeyer (2001: 63) report that "more than a half million children born each year in the United States have at least one additional nationality." Renshon (2001: 234) observes that the USA, like most countries, fails to keep track of how many of its citizens are dual nationals. He reports that between 1961 and 1997 a total of 17,437,607 immigrants entered the USA from nations that permitted dual nationality. Theoretically, all of these immigrants are potential dual nationals. At this point, we simply do not know how many of them have pursued this option; however, the figure suggests that the pool of those who might at some point in the future become a dual national is large and growing over time (Renshon 2001: 268–9).

Both Feldblum (2000: 478) and Zappala and Castles (2000: 56) concur that by the early twentieth century Australia had about 5 million dual nationals. This is a remarkable figure given that it represents nearly a quarter of the total Australian population. Koslowski (2003: 162) estimates that there are over a million French citizens who maintain dual nationality. Looking at Western Europe as a whole, Feldblum (2000: 478) estimates that the figure is "at least several million and rising." However imprecise these estimates are, they clearly point to the fact that dual nationality is a significant phenomenon in the world's liberal democracies, and is likely to increase in significance over time.

NESTED CITIZENSHIP

If dual citizenship is a pervasive feature of a majority of the world's nations, developed and developing states alike, nested citizenship is a far more limited and circumscribed phenomenon. It refers specifically to the newly emerging citizenship regime created by the constituent members of the European Union. What is nested citizenship? The image conjures up Russian dolls, with smaller dolls contained inside larger and larger dolls. Juan Díez Medrano and Paula Guitiérrez (2001: 757) succinctly describe the relationship in the following way: "Nested identities are lower- and higher-order identities such that the latter encompass the former." Nested citizenship is a form of multiple citizenship, but one in which multiple citizenship connotes full membership on multiple governance levels (Held 1995: Marks 1997; Faist 2001b; Faist and Ette forthcoming). Elizabeth Meehan (1993: 1) defines the new and evolving citizenship in the EU as "neither national nor cosmopolitan, but . . . multiple in the sense that the identities, rights, and obligations associated . . . with citizenship are expressed through an increasingly complex configuration of common community institutions, states, national and transnational voluntary associations, regions, and alliances of regions." The notion of nested citizenship presumes that the different levels of citizenship are interconnected, rather than operating autonomously.

Nested citizenship offers a perspective about what citizenship in the European Union means that differs from two competing perspectives, which we refer to as intergovernmentalism and postnationalism. The first position contends that EU citizenship is largely residual insofar as the primary function of the EU is to promote the market and to assist in the coordination of the economic activities of the member states. If this is true, it means that the EU is not to any significant extent engaged in policies aimed at redistribution or welfare provision, leaving such activities overwhelmingly to the member states. It is argued that the most notable involvement in the promotion of social rights has been regulatory in nature, such as the requirement for equal pay for equal work, health and safety standards, and migration policy. These activities can be seen as being chiefly designed to establish uniform standards across member states in order to achieve economic integration. However, in so doing, they have impacts that lead to greater similarities across states than would otherwise be the case. For this reason, it is our sense that the claim of residual rather than robust citizenship at the EU level ought to be viewed critically. The Treaty of Amsterdam will most likely over time add to the substance of EU membership by formally declaring that the basis of the EU lies in the recognition of fundamental human and social rights (Roche 1997; Faist and Ette forthcoming).

The second perspective is the antithesis of the former and it has had a larger influence in recent scholarly discourses on citizenship, generally under the rubric of postnationalism (Soysal 1994; Jacobson 1996). The central thesis of postnationalist thought is that the nation-state is weakening, being replaced by supranational constructs. Insofar as this is the case, the historic association of modern citizenship with the nation-state is seen as being eroded, while simultaneously supranational entities have stepped in to reconfigure and expand the territorial boundaries of citizenship. In this regard, the postnational musings that appeared on the scene during the past decade often suggested that we were witnessing the dawn of nationless era. A more modified form does not see the state as disappearing entirely, but its salience declining appreciably. This is the position advanced by Damian Tambini (2001: 212), who contends that: "No one can seriously propose that the nation as an institutional form is about to disappear. Neither, however, can it continue in the classical nineteenth-century form. Rather, the meaning and content of national belonging will be transformed as the structural basis of national citizenship continues to be undermined."

There are three main claims associated with this perspective. First, liberal democracies have increasingly come to respect the human rights of all persons irrespective of citizenship (Jacobson 1996). Second, international human rights discourses and international and supranational institutions have prompted nation-states to grant rights to previously excluded groups, such as immigrants from outside the EU who have taken up residence in one of its member states (Soysal 1994). Third, institutions such as the European Court of Justice (ECJ) have developed common rights for all residents, such that at present there are relatively few differences in social rights and the salience of social citizenship between permanent residents and citizens of EU member states. For this reason, the distinction between citizenship and what some have called denizenship has been blurred (Hammar 1990). When permanent legal residents who are not citizens – those dubbed denizens – acquire rights that are increasingly congruent with the rights traditionally associated with citizenship status, the salience of national citizenship is called into question.

The central idea is that the two prime components of citizenship – rights and obligations, on the one hand, and collective identity, on the other – have increasingly decoupled over the past few decades. Thus, for example, human rights, formerly tightly connected to nationality, nowadays also apply to noncitizen residents. In other words, settled noncitizens also have access to significant human, civil, and social rights. To the extent that this is true, citizenship as a "right to have rights" (Arendt 1968; Benhabib 2004: 49–69) is not any longer the fundamental basis for membership in political communities. Instead, discourses tied to interstate norms such as the various charters of the United Nations are viewed as contributing to postnational membership (Soysal 1994).

This is a problematic claim. There are, in fact, no supranational institutions conferring the status of formal membership irrespective of a prior nationality – not even the EU. The postnational perspective fails to appreciate the democratically legitimated aspect of citizenship status. As a consequence, it is no coincidence that analysts operating from this framework tend to speak of postnational membership instead of citizenship. For example, political rights are still almost exclusively tied to formal citizenship. The popular legitimation of membership in political communities, of utmost importance for any democratic regime, gets lost. Instead, the focus is on courts that uphold interstate norms, or what Jacobson (1996) refers to as "rights across borders."

If the intergovernmental approach downplays the significance of suprastate institutions, the postnational position treats such institutions as increasingly becoming more consequential than nation-states. From our perspective, neither offers a convincing portrait of the EU in its present form. Rather, it is our view that the idea of nested citizenship offers the most compelling account of the relationship between the EU and its constituent member states. At the same time, we should note that the EU has evolved over time, and continues to do so. With this proviso, the characteristics of nested citizenship become clearer when we look at an example of how the different levels interact in changing the "rules of the game."

This particular illustration concerns the increased portability of social rights across national borders for German retirees and beneficiaries of long-term care insurance. During the past two decades, on average about 30,000 pensioners from Germany have lived year-round in Spain. A problem arose when these pensioners became invalids and required increasing levels of healthcare. To be eligible for social assistance or long-term healthcare, they were expected to return to Germany. This changed when the European Court of Justice determined that the social benefits of EU member states are portable across national borders of member states. In this case, the ECJ had made a determination that required the German government to establish bureaucratic procedures designed to insure the portability of these particular social rights.

As this example suggests, nested citizenship entails an interactive system of political choices and policy decisions occurring at both the state and suprastate levels. The web of governance operates on multiple levels, and in the process the EU becomes the site of building new conceptions of rights. The EU does not function as a compensatory mechanism for deficiencies in the social rights regimes of the respective member states. It does, however, function to coordinate and harmonize those regimes. This can be seen in a variety of ways. For example, the EU is concerned with the regulation of safety and health policies, as well as those regulating the condition of economic production. As early as the agreement arrived at in Messina in 1955, there was an expressed attempt to harmonize social standards regarding the work week, overtime pay, vacation time, the free movement of labor, and the overall coordination of social policy (Moravcsik 1999). At the same time, the member states retain sole purview over their social security systems and the social service institutions tasked to oversee such provision. Indeed, most conventional social policies remain solidly ensconced within the borders of the respective member states, albeit with somewhat reduced levels of autonomy and sovereignty than before the creation of the EU.

What does this mean for EU citizenship? Are there rights that accrue to EU citizens that go beyond those possessed as a consequence of membership in a specific member state? It is worth quoting Benhabib's (2004: 148–9) summary of what individuals derive from EU membership:

> Not just a passive status, it is also intended to designate an active civic identity. Citizens of the EU states can settle anywhere in the union, take up jobs in their chosen countries, and vote as well as stand for office in local elections and in elections for the Parliament of Europe. They have the right to enjoy consular and diplomatic representation in the territory of a third country in which the member state whose nationals they are may not be represented. They have the right to petition the European Parliament and to apply to the European Ombudsman. As monetary and economic integration progresses, EU members are debating whether union citizenship should be extended to an equivalent package of social rights and benefits, such as unemployment compensation, health care, and old age pensions, which members of EU states would be able to enjoy whichever EU country they take up residency in.

All of this raises the question: how ought we to characterize the EU and to what extent is it meaningful to speak about EU citizenship? By introducing the term citizenship, the institution has been transformed into a polity, albeit one where the link between political rights and the articulation of those rights in terms of state boundaries since the Treaty of Westphalia has been, if not undone, at least partially uncoupled. As a multilevel governance system, the EU clearly reaches beyond a low-profile interstate regime, although it has not at this point developed into a coherent suprastate institution – a United States of Europe – as some of its elite proponents would prefer. Given its historical uniqueness, it is difficult to use traditional categories to describe the EU.

Reflective of this fact, while it is quite accurate to describe the EU as a suprastate and federative governance network with mixed intergovernmental and common authorities, such a description emphasizes the fact that the EU is sufficiently novel that our typical categories do not quite do it justice. The principal architects of the EU appear to have been aware of this situation when they created the European Economic Community (EEC) in the 1957 Treaty of Rome. Rather than attempting to create an explicitly suprastate institution, they opted for a more pragmatic approach, establishing instead an entity designed to foster the economic integration of Europe. Nevertheless, since that time the framework evolved from a purely economic institution to an intergovernmental one, becoming by the 1990s a collective actor on the global scene. Indeed, as Kalypso Nicolaidis (2005: 11) observes, "By the turn of the millennium, the EU had many prerogatives associated with sovereign states: various police powers, border controls, currency regulation, and cooperative (at least partly) foreign policy."

However, by introducing the idea of citizenship at a level that transcends the nation-state, the uniqueness of the EU comes into focus. As Benhabib (2004) emphasizes, the focus of much of the discussion about EU citizenship revolves around the question of rights – rights both for those who are already defined as citizens of member states and for those who are not. Insofar as this is the case, such a discourse highlights the fact that in its current form the EU suffers from a democratic deficit and from an imprecise understanding of collective affiliation. As long as the EU functioned well and questions of national sovereignty were not raised, these deficits were largely ignored. Many complained about the faceless bureaucrats in Brussels who were seen as the power behind the European Parliament. However, this did not deter the expansion of the role played by both the Parliament and the European Court of Justice.

The gulf between the ordinary citizens of the member states' perceptions of the rationale for the EU and that of the Eurocrats who run the institution has for some time been a topic of concern in some quarters. Thus, in British politics, a powerful strain of "Euroscepticism" has been evident in both the Tory and Labour parties, and recently led to the creation of a single-issue party led by a popular television presenter who wants the UK to exit the EU altogether. At the time of this writing, the gulf has taken, from the point of view of supporters of the EU, a disturbing turn. From its inception, the EU operated without a formal constitution. However, with the passage of the Treaty of Nice in 2000, not only did the member states agree to an expansion of the EU, but they also committed to the creation of a constitution – a constitution, as Nicolaidis (2005: 12) put it, "not for a nation but *among* nations."

This raised an interesting question, for it was not clear which voices were necessary to ratify the constitution – which proved to be a 300-page text, as befits a document written by bureaucrats. Many of the member states decided that their national legislatures would determine whether or not to approve the constitution, while in other cases it was decided that the decision would be put to the nation's voters in referenda. In the latter camp were two of the original members of the EEC, France and the Netherlands. After nearly half of the legislatures of the member states had approved the constitution, it appeared to be heading for approval. However, in the summer of 2005, the voters of France and the Netherlands resoundingly rejected the proposed constitution despite the coordinated efforts of political elites from the center left and center right in both countries to gain an electoral victory.

Despite victories among the voters in Spain and Luxemburg, there was a general sense that the proposed constitution had failed and, for the more pessimistic advocates of the EU, that the institution itself had entered into crisis that might spell the end of the EU as we have known it. This is a highly improbable scenario, given the fact that during its half-century of existence it has become institutionally embedded and cannot readily be undone. Indeed, despite the anti-EU stance of a minority in all of the member states, there is actually very little political will to pursue such a course. While some of the more pragmatically minded supporters of the EU are prepared to return to the status quo ante, arguing that a constitution is not necessary, others have instead suggested that if this version of the constitution is ultimately to be approved, it may be necessary to modify the rules required for approval.

At the same time, this impasse has prompted reflection about the distinctiveness of the EU. In an insightful commentary in the *Guardian*, sociologists Ulrich Beck and Anthony Giddens (2005: 28), both forceful defenders of the constitution and supporters of expansion, including the ultimate inclusion of Turkey, make the following bold claim:

> The European Union is the most original and successful experiment in political institution-building since the Second World War. It has reunited Europe after the fall of the Berlin Wall. It has influenced political change as far away as Ukraine and Turkey – not, as in the past, by military, but by peaceful means. Through its economic innovations, it has played a part in bringing prosperity to millions, even if its recent level of growth has been disappointing. It has helped one of the very poorest countries in Europe, Ireland, to become one of the richest. It has been instrumental in bringing democracy to Spain, Portugal, and Greece, countries that had previously been dictatorships.

They go on to make clear that they think the EU has much unfinished business to attend to, and that an inward-looking nationalism on the part of critics of the EU works against the best interests of the member states, individually and collectively. In making their case, Beck and Giddens (2005: 28) offer their own understanding of what precisely the EU is, suggesting that it ought not to be viewed as an "unfinished nation" or an "incomplete federal state." Stressing that the EU is not a threat to the sovereignty of the member nation states and neither signals a postnationalist institution that transcends the nation-state nor leads to cultural homogenization, they consider it to be "a new type of cosmopolitan project." We would only add that at this particular time, the pressing need is to create a new democratic legitimation of the project – one that manages to bridge the gulf between elite proponents and skeptical, apathetic, or antagonistic ordinary citizens.

There is one final point to make: although Beck and Giddens assert that the EU is a unique institutional project, they say nothing about the likelihood that it might be replicated elsewhere. Might, for example, the North American Free Trade Agreement, an economic pact linking Canada, Mexico, and the United States, over time evolve from a purely economic entity to one with political functions, in a parallel process to that which occurred with the EU? We think not. The United States is quite simply too large and powerful vis-à-vis the other two members for this to happen, combined with the fact that there is a huge difference in levels of economic development, with the USA and Canada as advanced industrial nations, on the one hand, and Mexico as a poor and developing nation, on the other. Moreover, beyond North America, there do not appear to be any other viable regional candidates for an EU-like experiment.

TOWARD GLOBAL CITIZENSHIP?

Given the current challenges confronting the EU, it would appear that any effort to expand the idea of citizenship to the global level has very little probability of success in the foreseeable future. Terms such as global or world citizenship are often used so indiscriminately that their meaning is far from clear. Certainly, in terms of law, including international law, there is no such status as a world or global citizen. Derek Heater (2002), one of the most ardent spokespersons on behalf of "world citizenship," is cognizant of this reality.

Nonetheless, he and other like-minded thinkers argue that there are incipient indications that such a prospect might in the long run take hold. For instance, in currently existing international law there do exist the rudiments of something resembling a world law, including important precedents that emerged out of the military tribunals that tried German and Japanese war criminals after the conclusion of World War II. The International War Crimes Tribunal and, more recently, the International Criminal Court constitute further developments along these lines – efforts, in effect, to articulate the content, the scope, and the nature of a universal human rights regime. Clearly, a landmark in this regard was the ratification of the Universal Declaration of Human Rights in 1948. It and its subsequent covenants on economic, social, and cultural rights likewise point to the seeds of a conceptualization of the global citizen.

Connected to the emergence of a global human rights framework is the growth of global civil society, for such institutions are viewed as primary carriers of a universal human rights regime. Considerable attention has been paid recently to the dramatic expansion of international nongovernmental organizations (INGOs), including human rights international nongovernmental organizations (HRINGOS), though the focus of such research has often been more concerned with their growth than with their impact on existing political regimes and cultural milieus (Tsutsui and Wotipka 2004). The assumption is that what has been evolving since the second half of the twentieth century is what Rainer Bauböck (2002) has referred to as a "political community beyond the nation state."

There are those who remain skeptical of the possibility of constructing citizenship regimes beyond the nation-state. Thus, Bryan Turner (2006) contends that:

> citizenship can only function within the nation-state, because it is based on contributions and a reciprocal relationship between duty and rights, unlike human rights for which there are as yet no explicit duties. To employ the notion of citizenship outside the confines of the nation-state is to distort the meaning of the term, indeed to render it meaningless. The idea of flexible citizenship is what we might call a political fiction. This criticism is not just a linguistic quibble. It implies that some terms are properly national and must remain so.

Given the incipient and protean character of the present situation, and the resistance of nation-states to challenges to their authority, it is not difficult to appreciate Turner's argument and his desire to preserve a certain precision in our usage of the term citizenship. Nevertheless, it is useful to be reminded of the fact that citizenship began at the level of the city-state; only centuries later was the boundary redefined as the nation-state. We do not find it inconceivable that in various ways the future might spell a similar redefinition that moves beyond the confines of the nation-state. That being said, it is difficult to predict where the future might lead. When considering the formidable challenges that any project aimed at promoting global citizenship inevitably faces, it is easy to sympathize with Jost Halfmann's (1998) contention that at present, "Kant's vision of a world civil society is a remote, if not highly improbable prospect in the future." In our conclusion, we shift from the past and present to sketch, in outline form, a consideration of what the future might hold for citizenship.

6

Future Trends

If we take seriously the disparate discourses on citizenship in the world's long-established democracies that we have analyzed in the preceding four chapters, we are led to ask what these discourses – individually and taken together – suggest about future trends of citizenship. To ask such a question is not the same as seeking to predict the future. We are acutely aware, as Erving Goffman (1983: 2) pointedly reminded us some time ago, that sociology (and the other social sciences) has had at best a checkered history as a predictive science. Indeed, we would argue (as he did) that, given the complexity and interactive nature of the key variables involved in shaping modern citizenship, attempting to predict the future is a fool's errand. That being said, this does not prevent us from drawing conclusions about certain trends that can be seen as path dependent or from identifying certain social factors that are playing a singularly prominent role in supporting or undermining democracy, and, in the process, in shaping the form and content of citizenship.

As the cumulative impact of the four discourses on citizenship indicates, its importance revolves around its capacity to establish who belongs and who is excluded from membership in a polity. This is crucial insofar as in the modern era nation-states have held a monopoly on defining the rights and obligations associated with belonging (Weber 1968 [1921]). In this regard, the chapters devoted to the discourses on inclusion, erosion, and withdrawal are concerned with developments that have occurred within the modern nation-state. They have focused on indications of social forces that have shaped and continue to reconfigure citizenship within the boundaries of particular states. The particular outcome of specific cases varies due to the differing configurations of forces at play. Nonetheless, our general sense is that to a large extent a convergence is occurring such that the similarities across states have become more pronounced over time.

Internal Factors Shaping Citizenship Regimes

Citizenship has evolved since the eighteenth century when the spirit of democratic revolution grew and took hold of the nations of Western Europe, North America, and elsewhere. However, as John Markoff (1996) has persuasively illustrated, the history of democracy cannot be described in terms of its slow, gradual, linear and progressive expansion, not only in terms of an expansion of the geography of democratic regimes, but also in terms of the depth and substance of democracy. Rather, as he contends, we ought to understand the history in terms of waves of democracy, waves that have been periodically threatened by anti-democratic movements. Thus, democracy ought not to be seen as a *fait accompli* in existing democracies and as the inevitable future of those parts of the world with little or no history of democratic penetration. Rather, it should be construed as an ongoing accomplishment. Democracy, to persist, must be perpetually reinvented, which requires an active citizenry committed to the practice of participatory democracy, being prepared to engage in, as Francesca Polletta (2004) puts it, "an endless meeting."

If this is the case, what do the three discourses concerned with internal factors contributing to the form and content of citizenship tell us about the prospects of democracy?

Inclusion

During the past two centuries or so, the efforts of elites to limit access to citizenship – using Weberian language, to effect closure – have been challenged by previously excluded groups. In particular, those who had heretofore been denied full citizenship status have challenged class, gender, and race/ethnicity as criteria for exclusion. As Chapter 2 indicated, the first successful challenges emanated from an organized working class (in the US case, the white working class). As an exemplar of a mobilized working class, the Chartist movement in Britain provided an articulate set of demands that were designed to permit the incorporation of the working class into the ranks of the citizenry, thereby giving voice to the concerns of those most adversely impacted by rapid industrialization and allowing them a say in the direction of social change. Although Chartism was a movement specific to one nation, its aspirations found parallel expression in the other industrializing nations of Western Europe and North America, along with Australia and New Zealand. By the beginning of the twentieth century, the trend was clear: class would no longer be a permissible ground for excluding people from the rights of citizenship. However, in this process of inclusion the state would extract a price from the working class in the form of the institutionalization and pacification of working-class militancy; inclusion into the polity represented an attempt to reduce challenges to the ruling class by an organized and radicalized working class (Mann 1987; Turner 2006: 147).

Although the inclusion of women and racial and ethnic minorities had been raised as an issue in the nineteenth century, gender and racial/ethnic criteria continued to be employed to exclude significant sectors of national populations from the rights of citizenship into the twentieth century – indeed, in many instances well into the century. Thus, although the first quarter of the last century witnessed a proliferation in the number of nations granting voting rights to women, in some instances this development occurred much later, with recalcitrant Swiss cantons holding out until as late as 1990. In the case of racial minorities, the situation was much the same. Thus, in the USA, although blacks were formally granted citizenship rights as a result of the post-Civil War amendments to the constitution, in fact a system of de facto racial subordination would emerge after the failure of reconstruction and blacks would be denied equal citizenship status for another century, until the impact of the civil rights movement began to be felt by the late 1960s (Katznelson 2005; Kivisto and Ng 2005: 181–91). In both Canada and Australia, the explicitly racist immigration policies of "white Canada" and "white Australia" persisted into the 1960s, as well (Kivisto 2002: 84–115). In the Australian case, the aboriginal residents of the continent were likewise denied full citizenship rights until the latter part of the twentieth century. The point is that these developments have occurred relatively recently, and their longer-term impacts are only now beginning to be felt.

One conclusion that might be drawn is that Parsons's (1971) characterization of modern societies as being more inclusive than their premodern counterparts is borne out by the empirical evidence. That being said, what we are speaking about here is inclusion in the formal sense alone. In other words, class, gender, and race/ethnicity are in principle no longer viewed by liberal democracies as appropriate aspects of identity in determining who is to be included and who excluded from citizenship. However, in current social practices, particularly evident in current debates about immigration, it is clear that reality often diverges from principle. Thus, unlike Parsons, we want to stress the incomplete and contradictory nature of inclusion. Once we turn to the more substantive aspect of inclusion, it is quite clear that the salience of these identities persists. If we look, for example, at the representation of people from working-class backgrounds, women, or racial/ethnic minorities in legislative bodies, it is clear that they remain underrepresented in positions of authority. Left unresolved in all of the liberal democracies is the matter of how it might be possible to remedy the historically embedded inequities that have, to borrow from Orwell (1987 [1945]: 90), created a situation in which some people "are more equal than others." In what ways is it possible to address the fact that people do not enter the public sphere with equal voices because of inequalities in financial resources, human capital, cultural capital, and social capital? Can equal opportunity be achieved without recourse to remedial and/or redistributive programs? We think not.

In this regard, the debates over affirmative action in the USA and its counterparts elsewhere point to the tensions and conflicts between those committed to forging more egalitarian democracies and those who are resistant to such a goal. While this conflict can be seen in all of the nations considered herein, the riots in France in the fall of 2005 offer a particularly poignant illustration of the potential for conflict due to high levels of inequality and marginalization. The riots were the result of anger created by the persistent exclusion of people of color from the French mainstream and from the daily confrontation with manifestations of racism (Ireland 2005). The official integrationist ideology of the nation, which asserts that citizenship is open equally to all who are prepared to embrace the ideals of the nation, has been forced to confront a reality quite at odds with that ideal. The question becomes how the nation ought to proceed to combat exclusionary practices shaped by racism. At this writing, the French government insists that anything that smacks of affirmative action is out of bounds. Whether or not the French political establishment – left and right – can continue to avoid confronting the disjunction between ideals and reality by resisting state intervention to insure equal opportunity remains an open question. In this regard, France is not alone. Both nations with affirmative action programs and those that have resisted them will confront demands from the excluded and marginalized to be incorporated into the society as full and equal partners. This constitutes one of the enduring fault lines of all these societies.

In this regard, as the second half of the chapter on inclusion indicates, a major challenge to existing polities arises from debates about what is construed to be the most appropriate mode of incorporation of excluded minorities, including immigrants, indigenous peoples, and ethnonationalist groups. Specifically, during the past three decades, the idea of multiculturalism as official state policy and/or as a practice emanating from a general sentiment that stresses the valorization of difference has become a major topic of disputation. Given the fact that multiculturalism means different things to different people and in different contexts, and that it can take different forms, we sought to clarify the terms of the debate. In so doing, we made use of the theoretical contributions to the topic offered by Alexander (2001) and Hartmann and Gerteis (2005). In summary, we concurred with their typologies, which in terms of actual state policies and

societal practices (as opposed to competing theories) can be seen as a divide
between incorporation regimes opposed to multiculturalism – in their
typology this is called assimilation – and varieties of multiculturalism.
Hartmann and Gerteis identify two types of real-world multiculturalism:
cosmopolitanism and interactive pluralism. We pointed to concrete cases
that most closely illustrated these types. France is the clearest example of
an assimilationist incorporation regime; Britain and the USA are instances
of cosmopolitan multiculturalism; and Canada and Australia are examples
of the interactive pluralist version of multiculturalism.

Multiculturalism remains highly contested, with significant challenges
arising in some nations that have embraced multicultural policies and/or
practices. Thus, after the murders of the populist politician Pym Fortuyn
and the controversial filmmaker Theo Van Gogh in the Netherlands, and
the series of bombings on London public transportation on July 7, 2005,
a growing chorus of commentators has declared multiculturalism to be a
failure. This emanated not only from the nationalist right, but in many
instances from the center left, as well. Assimilation was once again put
forth as a preferable alternative to multiculturalism. However, in the immediate aftermath of the riots in France, assimilation quickly lost its luster.

In a discussion in the Open Democracy Forum, Tariq Modood (2005b)
has offered a vigorous defense of multiculturalism. We concur with the
general thrust of his argument; as our discussion in Chapter 2 was meant
to indicate, if properly understood, multiculturalism serves a dual purpose:
(1) by promoting a politics of recognition, it valorizes difference and as
such recognizes heterogeneity as a characteristic feature of society that is
to be embraced rather than overcome; and (2) it provides a vehicle for the
incorporation or inclusion of individuals into full societal membership. It
is our view that in the foreseeable future, the debates over multiculturalism
will continue unabated, with some nations rejecting and others accepting
it as a mode of incorporation. When societies persist in resisting multiculturalism in any form, they will reinforce a sense of marginality and
exclusion on the part of minority group members. On the other hand, if
societies are prepared to promote a politics of recognition, they will find
themselves in a far more advantageous situation in their efforts to become
more inclusive.

Erosion

However, a politics of recognition is in itself insufficient to create a democratic society wherein citizens *qua* citizens are equals. As we noted in
Chapter 3, some on the democratic left, concurring with Nancy Fraser
(1995), have voiced concern about the prospect that a politics of recognition

has usurped a politics of redistribution. Put another way, the concern is that multiculturalism might be an essentially symbolic enterprise lacking any sustained attempts to overcome the inequalities generated by capitalist economies. If this is the case, citizenship ends up being devalued, and the significance attached to citizenship by T. H. Marshall (1964) and his progenitors is called into question.

The central focus of the Marshallian theory of citizenship is that there is a tension between the idea of democracy predicated on the equal status of citizenship and the inequalities created by capitalism. Marshall's thesis is that with the expansion of the rights associated with citizenship, particularly with the expansion of social rights during the twentieth century, it was possible to conceive of an historic compromise between contesting classes in capitalism. This is what he referred to as class abatement, a state in which the inequalities produced by an unfettered market are mitigated by government interventions that are designed to limit the range of inequality and to insure that those who are most disadvantaged are offered programs and policies that are designed to achieve equal opportunity. This, in short, became the rationale underpinning the welfare state, providing the basis for the claim that as citizens people were capable of functioning as equals while simultaneously the circumscribed inequalities in other spheres of life were regarded as legitimate and did not undermine the promise of equality among citizens.

It is precisely this historic compromise that has come under attack by neoliberal policies, which constitute a frontal assault on the welfare state. The result is that as neoliberal regimes have come to power, social rights have eroded. The redistributive goals of the welfare state have been challenged, with varied levels of success depending on how expansive and institutionally embedded the welfare state was in the first place. Thus, in the USA, with its comparatively weaker and thinner system of welfare provision, the rollback of the welfare state has been more successful. On the other hand, in the social democratic nations of Scandinavia, the welfare states have managed to date to remain relatively intact. In those nations where neoliberalism has been most successful, the result has been a substantial increase in levels of inequality – again the USA is the key example – while the social democracies have managed to maintain their egalitarianism.

Thus, the politics of redistribution is being played out over debates concerning the proper role of the state in remedying the inequalities produced by capitalism. It is by no means clear what the future portends. On the one hand, as the vaguely left-of-center Blair government in Britain suggests, "modernization" needs to be furthered, meaning that the older notion of the welfare state that arose after World War II needs to be replaced in significant ways. Blair's social policies are intended to effect this transformation. Likewise, the election of Angela Merkel in Germany suggests that even in this bastion of social democracy, neoliberal ideas are making deep inroads. On the other hand, it is not clear whether such policies have a limit in terms of what the electorate will permit. In the USA, Social Security has often been described as the "third rail" of American politics, which means that if one tampers with this New Deal program, it spells political death. While perhaps exaggerated, Ronald Reagan discovered that when he attempted to introduce "reforms" into Social Security, he was met with stiff opposition that forced him to climb down from his position. Two decades later, George W. Bush's efforts to partially privatize Social Security by creating individual retirement accounts has generated intense opposition that to date has been successful in stymieing such efforts. This suggests that the neoliberal experiment may be forced to confront the demands of an electorate for a continuing role for the state in protecting citizens from the vicissitudes of the market and the exigencies of life (e.g., illness, accidents, natural disasters).

In this regard, it is our view that the politics of multiculturalism are far more connected to debates over the erosion of social rights than is often appreciated. Indeed, as the debate over affirmative action suggests, a politics of recognition amounts to little more than a symbolic gesture if it is not accompanied by policies designed to offer the marginalized, new citizens and long-standing second-class citizens alike the varied forms of capital necessary to create an equal opportunity society.

Withdrawal

The emphasis in our language above has been on politics. Both multiculturalism and the welfare state are the products of political decision making, which in representative democracies relies not only on the actions of elected officials, but also on the involvement of the citizenry. The third discourse discussed in this book revolves around a widely held belief that in recent decades there has been an appreciable disinclination on the part of growing sectors of the citizenry to become involved in political and civic life. While the focus of much of this discussion has been on the USA, as is evident in the work of Bellah and his colleagues (1985) and the recent influential debates over "bowling alone" initiated by Putnam (1995, 2000), it has been seen as applicable in varying degrees to all of the world's liberal democracies.

As we indicated, part of the response to the withdrawal thesis is that it is overstated, that citizens today are perhaps less involved than was true in the recent past, but the differences between past and present have been overstated by Putnam and like-minded scholars (e.g., Skocpol 2003). This, for example, is the argument Turner (2001) makes, and moreover an argument that receives some confirmation in the comparative project edited by Putnam (2002). That being said, nobody appears prepared to argue that withdrawal has not occurred. The debate is primarily about the extent to which withdrawal has occurred. We are prepared to agree with Turner's general assessment. If one avoids romanticizing the past, as is Putnam's tendency, it can be argued that the problem with both past and present is that the opportunities for genuine engagement by the citizenry have been stymied by elites who benefit from a paucity of democratic involvement. To his credit, this appears to be something Giddens is aware of and it explains his call for the expansion and deepening of democratic participation.

In our discussion, the primary concern was with the explanations that have been proposed to account for why withdrawal is taking place. Specifically, we questioned Putnam's claim that the primary culprits are television and generational succession, arguing that his work is part of a tradition of social criticism that refuses to link what have been identified as social problems to the shifting nature of capitalist industrial society (this is a tendency evident in Bellah et al.'s work as well). Instead of accepting Putnam's description of capitalism as essentially static, we suggested that it ought to be viewed as having taken various forms throughout its fateful history. Indeed, as we pointed out, the rise of neoliberalism occurred during a period of capitalist restructuring that commenced in the 1960s and began to be felt in significant ways in the following decade. The widespread deindustrialization of the historic centers of capitalist industrial society – Manchester, Detroit, Lyon, the Ruhr Valley – during the heyday of manufacturing signaled the erosion of the power of the working class, especially through their chief instrument of political will, labor unions.

Michael Moore spotlighted the fate of Flint, Michigan, the birthplace of General Motors, in his documentary film *Roger and Me*. The experience of deindustrialization in that city can be seen as a synecdoche for manufacturing centers in general. Flint's history was intimately connected to the American automotive industry, and when GM slashed its American-based workforce, the city quickly entered a period of social decline. Unemployment, of course, rose dramatically. With it, myriad social problems increased, while the local resources to tackle those problems declined. As Steven Dandaneau's (1996) analysis of responses to the crisis revealed, nothing worked. Those who sought to return to the status quo ante, to the so-called "golden age" of the post-World War II decades (Michael Moore included), were engaged in romantic wishful thinking. Militant unionists found themselves as powerless as their mainstream union counterparts who hoped to negotiate with the corporation in order to salvage as many jobs as possible. Both militant and mainstream unions were incapable of challenging what had become a multinational corporation with more employees residing outside of the USA than inside. More utopian visions of freeing workers from the necessity of alienating work – reflected, for example, in the program advanced by University of Michigan philosopher Frithjof Bergmann – were similarly unsuccessful in gaining a voice in determining the economic future of the city. The boosterism of local middle-class civic leaders, seeking, for example, to make Flint a tourist destination, also failed.

It is not surprising that, in such a context, a growing feeling of powerlessness would be felt by Flint's citizens, the poor and working class first, but the rest of the community as well. What would become clear to many was that Flint's future was not going to be determined locally or even nationally. Instead, the city was enmeshed in an increasingly globalized economy that pitted workers rooted in particular places against footloose corporations that have become part of the transnational capitalist class (Sklair 2001). The consequence was that the rules of the game that had defined the inherent conflicts between capital and labor during the era of the historic compromise no longer pertained. The erosion of the working classes' political voice can go some way in explaining withdrawal from civic and political involvement. To the extent that a similar sense of political alienation penetrates the middle classes, a similar withdrawal could be expected.

While this takes us beyond Flint, the phenomenon known as corporate downsizing has increasingly placed white-collar professionals in a parallel situation to that which their working-class counterparts have confronted. The new corporate model is one in which employers no longer guarantee job security to their professional employees, who, therefore, can no longer assume that corporations will operate with a norm of reciprocity that is defined in terms of long-term expectations of mutual obligations. Insofar as this is the case, vulnerable sectors of the middle class, too, can come to view the world as increasingly beyond their control; the situation can go far to explain why increasing insecurity within the middle class might result in a tendency to withdraw from civic and political engagements.

CITIZENSHIP AND GLOBALIZATION

Chapter 5 was devoted to new modes of citizenship that have in various ways called into question the assumption that citizenship is a mode of identity and belonging that is linked solely to the nation-state. While we do not doubt but that the nation-state remains the most significant institution with the power to decide who is and who is not considered to be a member of a polity, and which defines rights and obligations, we have attempted to indicate that its historic monopoly is being challenged. Much of our effort was devoted to describing the two forms that this challenge has taken: (1) the dramatic expansion of dual (or multiple) citizenship; and (2) the European Union's project of nested citizenship.

Dual or multiple citizens do not question the legitimacy of states defining membership except insofar as that process of defining contends that an individual can be a member of one, and only one, state. Such a goal has never been achieved by any nation-state, due to the complex interplay of competing citizenship regimes. Many people were dual citizens by default. However, in recent years, with the expansion of transnational ties (Portes 1996; Faist 2000b; Kivisto 2001; Levitt 2003), where immigrants live with one foot in their homeland and one foot in the host society, and in the process create an ethnic community that transcends national boundaries, immigrants themselves have resisted efforts to force a severing of past ties as a prerequisite for achieving membership in a new polity. Moreover, nations of emigration have found that it is often in their own interest to permit their departing citizens to retain homeland membership even when naturalizing elsewhere. The result is that the number of individuals with dual or multiple citizenships has increased dramatically and we can reasonably assume that this trend will continue into the indefinite future.

The nested citizenship created by the European Union was depicted as a unique cosmopolitan experiment in which the national sovereignties of the EU's constituent states are not lost, but rather are reconfigured. Citizens remain members of distinct nations, but at the same time they share a common identity as citizens of Europe. Particularly with the expansion of the EU to the east, and the possible inclusion of Turkey, the EU has used the leverage it has to require that member states promote human rights in accordance with the Declaration of Human Rights. Thus, member states are expected to abolish the death penalty, to prohibit torture, and in other ways to insure that human rights are respected. At the same time, member states are expected to abide by the rule of law and in the process to weed out corruption. On the other hand, as critics often point out, the EU is a highly bureaucratic institution that appears to be quite distant from the lives of ordinary Europeans. This is the current challenge confronting the institution as it nears its half-century mark, a challenge that calls for becoming more democratically responsive to its members. While we do not think that a similar organization is likely to emerge elsewhere in the world, the EU's impact is felt well beyond its borders.

Turning to the issues that preoccupied us in Chapters 2, 3, and 4, which we described in terms of the internal dynamics of particular nations, it is clear to us that the factors shaping inclusion – the debates over multiculturalism, erosion, and withdrawal – are all increasingly being influenced by global factors. Multiculturalism, for example, is being shaped by transnationalism, with its border-transgressing features. The erosion of rights –

particularly social rights – that has been the hallmark of neoliberalism must be seen in terms of deindustrialization and the global restructuring of capitalism. Labor unions are discovering this fact. Whereas the union movement in the advanced industrial nations once sought to combat job losses by pressing for protectionist policies and by restricting immigration, now the futility of such efforts is becoming increasingly apparent. Thus, unions have come to recognize that their futures are tied to the unionization of workers in the nations of the South and to the promotion of decent wages and living standards for workers in those developing economies. Moreover, rather than restricting immigration, they have come to see immigrants as potential recruits to the union movement.

Likewise, the issue that we defined as withdrawal should be seen in terms of the impact of forces that transcend national borders. Put another way, one reason for explaining the withdrawal from civic and political involvements at the local and national level is that people increasingly feel that their ability to possess a genuine voice in decision making is constricted. Part of the reason for this feeling is that the decisions with the greatest impact on their lives can no longer be addressed satisfactorily simply at the level of the nation-state. In this regard, Derek Heater (2002: 24) provocatively points to the novelty of the present moment when he writes that, "there is mounting evidence that [the nation-state] cannot perform all of the functions it has accumulated since the seventeenth century: the Westphalian system is crumbling. If the state is not guaranteeing its citizens' rights, perhaps it also has not the strength to resist attempts to supplement its duties."

To the extent that he is right, what does this point to? If citizenship is to retain the salience accorded to it in varied ways by liberal, republican, and communitarian theorists, democracy needs to be deepened and strengthened in the existing liberal democracies, while at the same time democracy must expand beyond the boundaries of these discrete nations, penetrating into societies which heretofore have had no historical experience of democratic rule. We are at the cusp of a new era wherein the nation-state will no longer be the sole arbiter in defining the meaning of citizenship. What that world will look like will depend on the political will of those committed to self-rule and the outcome of their interaction with powerful opponents.

References

Abendroth, Wolfgang. 1972. *A Short History of the European Working Class*. New York: Monthly Review Press.

Abramsky, Sasah. 2000. "Barring Democracy." *Mother Jones*, October 17. www. motherjones.com/news/feature/2000/10/felonvote.html.

Addams, Jane. 1960. *Jane Addams: A Centennial Reader*. New York: Macmillan.

Aleinikoff, T. Alexander and Douglas Klusmeyer. 2001. "Plural Nationality: Facing the Future in a Migratory World," pp. 63–88 in T. Alexander Aleinikoff and Douglas Klusmeyer (eds.), *Citizenship Today: Global Perspectives and Practices*. Washington, DC: Carnegie Endowment for International Peace.

Alexander, Jeffrey C. 2001. "Theorizing the 'Modes of Incorporation': Assimilation, Hyphenation, and Multiculturalism as Varieties of Civil Participation." *Sociological Theory*, 19(3): 237–49.

Alexander, Jeffrey C. 2005. "Contradictions in the Societal Community: The Promise and Disappointment of Parsons's Concept," pp. 93–110 in Renée Fox, Victor M. Lidz, and Harold Bershady (eds.), *After Parsons: A Theory of Social Action for the Twenty-First Century*. New York: Russell Sage Foundation.

Alexander, Jeffrey C. 2006. *The Civil Sphere*. New York: Oxford University Press.

Alexander, Jeffrey C. and Neil J. Smelser. 1999. "Introduction: The Ideological Discourse of Cultural Discontent," pp. 3–18 in Neil J. Smelser and Jeffrey C. Alexander (eds.), *Diversity and Its Discontents: Cultural Conflict and Common Ground in Contemporary American Society*. Princeton, NJ: Princeton University Press.

Anderson, Elijah. 2000. *Code of the Street: Decency, Violence, and the Moral Life of the Inner City*. New York: W. W. Norton.

Antonio, Robert. 2000. "After Postmodernism: Reactionary Tribalism." *American Journal of Sociology*, 106(2): 40–87.

Appiah, Kwame Anthony. 2005. *The Ethics of Identity*. Princeton, NJ: Princeton University Press.

Arendt, Hannah. 1968 [1951]. *The Origins of Totalitarianism*. New York: Harcourt, Brace, and Jovanovich.

Armony, Ariel C. 2004. *The Dubious Link: Civic Engagement and Democratization*. Stanford, CA: University of California Press.

Aron, Raymond, 1974. "Is Multinational Citizenship Possible?" *Social Research*, 41(4): 638–72.

Bailyn, Bernard. 1967. *The Ideological Origins of the American Revolution*. Cambridge, MA: The Belknap Press of Harvard University Press.

Banfield, Edward. 1958. *The Moral Basis of a Backward Society*. Glencoe, IL: Free Press.

Barbalet, J. M. 1988. *Citizenship: Rights, Struggle, and Class Inequality*. Minneapolis, MN: University of Minnesota Press.

Barber, Benjamin. 1984. *Strong Democracy: Participatory Politics for a New Age*. Berkeley, CA: University of California Press.

Barry, Brian. 2001. *Culture and Equality*. Cambridge: Polity Press.

Bar-Yaacov, Nissim. 1961. *Dual Nationality*. New York: Frederick A. Praeger.

Bauböck, Rainer. 2002. "Political Community Beyond the Sovereign State, Supranational Federalism, and Transnational Minorities," pp. 110–36 in Steven Vertovec and Robin Cohen (eds.), *Conceiving Cosmopolitanism: Theory, Context, and Practice*. Oxford: Oxford University Press.

Bean, Frank D. and Gillian Stevens. 2003. *America's Newcomers and the Dynamics of Diversity*. New York: Russell Sage Foundation.

Beck, Ulrich and Anthony Giddens. 2005. "Nationalism has now Become the Enemy of Europe's Nations." *Guardian*, October 4: 28.

Béland, Daniel. 2005. "Insecurity, Citizenship, and Globalization: The Multiple Faces of State Protection." *Sociological Theory*, 23(1): 25–41.

Bell, Daniel. 1973. *The Coming of Post-Industrial Society: A Venture in Social Forecasting*. New York: Basic Books.

Bell, Daniel. 1976. *The Cultural Contradictions of Capitalism*. New York: Basic Books.

Bellah, Robert N., Richard Madsen, William M. Sullivan, Ann Swidler, and Steven M. Tipton. 1985. *Habits of the Heart: Individualism and Commitment in American Life*. Berkeley, CA: University of California Press.

Bellah, Robert N., Richard Madsen, William M. Sullivan, Ann Swidler, and Steven M. Tipton. 1991. *The Good Society*. New York: Alfred A. Knopf.

Bendix, Reinhard. 1964. *Nation-Building and Citizenship*. Berkeley, CA: University of California Press.

Benhabib, Seyla. 2002. *The Claims of Culture: Equality and Diversity in the Global Era*. Princeton, NJ: Princeton University Press.

Benhabib, Seyla. 2004. *The Rights of Others: Aliens, Residents, and Citizens*. Cambridge: Cambridge University Press.

Bibby, Reginald. 1990. *Mosaic Madness: Pluralism without a Cause*. Toronto: Stoddart.

Bissoondath, Neil. 2002. *Selling Illusions: The Cult of Multiculturalism in Canada*. Toronto: Penguin.

Bloemraad, Irene. 2004. "Who Claims Dual Citizenship? The Limits of Postnationalism, the Possibilities of Transnationalism, and the Persistence of Traditional Citizenship." *International Migration Review*, 38(2): 389–426.

Bloemraad, Irene. 2006. *Becoming a Citizen: Incorporating Immigrants and Refugees in the United States and Canada*. Berkeley, CA: University of California Press.

Bluestone, Barry and Bennett Harrison. 1982. *The Deindustrialization of America: Plant Closings, Community Abandonment, and the Dismantling of Basic Industry*. New York: Basic Books.

Bobbio, Norberto and Maurizio Viroli. 2003. *The Idea of the Republic*. Cambridge: Polity Press.

Bodnar, John. 1985. *The Transplanted*. Bloomington, IN: Indiana University Press.

Body-Gendrot, Sophie and Marilyn Gittell (eds.) 2003. *Social Capital and Social Citizenship*. Lanham, MD: Lexington Books.

Boggs, Carl. 2001. "Social Capital and Political Fantasy: Robert Putnam's *Bowling Alone*." *Theory and Society*, 30: 281–97.

Bonhoeffer, Dietrich. 1959. *The Cost of Discipleship*. New York: Macmillan.

Bourdieu, Pierre. 1986. "The Forms of Capital," pp. 241–58 in J. G. Richardson (ed.), *Handbook of Theory and Research for the Sociology of Education*. Westport, CT: Greenwood Press.

Bourque, Gilles and Jules Duchastel. 1999. "Erosion of the Nation-State and the Transformation of National Identities in Canada," pp. 183–98 in Janet L. Abu Lughod (ed.), *Sociology for the Twenty-First Century: Continuities and Cutting Edges*. Chicago, IL: University of Chicago Press.

Boynton, Robert S. 1997. "The Two Tonys: Why is the Prime Minister So Interested in What Anthony Giddens Thinks?" *The New Yorker*, October 6: 65–74.

Breton, Raymond. 1986. "Multiculturalism and Canadian Nation-Building," pp. 27–66 in Alan Cairns and Cynthia Williams (eds.), *The Politics of Gender, Ethnicity, and Language in Canada*. Toronto: University of Toronto Press.

Brokow, Tom. 1998. *The Greatest Generation*. New York: Random House.

Brubaker, Rogers. 1995. "Comments on 'Modes of Immigration Politics in Liberal Democratic States.'" *International Migration Review*, 29(4): 903–8.

Buechler, Steven M. 1990. *Women's Movements in the United States*. New Brunswick, NJ: Rutgers University Press.

Bulmer, Martin and Anthony M. Rees (eds.) 1996. *Citizenship Today: The Contemporary Relevance of T. H. Marshall*. London: UCL Press.

Calhoun, Craig. 1997. *Nationalism*. Milton Keynes, UK: Open University Press.

Callinicos, Alex. 2001. *Against the Third Way: An Anti-Capitalist Critique*. Cambridge: Polity Press.

Campbell, Angus, Philip E. Converse, Warren Miller, and Donald E. Stokes. 1976 [1960]. *The American Voter*. New York: John Wiley.

Cardoso, Fernando Henrique. 2000. "An Age of Citizenship." *Foreign Policy*, 119(Summer): 40–2.

Castles, Stephen. 1997. "Multicultural Citizenship: A Response to the Dilemma of Globalization and National Identity." *Journal of Intercultural Studies*, 18(1): 5–22.

Chaves, Mark. 2000. "Review of *Bowling Alone*." *Christian Century*, July 19: 42–3.

Childs, Marquis William. 1936. *Sweden: The Middle Way*. New Haven, CT: Yale University Press.

Cohen, Jean. 1999. "Does Voluntary Association Make Democracy Work?," pp. 263–91 in Neil J. Smelser and Jeffrey C. Alexander (eds.), *Diversity and Its Discontents: Cultural Conflict and Common Ground in Contemporary American Society*. Princeton, NJ: Princeton University Press.

Cohen, Lizabeth. 2003. *A Consumers' Republic: The Politics of Mass Consumption in Postwar America*. New York: Alfred A. Knopf.

Coleman, James S. 1988–9. "Social Capital in the Creation of Human Capital." *American Journal of Sociology*, 94(1): 95–120.

Coleman, James S. 1994. *Foundations of Social Theory*. Cambridge, MA: The Belknap Press of Harvard University Press.

Connor, Walker. 1994. *Ethnonationalism*. Princeton, NJ: Princeton University Press.

Coser, Lewis. 1974. *Greedy Institutions: Patterns of Undivided Commitment*. New York: Free Press.

Council of Europe. 1997. *European Convention on Nationality and Explanatory Report*. Strasbourg, France: Council of Europe.

Crenson, Matthew A. and Benjamin Ginsberg. 2004. *Downsizing Democracy: How America Sidelined Its Citizens and Privatized Its Public*. Baltimore, MD: The Johns Hopkins University Press.

Crouch, Colin, Klaus Eder, and Damian Tambini (eds.) 2001. *Citizenship, Markets, and the State*. New York: Oxford University Press.

Crozier, Michel. 1975. "Western Europe," pp. 11–57 in Michel Crozier, Samuel Huntington, and Jude Watanuki (eds.), *The Crisis of Democracy*. New York: New York University Press.

Dandaneau, Steven. 1996. *A Town Abandoned: Flint, Michigan Confronts Deindustrialization*. Albany, NY: SUNY Press.

Daniels, Roger. 2004. *Guarding the Golden Gate: American Immigration Policy and Immigrants since 1882*. New York: Hill and Wang.

Dean, Kathryn. 2003. *Capitalism and Citizenship: The Impossible Partnership*. London: Routledge.

Delanty, Gerard. 2000. *Citizenship in a Global Age: Society, Culture, Politics*. Milton Keynes, UK: Open University Press.

Delgado-Moreira, Juan M. 2000. *Multicultural Citizenship of the European Union*. Aldershot, UK: Ashgate.

Dower, Nigel. 2003. *An Introduction to Global Citizenship*. Edinburgh: Edinburgh University Press.

Drury, Shadia. 1999. *Leo Strauss and the American Right*. New York: St. Martin's Press.

Economist, The. 1999. "The New Establishment University of Downing Street." September 4: 30–1.

Edelman, Murray. 1985. *The Symbolic Uses of Politics*. Urbana, IL: University of Illinois Press.

Edwards, Bob and Michael W. Foley. 1998. "Civil Society and Social Capital Beyond Putnam." *American Behavioral Scientist*, 42(1): 124–39.

Edwards, Bob, Michael W. Foley, and Mario Diani (eds.) 2001. *Beyond Tocqueville: Civil Society and the Social Capital Debate in Comparative Perspective*. Hanover, NH: University Press of New England.

Elshtain, Jean Bethke. 1996. *Democracy on Trial*. New York: Basic Books.

Esping-Anderson, G. 1982. "The Incompatibilities of the Welfare State." *Working Papers for a New Society*, January.

Esping-Anderson, G. 1990. *The Three Worlds of Welfare Capitalism*. Cambridge: Polity Press.

Etzioni, Amitai. 1993. *The Spirit of Community: Rights, Responsibilities and the Communitarian Agenda*. New York: Crown.

Etzioni, Amitai. 1996. *The New Golden Rule: Community and Morality in a Democratic Society*. New York: Basic Books.

Etzioni, Amitai. 2000. "Community as We Know It." July 20. www.intellectualcapital.com/issues/issue393/item10109.asp.

Faist, Thomas. 2000a. "Social Citizenship in the European Union: Residual Post-National, and Nested Membership?" *Institute für Interkulturelle and Internationale Studien, Arbeitspapier* Wr. 17/2000.

Faist, Thomas. 2000b. *The Volume and Dynamics of International Migration and Transnational Social Spaces*. New York: Oxford University Press.

Faist, Thomas. 2000c. "Transnationalism in International Migration: Implications for the Study of Citizenship and Culture." *Ethnic and Racial Studies*, 23(2): 189–222.

Faist, Thomas. 2001a. "Beyond National and Post-national Models: Transnational Spaces and Immigrant Integration," pp. 277–312 in Luigi Tomasi (ed.), *New Horizons in Sociological Theory and Research*. Burlington, VT: Ashgate Publishing.

Faist, Thomas. 2001b. "Social Citizenship in the European Union: Nested Membership." *Journal of Common Market Studies*, 39(1): 39–60.

Faist, Thomas. 2004. "Dual Citizenship as Overlapping Membership," pp. 210–31 in Danièle Joly (ed.), *International Migration in the New Global Millennium: Global Movement and Settlement*. Burlington, VT: Ashgate Publishing.

Faist, Thomas (ed.) 2006. *Dual Citizenship in Europe*. Aldershot, UK: Ashgate.

Faist, Thomas and Andreas Ette (eds.) Forthcoming. *The Europeanization of National Immigration Policies: Between Autonomy and the European Union*. Basingstoke: Palgrave Macmillan.

Faist, Thomas and Peter Kivisto (eds.) Forthcoming. *Dual Citizenship in a Globalizing World*. Basingstoke: Palgrave Macmillan.

Falk, Richard. 1994. "The Making of Global Citizenship," pp. 42–61 in Bart Van Steenbergen (ed.), *The Condition of Citizenship*. London: Sage.

Faulks, Keith. 2000. *Citizenship*. London: Routledge.

Faux, Jeff. 1999. "Lost on the Third Way." *Dissent*, 46(2): 67–76.

Favell, Adrian. 1998. *Philosophies of Integration*. Basingstoke: Macmillan.

Feldblum, Miriam. 2000. "Managing Membership: New Trends in Citizenship and Nationality Policy," pp. 475–99 in T. Alexander Aleinikoff and Douglas Klusmeyer (eds.), *From Migrants to Citizens: Membership in a Changing World*. Washington, DC: Carnegie Endowment for International Peace.

Fenton, Steve and Stephen May (eds.) 2002. *Ethnonational Identities*. Basingstoke: Palgrave Macmillan.

Field, John. 2003. *Social Capital*. London: Routledge.

Flexnor, Eleanor and Ellen Fitzpatrick. 1996. *Century of Struggle: The Women's Rights Movement in the United States*. Cambridge, MA: The Belknap Press of Harvard University Press.

Foley, Michael W. and Bob Edwards. 1997. "Escape from Politics? Social Theory and the Social Capital Debate." *American Behavioral Scientist*, 40(5): 550–61.

Foner, Eric. 1988. *Reconstruction: America's Unfinished Revolution, 1863–1877*. New York: Harper and Row.

Ford, Richard Thompson. 2005. *Racial Culture: A Critique*. Princeton, NJ: Princeton University Press.

Frank, Robert H. and Philip J. Cook. 1995. *The Winner-Take-All Society*. New York: Free Press.

Fraser, Nancy. 1995. "From Redistribution to Recognition? Dilemmas of Justice in a Postsocialist Age." *New Left Review*, 212(August/September): 68–93.

Fraser, Nancy. 1996. *Justice Interruptus: Critical Reflections on the "Postsocialist" Condition*. London: Routledge.

Fredrickson, George M. 1995. *Black Liberation: A Comparative History of Black Ideologies in the United States and South Africa*. New York: Oxford University Press.

Freeman, Gary. 1995. "Modes of Incorporation Politics in Liberal Democratic States." *International Migration Review*, 29(4): 891–902.

Galbraith, John Kenneth. 1955. *The Affluent Society*. Boston, MA: Houghton, Mifflin.

Galloway, Donald. 2000. "The Dilemmas of Canadian Citizenship Law," pp. 82–118 in T. Alexander Aleinikoff and Douglas Klusmeyer (eds.), *From Migrants to Citizens: Membership in a Changing World*. Washington, DC: Carnegie Endowment for International Peace.

Galston, William. 1991. *Liberal Purposes: Goods, Virtues, and Duties in a Liberal State*. Cambridge: Cambridge University Press.

Gerson, Kathleen and Jerry A. Jacobs. 2004. "The Work–Home Crunch." *Contexts*, 3(4): 29–37.

Giddens, Anthony. 1973. *The Class Structure of the Advanced Societies*. New York: Harper Torchbooks.

Giddens, Anthony. 1982. *Profiles and Critiques in Social Theory*. London: Macmillan.

Giddens, Anthony. 1990. *The Consequences of Modernity*. Stanford, CA: Stanford University Press.

Giddens, Anthony. 1998. *The Third Way: The Renewal of Social Democracy*. Cambridge: Polity Press.

Giddens, Anthony. 1999. "Why the Old Left is Wrong on Inequality." *The New Statesman*, October 25: 25–7.

Giddens, Anthony. 2000a. *Runaway World: How Globalization is Reshaping Our Lives*. New York: Routledge.

Giddens, Anthony. 2000b. *The Third Way and Its Critics*. Cambridge: Polity Press.

Giddens, Anthony. 2002. *Where Now for New Labour?* Cambridge: Polity Press.

Giddens, Anthony. 2003. "Neoprogressivism: A New Agenda for Social Democracy," pp. 1–34 in Anthony Giddens (ed.), *The Progressive Manifesto*. Cambridge: Polity Press.

Giddens, Anthony and Patrick Diamond (eds.) 2005. *The New Egalitarianism*. Cambridge: Polity Press.

Gilbert, Neil. 2004. *Transformation of the Welfare State: The Silent Surrender of Public Responsibility*. New York: Oxford University Press.

Gilbertson, Greta and Audrey Singer. 2003. "The Emergence of Protective Citizenship in the USA: Naturalization among Dominican Immigrants in the Post-1966 Welfare Reform Era." *Ethnic and Racial Studies*, 26(1): 25–51.

Gitlin, Todd. 1995. *The Twilight of Common Dreams: Why America is Wracked by Culture Wars*. New York: Metropolitan Books.

Glassman, Ronald M., William H. Swatos, Jr., and Peter Kivisto. 1993. *For Democracy: The Noble Character and Tragic Flaws of the Middle Class*. Westport, CT: Greenwood Press.

Glazer, Nathan. 1997. *We Are All Multiculturalists Now*. Cambridge, MA: Harvard University Press.

Glenn, Evelyn Nakano. 2000. "Citizenship and Inequality: Historical and Global Perspectives." *Social Problems*, 47(1): 1–20.

Glenn, Evelyn Nakano. 2002. *Unequal Freedom: How Race and Gender Shaped American Citizenship and Labor*. Cambridge, MA: Harvard University Press.

Goffman, Erving. 1983. "The Interaction Order." *American Sociological Review*, 48(1): 1–17.

Goldberg, Chad Alan. 2001. "Social Citizenship and a Reconstructed Tocqueville." *American Sociological Review*, 66(2): 289–315.

Goldthorpe, John, David Lockwood, Frank Bechofer, and Jennifer Platt. 1968. *The Affluent Worker* (3 vols.) Cambridge: Cambridge University Press.

Granovetter, Mark. 1973. "The Strength of Weak Ties." *American Journal of Sociology*, 78(6): 1360–80.

Green, Philip. 1999. *Equality and Democracy*. New York: New Press.

Gregg, Benjamin. 2003. *Thick Moralities, Thin Politics: Social Integration across Communities of Belief*. Durham, NC: Duke University Press.

de Groot, Gerard-Rene. 2003. "Loss of Nationality: A Critical Inventory," pp. 201–99 in David A. Martin and Kay Hailbronner (eds.), *Rights and Duties of Dual Nationals: Evolution and Prospects*. The Hague: Kluwer Law International.

Guarnizo, Luis Eduardo, Alejandro Portes, and William J. Haller. 2003. "Assimilation and Transnationalism: Determinants of Transnational Political Action among Contemporary Migrants." *American Journal of Sociology*, 108(6): 1211–48.

Gutmann, Amy. 2003. *Identity in Democracy*. Princeton, NJ: Princeton University Press.

Habermas, Jürgen. 1975. *Legitimation Crisis*. Boston, MA: Beacon Press.

Habermas, Jürgen. 1998. *The Inclusion of the Other.* Cambridge: Polity Press.

Hagedorn, Heike. 2003. "Administrative Systems and Dual Nationality: The Information Gap," pp. 183–200 in David A. Martin and Kay Hailbronner (eds.), *Rights and Duties of Dual Nationals: Evolution and Prospects.* The Hague: Kluwer Law International.

Hailbronner, Kay. 2003. "Rights and Duties of Dual Nationals: Changing Concepts and Attitudes," pp. 19–26 in David A. Martin and Kay Hailbronner (eds.), *Rights and Duties of Dual Nationals: Evolution and Prospects.* The Hague: Kluwer Law International.

Halfmann, Jost. 1998. "Citizenship, Universalism, Migration and the Risks of Exclusion." *The British Journal of Sociology,* 49(4): 513–33.

Hall, Peter A. 2002. "Great Britain: The Role of Government and the Distribution of Social Capital," pp. 21–57 in Robert D. Putnam (ed.), *Democracies in Flux: The Evolution of Social Capital in Contemporary Society.* New York: Oxford University Press.

Hammar, Tomas. 1990. *Democracy and the Nation-State: Aliens, Denizens, and Citizens in a World of International Migration.* Aldershot, UK: Gower.

Hansen, Randall. 2002. "The Dog that Didn't Bark: Dual Nationality in the United Kingdom," pp. 179–90 in Randall Hansen and Patrick Weil (eds.), *Dual Nationality, Social Rights, and Federal Citizenship in the US and Europe: The Reinvention of Citizenship.* New York: Berghahn Books.

Hansen, Randall and Patrick Weil. 2002. "Dual Citizenship in a Changed World: Immigration, Gender and Social Rights," pp. 1–15 in Randall Hansen and Patrick Weil (eds.), *Dual Nationality, Social Rights and Federal Citizenship in the US and Europe: The Reinvention of Citizenship.* New York: Berghahn Books.

Harles, John C. 1997. "Integration before Assimilation: Immigration, Multiculturalism, and the Canadian Polity." *Canadian Journal of Political Science,* 30(4): 711–36.

Harris, Jose. 1998. *William Beveridge: A Biography.* Oxford: Oxford University Press.

Hartmann, Douglas and Joseph Gerteis. 2005. "Dealing with Diversity: Mapping Multi-culturalism in Sociological Terms." *Sociological Theory,* 23(2): 218–40.

Harvey, David. 1989. *The Condition of Postmodernity: An Enquiry into the Origins of Cultural Change.* Oxford: Blackwell.

Hauerwas, Stanley. 1981. *A Community of Character.* South Bend, IN: University of Notre Dame Press.

Heater, Derek. 1999. *What is Citizenship?* Cambridge: Polity Press.

Heater, Derek. 2002. *World Citizenship: Cosmopolitan Thinking and Its Opponents.* London: Continuum.

Heater, Derek. 2004. *A Brief History of Citizenship.* New York: New York University Press.

Held, David. 1995. *Democracy and the Global Order: From the Modern State to Cosmopolitan Governance.* Cambridge: Polity Press.

Hemerijck, Anton. 2001. "Prospects for Effective Social Citizenship in an Age of Structural Inactivity," pp. 134–70 in Colin Crouch, Klaus Eder, and Damian

Tambini (eds.), *Citizenship, Markets, and the State*. New York: Oxford University Press.

Higham, John. 1955. *Strangers in the Land: Patterns of American Nativism, 1860–1925*. New Brunswick, NJ: Rutgers University Press.

Hobsbawm, E. J. 1962. *The Age of Revolution, 1789–1848*. New York: Mentor Books.

Hobsbawm, E. J. 1965. *Labouring Men: Studies in the History of Labour*. New York: Basic Books.

Hobsbawm, E. J. 1969. *Industry and Empire*. New York: Penguin Books.

Hochschild, Arlie Russell. 1997. *The Time Bind: When Work Becomes Home and Home Becomes Work*. New York: Henry Holt.

Hodgson, Godfrey. 2004. *More Equal than Others: America from Nixon to the New Century*. Princeton, NJ: Princeton University Press.

Hoffman, John. 2004. *Citizenship Beyond the State*. London: Sage Publications.

Hufton, Olwen H. 1992. *Women and the Limits of Citizenship in the French Revolution*. Toronto: University of Toronto Press.

Hunter, James Davidson. 2000. "Bowling with the Social Scientists: Robert Putnam Surveys America." *The Weekly Standard*, 5(47), August 28/September 4: 1–10.

Huntington, Samuel. 1976. "The Democratic Distemper," pp. 9–38 in Nathan Glazer and Irving Kristol (eds.), *The American Commonwealth*. New York: Basic Books.

Huntington, Samuel. 2004. *Who Are We? The Challenges to America's National Identity*. New York: Simon and Schuster.

Ireland, Doug. 2005. "Why is France Burning?" *The Nation*, November 28: 29–30.

Iriye, Akira. 2002. *Global Community: The Role of International Organizations in the Making of the Contemporary World*. Berkeley, CA: University of California Press.

Isin, Engin F. and Patricia K. Wood. 1999. *Citizenship and Identity*. Thousand Oaks, CA: Sage.

Jacobson, David. 1996. *Rights Across Borders: Immigration and the Decline of Citizenship*. Baltimore, MD: The Johns Hopkins University Press.

Jameson, Fredic. 1991. *Postmodernism, or, the Cultural Logic of Late Capitalism*. Durham, NC: Duke University Press.

Janoski, Thomas. 1998. *Citizenship and Civil Society: A Framework of Rights and Obligations in Liberal, Traditional, and Social Democratic Regimes*. Cambridge: Cambridge University Press.

Janowitz, Morris. 1980. "Observations on the Sociology of Citizenship: Obligations and Rights." *Social Forces*, 59(1): 1–24.

Jelin, Elizabeth. 2000. "Towards a Global Environmental Citizenship." *Citizenship Studies*, 4(1): 47–63.

Johnston, Paul. 2001. "The Emergence of Transnational Citizenship among Mexican Immigrants in California," pp. 253–77 in T. Alexander Aleinikoff and Douglas Klusmeyer (eds.), *Citizenship Today: Global Perspectives and Practices*. Washington, DC: Carnegie Endowment for International Peace.

Jones-Correra, Michael. 2001. "Under Two Flags: Dual Nationality in Latin America and its Consequences for the United States." *International Migration Review*, 35: 997–1029.

Joppke, Christian. 2001. "Multicultural Citizenship: A Critique." *European Journal of Sociology*, 42(2): 431–47.

Joppke, Christian. 2005. *Selecting by Origin: Ethnic Migration in the Liberal State*. Cambridge, MA: Harvard University Press.

Joppke, Christian and Ewa Morawska (eds.) 2003. *Toward Assimilation and Citizenship: Immigrants in Liberal Nation States*. Basingstoke: Palgrave Macmillan.

Kastoryano, Riva. 2002. *Negotiating Identities: States and Immigrants in France and Germany*. Princeton, NJ: Princeton University Press.

Katznelson, Ira. 2005. *When Affirmative Action was White: An Untold History of Racial Inequality*. New York: W. W. Norton.

Katznelson, Ira and Aristide R. Zolberg (eds.) 1986. *Working-Class Formation: Nineteenth-Century Patterns and the United States*. Princeton, NJ: Princeton University Press.

Kelly, Jack. 2002. "Number of Dual Citizens in US Soaring." www.post-gazette.com/nation/200205/dual0515p4.asp

Kelly, Paul (ed.) 2002. *Multiculturalism Reconsidered*. Cambridge: Polity Press.

Kerber, Linda. 1997. "The Meanings of Citizenship." *Dissent*, 44(Fall): 33–7.

Kessler-Harris, Alice. 2001. *In Pursuit of Equality: Women, Men, and the Quest for Economic Citizenship in Twentieth-Century America*. New York: Oxford University Press.

Kimmel, Barbara Brooks and Alan M. Lubiner. 2003. *Citizenship Made Simple: An Easy-to-Read Guide to the US Citizenship Process*. Chester, NJ: Next Decade.

Kivisto, Peter. 1984. *Immigrant Socialists in the United States: The Case of Finns and the Left*. Rutherford, NJ: Fairleigh Dickinson University Press.

Kivisto, Peter. 2001. "Theorizing Transnational Immigration: A Critical Review of Current Efforts. *Ethnic and Racial Studies*, 24(4): 549–77.

Kivisto, Peter. 2002. *Multiculturalism in a Global Society*. Malden, MA: Blackwell Publishing.

Kivisto, Peter (ed.) 2005. *Incorporating Diversity: Rethinking Assimilation in a Multicultural Age*. Boulder, CO: Paradigm Publishers.

Kivisto, Peter and Wendy Ng. 2005. *Americans All: Race and Ethnic Relations in Historical, Structural, and Comparative Perspectives*, 2nd edn. Los Angeles: Roxbury Publishing.

Kivisto, Peter and Elizabeth Hartung (eds.) 2007. *Intersecting Inequalities: Class, Race, Sex and Sexualities*. Upper Saddle River, NJ: Pearson Prentice Hall.

Kloosterman, Robert and Jan Rath (eds.) 2003. *Immigrant Entrepreneurs: Venturing Abroad in the Age of Globalization*. Oxford: Berg.

Kohn, Hans. 1944. *The Age of Nationalism*. New York: Harper and Row.

Korpi, Walter. 1983. *The Democratic Class Struggle*. London: Routledge and Kegan Paul.

Koslowski, Rey. 2003. "Challenges of International Cooperation in a World of Increasing Dual Nationality," pp. 157–82 in David A. Martin and Kay

Hailbronner (eds.), *Rights and Duties of Dual Nationals: Evolution and Prospects*. The Hague: Kluwer Law International.

Kreuzer, Christine. 2003. "Double and Multiple Nationality in Germany after the Citizenship Reform Act of 1999," pp. 347–59 in David A. Martin and Kay Hailbronner (eds.), *Rights and Duties of Dual Nationals: Evolution and Prospects*. The Hague: Kluwer Law International.

Kymlicka, Will. 1995. *Multicultural Citizenship*. New York: Oxford University Press.

Kymlicka, Will. 1998. *Finding Our Way: Rethinking Ethnocultural Relations in Canada*. Toronto: Oxford University Press.

Kymlicka, Will. 2001. *Politics in the Vernacular: Nationalism, Multiculturalism, and Citizenship*. New York: Oxford University Press.

Kymlicka, Will. 2003. "Immigration, Citizenship, Multiculturalism: Exploring the Links," pp. 195–208 in Sarah Spencer (ed.), *The Politics of Migration: Managing Opportunity, Conflict and Change*. Malden, MA: Blackwell Publishing.

Lash, Scott and John Urry. 1987. *The End of Organized Capitalism*. Cambridge: Polity Press.

Latham, Robert and Saskia Sassen (eds.) 2005. *Digital Formations: IT and New Architectures in the Global Realm*. Princeton, NJ: Princeton University Press.

Lechner, Frank and John Boli. 2005. *World Culture: Origins and Consequences*. Malden, MA: Blackwell Publishing.

Legomsky, Stephen. 2003. "Dual Nationality and Military Service: Strategy Number Two," pp. 79–126 in David A. Martin and Kay Hailbronner (eds.), *Rights and Duties of Dual Nationals: Evolution and Prospects*. The Hague: Kluwer Law International.

Leland, John. 2005. "A Church that Packs them in, 16,000 at a Time." *New York Times*, July 18: A6.

Lemann, Nicholas. 1992. *The Promised Land: The Great Black Migration and How It Changed America*. New York: Vintage Books.

Lenin, V. I. n.d. *On Britain*. Moscow: Foreign Language Publishing House.

Levitt, Peggy. 2003. "Keeping Feet in Both Worlds: Transnational Practices and Immigrant Incorporation in the United States," pp. 177–94 in Christian Joppke and Ewa Morawska (eds.), *Toward Assimilation and Citizenship*. New York: Palgrave Macmillan.

Li, Yaojun, Mike Savage, and Andrew Pickles. 2003. "Social Capital and Social Exclusion in England and Wales (1972–1999)." *British Journal of Sociology*, 54(4): 497–526.

Lichtenstein, Neil. 2003. *State of the Union: A Century of American Labor*. Princeton, NJ: Princeton University Press.

Lin, Nan. 2001. *Sociology Capital: A Theory of Social Structure and Action*. Cambridge: Cambridge University Press.

Lindblom, Charles E. 1997. *Politics and Markets: The World's Political–Economic Systems*. New York: Basic Books.

Linkater, Andrew. 1998. "Cosmopolitan Citizenship." *Citizenship Studies*, 2(1): 23–41.

Lipset, Seymour Martin. 1963. *Political Man: The Social Bases of Politics*. Garden City, NY: Anchor Books.

Lipset, Seymour Martin and Gary Marks. 2000. *It Didn't Happen Here: Why Socialism Failed in the United States*. New York: W. W. Norton.

Lipset, Seymour Martin and Isabelle Hausser. 2001. "The Americanization of the European Left." *Commentaire*, 24(Autumn): 579–88.

Lister, Ruth. 1997. *Citizenship: Feminist Perspectives*. New York: New York University Press.

Lister, Ruth. 2004. *Poverty*. Cambridge: Polity Press.

Litwack, Leon. 1998. *Trouble in Mind: Black Southerners in the Age of Jim Crow*. New York: Alfred A. Knopf.

Lowenstein, Roger. 2005. "The End of Pensions?" *New York Times*, October 30: 56–90.

Luckmann, Thomas. 1967. *The Invisible Religion: The Problem of Religion in Modern Society*. New York: Macmillan.

Luhmann, Niklas. 1995. *Social Systems*, trans. John Bednarz, Jr. and Dirk Baecker. Palo Alto, CA: Stanford University Press.

Lyman, Stanford M. 1991. "The Race Question and Liberalism: Casuistries in American Constitutional Law." *International Journal of Politics, Culture, and Society*, 5(2): 183–247.

Lyman, Stanford M. 1993a. "Marginalizing the Self: A Study of Citizenship, Color, and Ethnoracial Identity in American Society." *Symbolic Interaction*, 16(4): 379–93.

Lyman, Stanford M. 1993b. "The Chinese before the Courts: Ethnoracial Construction and Marginalization." *International Journal of Politics, Culture, and Society*, 6(3): 443–62.

MacIntyre, Alasdair. 1984. *After Virtue*. South Bend, IN: University of Notre Dame Press.

Macpherson, Crawford B. 1964. *The Political Theory of Possessive Individualism: Hobbes to Locke*. New York: Oxford University Press.

Madrick, Jeff. 2003. "Health for Sale." *New York Review of Books*, December 18: 71–4.

Malik, Kenan. 2002. "Against Multiculturalism." *New Humanist* (Summer). http://www.Rationalist.org.uk/newhumanist/issue02summer/malik.shtml.

Mann, Michael. 1987. "Ruling Class Strategies and Citizenship." *Sociology*, 21(3): 339–52.

Markoff, John. 1996. *Waves of Democracy*. Thousand Oaks, CA: Pine Forge Press.

Marks, Gary. 1997. "A Third Lens: Comparing European Integration and State Building," pp. 23–44 in Jytte Klausen and Louise Tilly (eds.), *European Integration in Social and Historical Perspective: From 1850 to the Present*. Lanham, MD: Rowman & Littlefield.

Marshall, T. H. 1964. *Class, Citizenship, and Social Development*. Garden City, NY: Doubleday.

Marshall, T. H. 1975. *Social Policy in the Twentieth Century*. London: Hutchinson.

Martin, David A. 2003. "Introduction: The Trend Toward Dual Nationality," pp. 3–18 in David A. Martin and Kay Hailbronner (eds.), *Rights and Duties of Dual Nationals: Evolution and Prospects*. The Hague: Kluwer Law International.

Massey, Douglas S. 1996. "The Age of Extremes." *Demography*, 33(4): 395–412.

McAdam, Doug. 1982. *Political Process and the Development of Black Insurgency*. Chicago, IL: University of Chicago Press.

Medrano, Juan Díez and Paula Gutiérrez. 2001. "Nested Identities: National and European Identity in Spain." *Ethnic and Racial Studies*, 24(5): 753–78.

Meehan, Elizabeth. 1993. *Citizenship and the European Community*. London: Sage.

Merton, Robert K. 1968. *Social Theory and Social Structure*. New York: The Free Press.

Miliband, Ralph. 1964. *Parliamentary Socialism*. New York: Monthly Review Press.

Milkman, Ruth and Kim Voss (eds.) 2004. *Rebuilding Labor: Organizing and Organizers in the New Union Movement*. Ithaca, NY: ILR Press.

Miller, Mark J. 1991. "Dual Citizenship: A European Norm?" *International Migration Review*, 33(4): 945–50.

Modood, Tariq. 2001. "Their Liberalism and Our Multiculturalism?" *British Journal of Politics and International Relations*, 3: 245–57.

Modood, Tariq. 2005a. *Multicultural Politics: Racism, Ethnicity, and Muslims in Britain*. Minneapolis, MN: University of Minnesota Press.

Modood, Tariq. 2005b. "Rethinking Multiculturalism after 7/7." Open Democracy Forum. www.openDemocracy.net/conflict-tension/multiculturalism_2879.jsp.

Montgomery, David. 1987. *The Fall of the House of Labor: The Workplace, the State, and American Labor Activism*. Cambridge: Cambridge University Press.

Moravcsik, Andrew. 1999. *The Choice for Europe: Social Purpose and State Power from Messina to Maastricht*. Ithaca, NY: Cornell University Press.

Morin, Richard. 2000. "On Pins and Needles." *The Washington Post*, July 15: A3.

Morris, Aldon. 1984. *The Origins of the Civil Rights Movement*. New York: The Free Press.

Mouffe, Chantal. 1998. "The Radical Center: Politics without an Adversary." *Soundings*, 9: 11–23.

Münch, Richard. 2001. *National Citizenship in the Global Age: From National to Transnational Ties and Identities*. Basingstoke: Palgrave Macmillan.

Nagel, Joane. 2003. *Race, Ethnicity, and Sexuality: Intimate Intersections, Forbidden Frontiers*. New York: Oxford University Press.

Nairn, Tom. 2000. *After Britain*. London: Granta.

Nicolaidis, Kalypso. 2005. "The Struggle for Europe." *Dissent*, Fall: 11–17.

Nisbet, Robert. 1974. "Citizenship: Two Traditions." *Social Research*, 41(4): 612–37.

Novak, Michael. 1972. *The Rise of the Unmeltable Ethnics: Politics and Culture in the Seventies*. New York: Macmillan.

O'Conner, James. 2003. *The Fiscal Crisis of the State*. Somerset, NJ: Transaction.

Offe, Claus. 1984. *Contradictions of the Welfare State*. Cambridge, MA: MIT Press.

Offe, Claus. 1985. *Disorganized Capitalism*. Cambridge, MA: MIT Press.

Offen, Karen. 1997. "Women, Citizenship, and Suffrage in France since 1789," pp. 125–41 in William B. Cohen (ed.), *The Transformation of Modern France: Essays in Honor of Gordon Wright*. Boston, MA: Houghton Mifflin.

Okin, Susan Moller (ed.) 1999. *Is Multiculturalism Bad for Women?* Princeton, NJ: Princeton University Press.

Olzak, Susan. 1992. *The Dynamics of Ethnic Competition and Conflict*. Stanford, CA: Stanford University Press.

Omi, Michael and Howard Winant. 1986. *Racial Formation in the United States: From the 1960s to the 1980s*. New York: Routledge and Kegan Paul.

Ong, Aihwa. 1999. *Flexible Citizenship: The Cultural Logic of Transnationality*. Durham, NC: Duke University Press.

Organski, A. F. K. 1965. *The Stages of Political Development*. New York: Alfred A. Knopf.

Orwell, George. 1987 [1945]. *Animal Farm*. Vol. 8 in *The Complete Works of George Orwell*. London: Secker and Warburg.

Papastergiadis, Nikos. 2000. *The Turbulence of Migration*. Cambridge: Polity Press.

Parekh, Bhikhu. 2000a. *The Future of Multi-Ethnic Britain: The Parekh Report*. London: Profile Books.

Parekh, Bhikhu. 2000b. *Rethinking Multiculturalism: Cultural Diversity and Political Theory*. Cambridge, MA: Harvard University Press.

Parekh, Bhikhu. 2005. "British Commitments." *Prospect*, 114(September): 36–40.

Parkin, Frank. 1979. *Marxism and Class Theory: A Bourgeois Critique*. New York: Columbia University Press.

Parsons, Talcott. 1971. *The System of Modern Societies*. Englewood Cliffs, NJ: Prentice-Hall.

Pateman, Carole. 1988. *The Sexual Contract*. Stanford, CA: Stanford University Press.

Pearson, David. 2001. *The Politics of Ethnicity in Settler Societies: States of Unease*. New York: Palgrave.

Pearson, David. 2002. "Theorizing Citizenship in British Settler Societies." *Ethnic and Racial Studies*, 25(6): 989–1012.

Perrot, Michelle. 1986. "On the Formation of the French Working Class," pp. 71–110 in Ira Katznelson and Aristide R. Zolberg (eds.), *Working-Class Formation: Nineteenth-Century Patterns in Western Europe and the United States*. Princeton, NJ: Princeton University Press.

Pitkin, Hanna Fenichel and Sara M. Shumer. 1982. "On Participation." *Democracy*, Fall: 43–54.

Plummer, Ken. 2003. *Intimate Citizenship: Private Decisions and Public Dialogues*. Seattle: University of Washington Press.

Polletta, Francesca. 2004. *Freedom is an Endless Meeting: Democracy in American Social Movements*. Chicago, IL: University of Chicago Press.

Porter, John. 1965. *The Vertical Mosaic: An Analysis of Social Class and Power in Canada*. Toronto: University of Toronto Press.

Portes, Alejandro. 1996. "Transnational Communities: Their Emergence and Significance in the Contemporary World-System," pp. 151–68 in Roberto Korzeniewicz and William Smith (eds.), *Latin America in the World Economy*. Westport, CT: Greenwood Press.

Portes, Alejandro. 1998. "Social Capital: Its Origins and Applications in Modern Sociology." *Annual Review of Sociology*, 24: 1–24.

Portes, Alejandro, William J. Haller, and Luis Eduardo Guarnizo. 2002. "Transnational Entrepreneurs: An Alternative Form of Immigrant Economic Adaptation." *American Sociological Review*, 67(2): 278–98.

de la Pradelle, Géraud. 2002. "Dual Nationality and the French Citizenship Tradition," pp. 191–212 in Randall Hansen and Patrick Weil (eds.), *Dual Nationality, Social Rights, and Federal Citizenship in the US and Europe: The Reinvention of Citizenship*. New York: Berghahn Books.

Putnam, Robert D. 1993. *Making Democracy Work: Civic Traditions in Modern Italy*. Princeton, NJ: Princeton University Press.

Putnam, Robert D. 1995. "Bowling Alone? America's Declining Social Capital." *Journal of Democracy*, 6: 65–78.

Putnam, Robert D. 2000. *Bowling Alone: The Collapse and Revival of American Community*. New York: Simon & Schuster.

Putnam, Robert D. (ed.). 2002. *Democracies in Flux: The Evolution of Social Capital in Contemporary Society*. New York: Oxford University Press.

Rand, Ayn. 1964. *The Virtue of Selfishness: A New Concept of Egoism* (with additional articles by Nathaniel Branden). New York: New American Library.

Rees, Anthony M. 1996. "T. H. Marshall and the Progress of Citizenship," pp. 1–23 in Martin Bulmer and Anthony M. Rees (eds.), *Citizenship Today: The Contemporary Relevance of T. H. Marshall*. London: UCL Press.

Renshon, Stanley A. 2001. "Dual Citizenship + Multiple Loyalties = One America?" pp. 232–82 in Stanley A. Renshon (ed.), *One America? Political Leadership, National Identity, and the Dilemmas of Diversity*. Washington, DC: Georgetown University.

Rieff, Philip. 1966. *The Triumph of the Therapeutic: Uses of Faith after Freud*. New York: Harper and Row.

Ringer, Benjamin B. 1983. *We the People and Others: Duality and America's Treatment of Its Racial Minorities*. New York: Tavistock.

Roche, Maurice. 1992. *Rethinking Citizenship: Welfare, Ideology and Change in Modern Society*. Cambridge: Polity Press.

Roche, Maurice. 1997. "Citizenship and Exclusion: Reconstructing the European Union," pp. 3–22 in Maurice Roche and Rik van Berkel (eds.), *European Citizenship and Social Exclusion*. Aldershot, UK: Ashbury.

Roediger, David R. 1991. *The Wages of Whiteness: Race and the Making of the American Working Class*. London: Verso.

Roediger, David R. 2005. *Working Toward Whiteness: How American Immigrants Became White: The Strange Journey from Ellis Island to the Suburbs.* New York: Basic Books.

Roof, Wade Clark. 1999. *Spiritual Marketplace: Baby Boomers and the Remaking of American Religion.* Princeton, NJ: Princeton University Press.

Rorty, Richard. 1997. *Achieving Our Country: Leftist Thought in Twentieth-Century America.* Cambridge, MA: Harvard University Press.

Rosenau, James N. 2003. *Distant Proximities: Dynamics Beyond Globalization.* Princeton, NJ: Princeton University Press.

Rosenau, Pauline (ed.) 2000. *Public–Private Policy Partnerships.* Cambridge, MA: MIT Press.

Rubin, Beth. 1995. *Shifts in the Social Contract: Understanding Change in American Society.* Thousand Oaks, CA: Pine Forge Press.

Rueschemeyer, Dietrich, Evelyn H. Stephens, and John D. Stephens. 1992. *Capitalist Development and Democracy.* Chicago, IL: University of Chicago Press.

Ryan, Alan. 1999. "Britain: Recycling the Third Way." *Dissent*, Spring: 77–80.

Sandel, Michael. 1998. *Democracy's Discontent: America in Search of a Public Philosophy.* Cambridge, MA: The Belknap Press of Harvard University Press.

Sassen, Saskia. 1996. *Losing Control? Sovereignty in an Age of Globalization.* New York: Columbia University Press.

Sassen, Saskia. 1999. *Guests and Workers.* Chicago, IL: University of Chicago Press.

Savas, E. S. 1999. *Privatization and Public–Private Partnerships.* Washington, DC: CQ Press.

Saxton, Alexander. 1990. *The Rise and Fall of the White Republic: Class, Politics, and Culture in Nineteenth-century America.* London: Verso.

Schlesinger, Arthur, Jr. 1992. *The Disuniting of America: Reflections on a Multicultural Society.* New York: W. W. Norton.

Schneider, Dorothee. 2001. "Naturalization and United States Citizenship in Two Periods of Mass Migration, 1890–1930, 1965–2000." *Journal of American Ethnic History*, 21(1): 50–82.

Schuck, Peter H. 2002. "Plural Citizenships," pp. 61–99 in Randall Hansen and Patrick Weil (eds.), *Dual Nationality, Social Rights and Federal Citizenship in the US and Europe.* New York: Berghahn Books.

Schultz, David A. 2002. "The Phenomenology of Democracy: Putnam, Pluralism and Voluntary Associations," pp. 74–98 in Scott L. McLean, David A Schultz, and Manfred B. Steger (eds.), *Social Conflict: Critical Perspectives on Community and "Bowling Alone."* New York: New York University Press.

Schwartz, Barry. 1999. "Capitalism, the Market, 'the Underclass,' and the Future." *Society*, 37(1): 37.

Sciortino, Guiseppe. 2003. "From Homogeneity to Difference? Comparing Multiculturalism as a Description and a Field for Claim-Making." *Comparative Social Research*, 22: 263–85.

Scobey, David. 2001. "The Specter of Citizenship." *Citizenship Studies*, 5(1): 11–26.

Seidman, Gay. 1999. "Gendered Citizenship: South Africa's Democratic Transformation and the Constitution of a Gendered State." *Gender & Society*, 13(3): 287–307.

Selznick, Philip. 1992. *The Moral Commonwealth: Social Theory and the Promise of Community*. Berkeley, CA: University of California Press.

Sennett, Richard. 1992. *The Fall of Public Man*. New York: W. W. Norton.

Sennett, Richard. 1998. *The Corrosion of Character: The Personal Consequences of Work in the New Capitalism*. New York: W. W. Norton.

Sennett, Richard. 2006. *The Culture of the New Capitalism*. New Haven, CT: Yale University Press.

Shklar, Judith N. 1991. *American Citizenship: The Quest for Inclusion*. Cambridge, MA: Harvard University Press.

Shweder, Richard A., Martha Minow, and Hazel Rose Markus (eds.) 2002. *Engaging Cultural Differences: The Multicultural Challenge to Liberal Democracies*. New York: Russell Sage Foundation.

Singer, Peter. 2002. *One World: The Ethics of Globalization*. New Haven, CT: Yale University Press.

Skinner, Quentin. 1998. *Liberty before Liberalism*. Cambridge: Cambridge University Press.

Sklair, Leslie. 2001. *The Transnational Capitalist Class*. Malden, MA: Blackwell.

Skocpol, Theda. 1992. *Protecting Soldiers and Mothers: The Political Origins of Social Policy in the United States*. Cambridge, MA: The Belknap Press of Harvard University Press.

Skocpol, Theda. 2003. *Diminished Democracy: From Membership to Management in American Civil Life*. Norman, OK: University of Oklahoma Press.

Skrentny, John D. 2002. *The Minority Rights Revolution*. Cambridge, MA: The Belknap Press of Harvard University Press.

Slater, Philip. 1970. *The Pursuit of Loneliness*. Boston, MA: Beacon Press.

Smith, Anthony. 1986. *The Ethnic Origins of Nations*. Oxford: Blackwell.

Sniderman, Paul M. and Thomas Piazza. 1993. *The Scar of Race*. Cambridge, MA: Harvard University Press.

Solomos, John. 2003. *Race and Racism in Britain*, 3rd edn. Basingstoke: Palgrave Macmillan.

Sombart, Werner. 1976 [1906]. *Why is There No Socialism in the United States?* London: Macmillan.

Sommers, Margaret. 2001. "Romancing the Market, Reviling the State: Historicizing Liberalism, Privatization, and the Compelling Claims to Civil Society," pp. 23–48 in Colin Crouch, Klaus Eder, and Damian Tambini (eds.), *Citizenship, Markets, and the State*. New York: Oxford University Press.

Soysal, Yasemin. 1994. *Limits of Citizenship: Migrants and Postnational Membership in Europe*. Chicago, IL: University of Chicago Press.

Spiro, Peter. 2002. "Embracing Dual Nationality," pp. 19–33 in Randall Hansen and Patrick Weil (eds.), *Dual Nationality, Social Rights, and Federal Citizenship in the US and Europe: The Reinvention of Citizenship*. New York: Berghahn Books.

Starr, Paul. 2000. "The Public Vanishes." *The New Republic*, August 14: 35–7.

Stevenson, Nick. 1997. "Globalization, Natural Cultures, and Cultural Citizenship." *The Sociological Quarterly*, 38(1): 41–66.

Stewart, Angus. 1995. "Two Conceptions of Citizenship." *The British Journal of Sociology*, 46(1): 63–78.

Sumner, William Graham. 1925. *What Social Classes Owe Each Other*. New Haven, CT: Yale University Press.

Tambini, Damian. 1997. "Universal Cybercitizenship," pp. 84–109 in R. Tsagarousiannou, D. Tambini, and C. Bryan (eds.), *Cyberdemocracy: Technology, Cities, and Civic Networks*. London: Routledge.

Tambini, Damian. 2001. "Post-national Citizenship." *Ethnic and Racial Studies*, 24(2): 195–212.

Taylor, Charles, with commentary by Amy Gutmann, Steve C. Rockefeller, Michael Walzer, and Susan Wolf. 1992. *Multiculturalism and the "Politics of Recognition."* Princeton, NJ: Princeton University Press.

Taylor, Charles. 2002. "Modern Social Imaginaries." *Public Culture*, 14(1): 91–123.

Thompson, E. P. 1963. *The Making of the English Working Class*. New York: Vintage Books.

Tichenor, Daniel J. 2002. *Dividing Lines: The Politics of Immigration Control in America*. Princeton, NJ: Princeton University Press.

Tilly, Charles. 1985. "War Making and State Making as Organized Crime," pp. 169–91 in P. B. Evans, D. Rueschmeyer, and T. Skocpol (eds.), *Bringing the State Back In*. Cambridge: Cambridge University Press.

Tilly, Charles. 1990. *Coercion, Capital, and European States, AD 990–1992*. Malden, MA: Blackwell Publishing.

Tilove, Jonathan. 2002. "Rethinking Dual Citizenship in the Post-September 11 World. www.newhouse.com/archieve/story/a062002.html.

Tiryakian, Edward A. 2004. "Assessing Multiculturalism Theoretically: *E Pluribus Unum, Sic et Non*," pp. 1–18 in John Rex and Gurharpal Singh (eds.), *Governance in Multicultural Societies*. Burlington, VT: Ashgate Publishing.

Tocqueville, Alexis de. 1969 [1853]. *Democracy in America*, edited by J. P. Mayer. Garden City, NY: Doubleday.

Torpey, John. 2000. *The Invention of the Passport: Surveillance, Citizenship, and the State*. Cambridge: Cambridge University Press.

Touraine, Alain. 1971. *Post-Industrial Society*. New York: Random House.

Touraine, Alain. 1981. *The Voice and the Eye: An Analysis of Social Movements*. Cambridge: Cambridge University Press.

Touraine, Alain. 1997. *What is Democracy?* Boulder, CO: Westview Press.

Touraine, Alain. 2001. *Beyond Neoliberalism*. Cambridge: Polity Press.

Tsutsui, Kiyoteru and Christine Min Wotipka. 2004. "Global Civil Society and the International Human Rights Movement: Citizen Participation in Human Rights International Nongovernmental Organizations." *Social Forces*, 83(2): 587–620.

Tully, James. 2002. "Reimagining Belonging in Circumstances of Cultural Diversity: A Citizen Approach," pp. 152–77 in Ulf Hedetoft and Mette Hjort (eds.),

The Postnational Self: Belonging and Identity. Minneapolis, MN: University of Minnesota Press.

Turner, Bryan S. 1986. *Citizenship and Capitalism*. London: Allen & Unwin.

Turner, Bryan S. 1993. "Contemporary Problems in the Theory of Citizenship," pp. 1–18 in Bryan S. Turner (ed.), *Citizenship and Social Theory*. London: Sage.

Turner, Bryan S. 2001. "The Erosion of Citizenship." *British Journal of Sociology*, 52(2): 189–209.

Turner, Bryan S. 2006. "Classical Sociology and Cosmopolitanism: A Critical Defence of the Social." *British Journal of Sociology*, 57(1): 133–51.

Twine, Fred. 1994. *Citizenship and Social Rights: Aliens, Residents, and Citizens: The Interdependence of Self and Society*. London: Sage.

Ward, Russel. 1978. *The Australian Legend*. Melbourne: Oxford University Press.

Weber, Max. 1968 [1921]. *Economy and Society*, vols. 1–3. Berkeley, CA: University of California Press.

Weil, Patrick. 2001. "Access to Citizenship: A Comparison of Twenty-Five Nationality Laws," pp. 17–35 in T. Alexander Aleinikoff and Douglas Klusmeyer (eds.), *Citizenship Today: Global Perspectives and Practices*. Washington, DC: Carnegie Endowment for International Peace.

White, Robert and Jed Donoghue. 2003. "Marshall, Mannheim, and Contested Citizenship." *British Journal of Sociology*, 54(3): 391–406.

Wiedemann, Marianne. 2003. "Development of Dual Nationality under German Law," pp. 335–45 in David A. Martin and Kay Hailbronner (eds.), *Rights and Duties of Dual Nationals: Evolution and Prospects*. The Hague: Kluwer Law International.

Wieviorka, Michel. 1998. "Is Multiculturalism the Solution?" *Ethnic and Racial Studies*, 21(5): 881–910.

Wilentz, Sean. 1984. *Chants Democratic: New York City and the American Working Class, 1788–1850*. New York: Oxford University Press.

Wills, Garry. 2000. "Putnam's America." *The American Prospect*, 11(16): 14–15.

Wilson, William Julius. 1987. *The Truly Disadvantaged: The Inner City, the Underclass, and Public Policy*. Chicago, IL: University of Chicago Press.

Withol de Wenden, Catherine. 2004. "Multiculturalism in France," pp. 70–80 in John Rex and Gurharpal Singh (eds.), *Governance in Multicultural Societies*. Burlington, VT: Ashgate Publishing.

Wolfe, Alan. 2003. "The Costs of Citizenship: Assimilation v. Multiculturalism in Liberal Democracies." *The Responsive Community*, 13(3): 23–33.

Wood, Patricia K. and Gilbert Liette. 2005. "Multiculturalism in Canada: Accidental Discourse, Alternative Vision, Urban Practice." *International Journal of Urban and Regional Research*, 29(3): 679–91.

Wuthnow, Robert. 2002. "The United States: Bridging the Privileged and the Marginalized?," pp. 59–102 in Robert D. Putnam (ed.), *Democracies in Flux: The Evolution of Social Capital in Contemporary Society*. New York: Oxford University Press.

Young, Iris Marion. 1989. "Polity and Group Difference: A Critique of the Ideal of Universal Citizenship." *Ethics*, 99 (January): 250–74.

Young, Iris Marion. 1990. *Justice and the Politics of Difference*. Princeton, NJ: Princeton University Press.

Young, Iris Marion. 2000. *Inclusion and Democracy*. New York: Oxford University Press.

Yuval-Davis, Nira. 2000. "Multi-layered Citizenship and the Boundaries of the 'Nation-State.' " *International Social Science Review*, 1(1): 112–27.

Zappala, Gianni and Stephen Castles. 2000. "Citizenship and Immigration in Australia," pp. 32–81 in T. Alexander Aleinikoff and Douglas Klusmeyer (eds.), *From Migrants to Citizens: Membership in a Changing World*. Washington, DC: Carnegie Endowment for International Peace.

Index